Jewish Law and International Law

Jewish Law and International Law

Sovereignty and Exogenous Authority in a Transnational World

MICHAEL J. BROYDE

Professor of Law, Emory University School of Law, Atlanta, GA, USA

YEHONATAN ELAZAR-DE MOTA

Senior Research Fellow, Center for the Study of Law and Religion, Emory University, Atlanta, GA, USA

OXFORD
UNIVERSITY PRESS

OXFORD
UNIVERSITY PRESS

Oxford University Press is a department of the University of Oxford. It furthers the University's objective of excellence in research, scholarship, and education by publishing worldwide. Oxford is a registered trade mark of Oxford University Press in the UK and in certain other countries.

Published in the United States of America by Oxford University Press
198 Madison Avenue, New York, NY 10016, United States of America.

Library of Congress Cataloging-in-Publication Data
Names: Broyde, Michael J., author. | Elazar-De Mota, Yehonatan, 1981– author.
Title: Jewish law and international law : sovereignty and exogenous authority in a transnational world / Michael J. Broyde and Yehonatan Elazar-De Mota.
Description: New York : Oxford University Press, 2025. |
Includes bibliographical references and index.
Identifiers: LCCN 2024055757 (print) | LCCN 2024055758 (ebook) |
ISBN 9780197805244 (hardback) | ISBN 9780197805268 (updf) | ISBN 9780197805275 (online) |
ISBN 9780197805251 (epub)
Subjects: LCSH: International law (Jewish law) | Jewish law. |
International law. | International law—Religious aspects—Judaism.
Classification: LCC KBM524.15.B76 2025 (print) | LCC KBM524.15 (ebook) |
DDC 340.5/8—dc23/eng/20241121
LC record available at https://lccn.loc.gov/2024055757
LC ebook record available at https://lccn.loc.gov/2024055758

DOI: 10.1093/9780197805275.001.0001

Printed by Marquis Book Printing, Canada

Contents

Preface

In an era marked by rising antisemitism and increasing tensions between Israel and the international community, this book offers a timely and necessary exploration of the intricate relationship between Jewish law and international law. Our goal is to illuminate the commonalities and potential harmonies between these two systems, both of which transcend territorial boundaries and hold significant jurisprudential and methodological parallels.

This work comes at a crucial moment. The current climate of antisemitism globally necessitates a deeper understanding and appreciation of the contributions of Jewish law to the broader legal landscape. While Israel is fundamentally a Jewish state, it does not operate strictly under Jewish law. However, understanding the intersections and divergences between Jewish law and international law can foster a more nuanced perspective on both systems and promote greater mutual respect and integration.

The eight chapters of this book are designed to weave together the connections between Jewish law and international law. The first chapter introduces the foundational concepts and histories of both legal systems, establishing their shared values and transcendent nature. The second chapter examines the incorporation of secular law into Jewish law, outlining the conditions and justifications for such integration.

In the third chapter, we present a crucial example of Jewish law's engagement with international law through the lens of war and humanitarian law, highlighting the ethical and legal considerations that guide such interactions. The fourth chapter shifts focus to more mundane but equally significant areas, such as copyright and bankruptcy, demonstrating the practical applications of Jewish law in contemporary legal contexts.

Chapter 5 offers a historical account of the co-development of Jewish law and international law over the past century and a half, setting the stage for the present-day analysis in chapter 6. That chapter surveys the current relationship between the two legal systems, emphasizing the intellectual contributions and ongoing dialogues within Israeli rabbinic circles.

The penultimate chapter, chapter 7, addresses the pressing issue of antisemitism within legal systems and how Jewish law confronts and navigates these challenges. We argue that recognizing and combating antisemitic elements in international law is not only necessary but imperative for the pursuit of justice and equity.

Finally, chapter 8 envisions a future where Jewish law and international law collaborate more effectively, learning from each other to build a more just and harmonious world order. We reflect on what both legal systems can gain from their interactions and how they can work together to address the global challenges ahead.

In summary, this book is both a theoretical examination and a call to action. By fostering a deeper understanding of Jewish law and its relevance to international law, we hope to contribute to a more just and equitable world where legal systems work in concert rather than in conflict. We invite readers to engage with these ideas and join us in this important conversation.

Acknowledgments and Dedications

This book was a complex, multiyear project that began during the COVID-19 pandemic and concluded during the war that started on October 7, 2023, in Israel. As Emily Dickinson once wrote, "Hope is the thing with feathers that perches in the soul." This project is grounded in hope but written amidst tragedy, echoing the words of Aristotle: "The aim of the wise is not to secure pleasure, but to avoid pain."

Many people have contributed to our intellectual vision and this presentation. We extend our heartfelt thanks to Drs. Michael Berger, David Blumenthal, and Don Seeman and our colleagues at the Emory University Center for the Study of Law and Religion, where this project was discussed numerous times. Special thanks go to the Center's leading scholar, Professor John Witte, Jr., without whom this project would not have been possible. We also gratefully acknowledge the support of the Summer Research Grant program at Emory Law School and thank both the previous dean, Mary Anne Bobinski, and the current dean, Richard D. Freer, for their unwavering support. A special thanks to Jesse Lempel, Esq. as well.

We dedicate this work to our teachers, in both rabbinics and law, as well as to our families. Specifically, we wish to dedicate this to our wives, Channah S. Broyde and Hannah Abreu de Elazar, whose support has been invaluable. As it is said in Proverbs 31:10, "A woman of valor, who can find? For her worth is far above rubies." Your unwavering support, love, and dedication have been our guiding light throughout this journey.

About the Authors

Michael J. Broyde is a Professor of Law, the director of its SJD program, the Berman Projects Director in the Center for the Study of Law and Religion ant and a Professor of Jewish Law at the Tam Institute of Jewish Studies, all at Emory. He is also an adjunct professor of Law at Columbia University School of Law, where he teaches advanced Jewish Law. He has been a synagogue rabbi, *rosh kollel* and judge (*dayyan*) in a rabbinical court (*bet din*) previously.

Yehonatan Elazar-De Mota is a Senior Research Fellow at the Center for the Study of Law and Religion at Emory University's Law School. He holds a master's degree in Anthropology and Religious Studies from Florida International University and a PhD in International Law from the University of Amsterdam. He is *rosh yeshiba* of Beth Midrash Eleazar and judge (*ab beth din*) of Beth Din Zedek of the Dominican Republic. In 2020 and the beginning of 2021, Elazar-De Mota was a visiting lecturer at Universidade Lusófona Porto, at the department of European Studies and Political Science. In 2022, he continued post-doctoral research at the Political History department at the University of Antwerp.

Glossary of Hebrew Terms

Ab beth din chief judge of the Jewish tribunal

Abodah zarah illicit cult

Anus under duress due to *force majeure*

Berirah arbitral sentence

Berith covenant, pact, or treaty

Beth din Jewish tribunal

Darke shalom the ways of peace

Din melekh the law of the monarch

Dinim law enforcement

Dina demalkhuta dina the law of the land is the law

Erubin city limits

Ger ṣedeq Jewish proselyte

Ger toshab a resident stranger who is not Jewish

Geṭ bill of divorce

Gezerah legal decree

Hakhamim rabbinic jurists

Halakhah practical Jewish law or jurisprudence

Hassagath gebul unlawful taking of another's land

Ḥazaqah legal presumption

Ketubah prenuptial agreement

Ma'amad governing body of the Sephardic community

Malshinim accusers

Mideoraita scriptural law

Miderabbanan rabbinic law

Midrash · an exegetical study of the Hebrew Bible

Midresheth halakhah exegetical process for deriving law from the Scripture

Milḥemeth ha-reshuth war of territorial expansion

Milḥemeth miṣwah the biblical injunction to make war with the seven Canaanite nations

Minhagim customs

Miqveh a bath used to remove ritual/ceremonial impurity

Mishnah is the first major written collection of the Jewish oral legal traditions

Parnassim trustees of the Jewish community

Pesaq rabbinical decision

Pesharah agreement

Poseq rabbinican decisor

Qinyan the transfer of title to property

Sanhedrin Jewish Senate

Shaliaḥ agent, power of attorney

Shebu'ah oath

Shebu'ah piqadon an oath about deposits

Shemad general persecution

Sheṭar serub a writ of contempt

Sittumta binding custom

Sugya legal discussion within the Talmud

Talmud body of Jewish law comprised of 63 volumes

Tanḥuma three different collections of exegetical studies and stories based on the Pentateuch

Tam'e/teme'a the status of ritual impurity

Taqanah legal enactment

Tebilah ritual immersion

Tena'im conditions, stipulations

Tiqqun 'olam reparation of the world order

Torah the Law of Moses. Known as the Pentateuch in Christian tradition

Yaḥid Jewish community member

1

An Introduction to Jewish Law and an Introduction to International Law: Two Legal Systems that Transcend Territoriality

Introduction

The rule of law is often considered a legacy of the ancient Roman Empire. Instead of an emperor or universal ruler, Rome had a different vision, focusing on the rule of law. Rome espoused a vision of law as an impersonal and abstract idea, a universal law known as *ius naturale* and *ius gentium*. International law was born from the clashes between different versions and understandings of what constituted natural law and the law of nations. The New World exploration by Iberian travelers and the exploitation of Africans and Native Americans was grounded on European reasonings of natural law and the law of nations. Relations between Europeans, Ottomans, and Chinese merchants posed challenges to the universal law conceived by European jurists and rulers, who now sought various ways to accommodate these differences. The rise of positivism in the nineteenth century led to the world order we recognize today.

Legal positivism led to the theorization of a rule of law based on agreements and treaties between states. Subsequently, the German *Rechtsstaat* (law state) developed from the idea that a state should, of its own free will, elect to operate according to the rule of law. The Vienna School, championed by Hans Kelsen (1881–1973), sought to devise a master system of norms. Contrary to this endeavor, constitutionalists envisioned a system of specific, substantive, and concrete rules. After the League of Nations failed, legal realists entered the scene. If legal idealists think in terms of ethics, then realists think in terms of power. The tension between these two stances became evident during the Cold War when political rivalry weakened the International Court of Justice. It was not until the 1990s that the rule of law in international affairs

Jewish Law and International Law. Michael J. Broyde and Yehonatan Elazar-De Mota, Oxford University Press.
 DOI: 10.1093/9780197805275.003.0001

appeared to be making progress. Amid the crisis precipitated by Iraq's invasion of Kuwait in 1990, former UN ambassador and then US President George H. W. Bush announced that a New World Order was on its way.

Bush's New World Order was fueled by constitutionalism, which aimed to establish global governance that protected human rights, democracy, and the environment and sought to reduce poverty and inequality. Focusing on the rule of law, global administrative law gives little importance to legislative or judicial aspects of governance. Instead, it seeks to accomplish its goal through international organizations. Cynicism within a group of international legal scholars who viewed these efforts skeptically led to the critical legal studies movement. David Kennedy and Martti Koskenniemi, two leaders of this movement, utilize history to critique international legal theory. This movement maintains that human dignity will prevail around the globe as victims triumph over oppressors. This movement thus does not seek global governance through a world rule of law.

As the need for cordial and productive international relations between world powers increased during the early modern era, international law emerged as a product of European legal theory, extending its reach to other regions of the world. However, thousands of years before European jurists began reworking Roman legal notions, Jews had developed their own version of international law, as recorded in the Hebrew Bible and the Talmud. During the Biblical period, the nation of Israel encountered various other nations: Canaan, Moab, Ammon, Midian, Amaleq, Sidon, Tyre, Assyria, Babylon, and Medo-Persia. The Hebrew Bible records the establishment of treaties between nations and intricate details of humanitarian and military law. Contact with the Greeks and Romans during the second Jewish commonwealth led Talmudic legislators to further develop Jewish law. The Talmud details various laws pertaining to international relations under the auspices of *darke shalom* (the ways of peace) and *tiqqun 'olam* (reparation of the world order).

Outsiders often categorize the Jewish tradition as a religion. However, after a deeper look, one discovers the intricate details of law and jurisprudence, which are found at the core of Jewish ritual and ethos. The Jewish tradition is essentially a religious civilization with a legal system. Its legal system shares many similarities with Roman, Islamic, and international law. While the first two may seem obvious to rabbinic scholars, the connection with international law is often overlooked because it is viewed by some Jews as the product of Christian civilization and, therefore, rendered not relevant to rabbinic study and unimportant for this book. Most scholars of international law are oblivious to Jewish law and are not able to see the relationship between both legal systems.

Thinking about International Law and Jewish Law Together

Our leading argument is that international law and Jewish law are most similar in that they are both nonterritorial legal systems. Thus, they both depend on the role of judges to interpret the rule of law. In finding common ground between the two legal systems, scholars of international law and rabbinic jurists could gain insight into how each legal system might contribute to the other and lend a helping hand where the other may be blind or truncated. Our book attempts to stimulate discourse between scholars of Jewish law and scholars of international law. In doing so, we aim to initiate a long-lasting relationship whereby scholars of the respective fields may consult each other to tackle the problems that Jews and non-Jews alike face daily.

Scholars of the critical legal studies movement have criticized the polarized nature of international law. Martti Koskenniemi, professor of international law and former Finnish diplomat, asserts, "International law is a process of articulating political preferences into legal claims that cannot be detached from the conditions of political contestation in which they are made" (Koskenniemi 2011, 221). He maintains that international law is a technique that presents a particular hegemony as the universal preference (ibid.). Moreover, he argues that in the nineteenth century, legal historians with Protestant European backgrounds began to write the history of international law and that this history is not inclusive of minorities and marginalized communities (Koskenniemi 2019, 221).

Antony Anghie, an international law professor at the National University of Singapore, posits that international law is based on colonialism. Furthermore, he argues that European structures of colonialism in the non-European world continuously repeat themselves at various stages of international law. In focusing on the civilizing mission of international law, Anghie highlights "cultural difference" (Anghie 2004, 3). Overall, he argues that different versions of the civilizing mission were mobilized by imperialist actors (ibid., 96).

In response to the issues raised by Anghie, Arnulf Becker-Lorca, an expert in the global intellectual history of international law, argues that "a different narrative of the history of international law will challenge the Western standpoint and may clear up space for new and more emancipatory international legal practices tomorrow" (Becker-Lorca 2014, 22). Becker-Lorca asserts, "[T]he expression *Mestizo international law* reminds us of the historical association between Western colonial expansion and European international law" (ibid.). The term *mestizo* implies a hybrid origin of international law formed through the combination of Western and non-Western attitudes and the globalization of European international legal thought (ibid.). Essentially, Becker-Lorca's work is a deconstructive project of international law.

In recent decades, some Jewish scholars have published works on the relationship between Jewish law and international law. Some of these works include comparative analyses between the two systems. Emory law professor Michael J. Broyde maintains that Jewish law and international law are very similar, as they both utilize the notion of treaties to ensure peaceful relations between nations. He explores how the so-called Noahide laws (the law given by God to Noah in the book of Genesis) are a form of universal law, binding upon non-Jews and Jews alike. This legal system contains an obligation to create *dinim*, that is, law enforcement or a system of judgment (Broyde 2012, 363–68).

Other scholars deal with the contribution of Jews to the development of international law. Canadian law professor Betina Kuzmarov examines the relationship between the Jewish laws of war and international law. She criticizes the othering of Jews and Jewish law within the historiography of international law. If international law claims to be international, it cannot disparage non-European and non-Christian legal traditions, she asserts. Kuzmarov argues that European jurists appropriated Jewish intellectual thought. Consequently, although Jewish ideas were mobilized within the laws of war, Jewish thinkers were left out of the picture.

In his Nacão Legal Consciousness (2021), Yehonatan Elazar-DeMota contends that the contribution of seventeenth-century Portuguese Jews in the discourse of the law of nations and nature was overlooked because of their ethnoreligious identities (Elazar-DeMota 2021, 11). He argues that jurists, philosophers, and merchants of the Eẓ Ḥaim community of Amsterdam not only mobilized the language and legal concepts of the School of Salamanca but also influenced the legal discourse concerning the intersection of private and public international law (ibid., 268). His work focuses on intracommunal and extracommunal discussions concerning slavery and the slave trade. Elazar-DeMota fleshes out how Nacão participants translate the halakhah of slavery into Iberian-Roman law and Dutch-Roman law (ibid., 212).

Israel scholar of international law Reut Yael Paz (2012) posits that Hersch Lauterpacht's training in Jewish law contributed to his "Kelsian twist" toward the individual and nation-state sovereignty. She rereads Lauterpacht in light of a Talmudic passage to explain how he may have deconstructed Hegelian political thought. Her current work explores antisemitism in international law. She advances the claim that while law can be utilized to combat antisemitism, it often reinforces antisemitic stereotypes. Her analysis of court cases highlights the role of law in the neutralization and universalization of human rights and antisemitism.

Legal historian James Loeffler and law professor Moriah Paz (2022) collaborated on a monumental work entitled *The Law of Strangers: Jewish Lawyers and International Law in the Twentieth Century*, in which they survey the contributions of Jewish lawyers to the development of international law from the Nuremberg Trials to the present day. Through biographical sketches, they flesh out connections between the Jewish heritage and the legal thought of selected actors. This work answers the question of why so many leading twentieth-century international lawyers were Jewish and how their identity helped shape international law.

Finally, other works explore the attitudes of contemporary Jewish jurists toward international law. In his doctoral dissertation, Israeli scholar of international law Amos Israel-Vleeschhouwer tackles the challenge of organizing a general theory of the attitude of Jewish law toward international law. He brings various rabbinic opinions and positions to the discourse and systematically categorizes them. He describes and analyzes contemporary Jewish materials and their respective legal processes. He aims to survey the development of Jewish international law and the legal tools and concepts used in arguing each position regarding international law. Ultimately, Israel-Vleeschhouwer trailblazes a path that others are currently following.

How We Think about International Law

At the outset, it is crucial for us to define international law to a rabbinic audience. When describing international law, it is important to distinguish between two branches of international law: public international law and private international law. Public international law deals with a set of norms aiming to regulate the interaction of states that participate in international relations and their subjects. These norms establish a common framework by which states may contribute to the coexistence of stable, ordered, and consistent international relations. Accordingly, international relations and international law go hand in hand. Public international law governs the domain of human rights, international criminal law, and international humanitarian law.

It is worth noting that sovereign states subject themselves to resolutions by the United Nations Security Council without coercion. While there is an International Court of Justice (ICJ) in the Hague, Netherlands, this court has no enforcing authority over any sovereign nation. Thus, public international law promotes the reinforcement of equality among all states and seeks to prevent them from pursuing actions that may lead to sanctions, international censorship, or military action. In general, nation-states that submit to resolutions, conventions, and treaties resulting from international legal consensus do so voluntarily.

Public international law has many sources, including both customary law and codified law. Customary law refers to state practices that "appear to be sufficiently widespread, representative as well as consistent," and where the rule in question has been relied on by a majority of states and has not been rejected by a significant number of states (Wood 2014, 45). Another condition of customary law is that states have been motivated by the belief that they were legally compelled to accept the legitimacy of a rule in question (*opinion juris*). Thus, customary law is independent of treaty law. In today's climate of conflict, customary international humanitarian rights law strengthens the protection offered to victims where treaty law fails to protect them.

Another branch of international law deals with codified law, ordering the conflicts between private citizens of different countries. Private international law must determine jurisdiction, the rule of law, and the enforcement of judgments on foreign soil. Most of the sources of private international law come from domestic laws of the countries involved. Today, most private international law gravitates toward specific subjects, such as contracts or family law. While there is no well-defined body of private international law, there are treaties, conventions, legal guides, and other instruments that govern it.

In any discussion of jurisdiction in private international law, five bases must be considered. First, a nation may be granted jurisdiction if a conflict occurs within its borders. Second, if a country has been harmed, it may claim passive personality, the principle that bases criminal jurisdiction on the status of the victim of crime as a national of the state exercising jurisdiction. Third, a nation may be granted jurisdiction when one of its citizens has perpetrated wrongs. Fourth, a court may grant protective jurisdiction when a nation's security is threatened. Finally, in extreme cases, universal jurisdiction may be established by intrinsic rejection by the international community.

How We Think about Jewish Law

Equally important to defining international law for Jewish scholars, we must define Jewish law (halakhah) for an audience of legal experts who may have little to no knowledge about it.

Like international law, Jewish law has two branches: public and private. Public Jewish law deals with everything from the laws of war, treaties, and oaths undertaken between the nation of Israel and bordering nations to the seven Noahide laws by which resident-foreigners are governed in the Holy Land to those activities performed in the public domain, which affect everyone. Hence, within the sphere of public Jewish law, one may find laws that define the parameters of illicit cult (*abodah zarah*), city limits (*erubin*), or where land for a cemetery may be set aside.

Private Jewish law, on the other hand, deals with family law and business law. These laws govern dealings between individuals, including contracts, property damage, theft, neighbors, agents, partners, slaves, and more. Thus, within this domain, one may discuss cases involving creditors and debtors, loans and deposits, or inheritances. Therefore, private Jewish law constitutes the civil legal system of the Jewish people.

When rabbinic jurists speak about halakhah, they distinguish between scriptural law (*mideoraita*) and rabbinic law (*miderabbanan*). The Jewish tradition teaches that Moses received a written Torah and an oral Torah at Sinai. The written Torah is contained within the five books of Moses: Genesis, Exodus, Leviticus, Numbers, and Deuteronomy. The oral Torah was transmitted orally from the time of Moses until it was compiled by Yehudah Ha-Nasi (b. 135 CE). The compilation of the oral Torah comprises six orders: agricultural laws, laws about holidays, family laws, laws about damages, sacrificial laws, and purity laws. This body of law, known as the Mishnah, was codified with succinct language to facilitate memorization. The judges and teachers of the Mishnah lived in Palestine and were called Tannaim. The period of the Tannaim lasted until about the year 220 CE.

After the compilation of the Mishnah, jurists, and legislators living in Palestine and Babylon expanded on the rulings of the Mishnah. Their work, completed between the third century and fifth centuries CE, is called the Gemara. The study of the Mishnah and the Gemara is known as the Talmud (the Study).

According to Talmudic law, the halakhah is established through Rabbi Ishmael's (95–135 CE) thirteen hermeneutical rules (Ouaknin 1998, 72). Talmudic jurists analyze the language of the written Torah and interpret its meaning through a process of exegesis known as *midresheth halakhah*. This is essentially what rabbinic law is. The Jerusalem Talmud (c. 375 CE) and the Babylonian Talmud (c. 500 CE) contain the legal discussions and decisions made by the High Court of the Jewish People (Zelcer 2002, 49). Until the fifth century CE, national law was decided by the Jewish Senate, namely the Sanhedrin (seventy-one Supreme Court judges). After the compilation and close of the Babylonian Talmud, with the legal decisions of Rab Ashe (352–427 CE) and Rab ʻEna (d. 427 CE), there could be no new national legislations for the Jewish people (Brody 1998, 5).

Apart from scriptural and rabbinic law, Talmudic law also contains customary law. It includes the customs and ordinances that were ordained or practiced in each generation according to the ruling of the governing court of that generation. After the close of the Talmudic era, every court established thereafter, regardless of the country in which it was established, issued decrees, enacted ordinances, and established customs for the people of that country or those of several countries. These practices, however, were not accepted universally by the Jewish people because of the distances and inadequate communication between their different settlements. Since each of these courts was considered to be authoritative only in its region, and the Sanhedrin had been defunct for many years, people in one country could not be compelled to follow the practices of another country, nor was one court required to sanction decrees declared by another court in its locale.

Similarities between International Law and Jewish Law: Three Talmudic Cases

Comparing international law to Jewish law highlights many similarities between them. The most important similarity is that both legal systems lack jurisdiction and law enforcement. Jewish law recurs to the legal device of bans, while the international legal consensus may utilize sanctions against countries that do not conform to the rule of law. Beyond these measures, both Jewish law and international law lack teeth. One could say that Jewish law and international law both depend on trust in the rule of law. In the case of the former, trust is based on the idea of nationhood and the treaty between God and the Israelite nation at Sinai. Trust in the rule of law within the realm of international law is based on treaties made between sovereign states. (Both international law and Jewish law are divided into branches of private, public, and customary law. This convention permits individuals to become experts in specific fields of law.)

The next significant similarity between international law and Jewish law is that they are both nonterritorial legal systems. Where a living legislator is lacking, customary law will naturally develop. Whereas in American law, French law, or even common law, there is a codified law for everything (statutory law), both international law and Jewish law rely on reasonability and proportionality. Indeed, private commercial international law functions much like Jewish law. While territorial legal systems seek definitive codification of law, nonterritorial legal systems like international law and Jewish law work in gray areas.

Rabbi and professor of law Elliot Dorff has argued:

> Customs also serve to decide what the law is when the legal authorities differ. When customs act in this way, however, they are in effect acting in the absence of law, because in some areas of Jewish law, when the jurists disagree, there effectively is no law. This situation does not arise in American law because there are definite methods for reconciling such disputes, but such methods have not existed in many periods of Jewish history. Both the Babylonian and Jerusalem Talmuds record instances when conflicts between laws were settled by the rule, "Go check the practice of the people." In post-Talmudic times, most Rabbis followed the rule that in disputes about Biblical law the more stringent view was to be followed but that, if the dispute concerned Rabbinic legislation, the more lenient rule prevailed. (Dorff 1978, 1344)

It would seem that differing opinions are foundational to Jewish law. Divergence in legal opinions leads to the development of customs, and in turn, customs can produce law or operate in its place.

The Talmud is replete with cases where custom influences halakhah in the absence of law. For instance, where it is necessary to set aside tithes from fruit trees in their fourth year (*orlah*), the Jerusalem Talmud states, "When there is no clearly established law on any matter before the court and you do not know what its true nature is, go and ascertain the custom of the people and act accordingly, and we see that the public does not set aside tithes in this case" (*y.Pe'ah* 7:6; *y.Ma'aser Sheni* 5:3). This is a clear instance of customary law operating in the absence of codified law in the Bible or the Mishnah.

Another passage of the Talmud discusses a discrepancy between rabbinic opinions and whether one should recite a blessing for drinking water. A legal precedent is cited by one authority, where someone was choking over a piece of meat and drank water to flush it down. When asked about the law on this matter, one rabbinic jurist replies, "Go out and observe what the people are doing and act accordingly" (*b.Berakhoth* 44b–45a). It is evident that there was no previously existing convention on this matter, so that the authorities had to resort to the practice of the people.

A third case in the Talmud deals with the requisite distance between two side posts to render an alleyway fit for transporting within it. One authority claims that the distance can be any length. A contrary opinion states that the distance between the side posts must be at least three handbreadths. At the resolution of this case, as in the previous cases, the leading justice said, "Go out and observe what the people are doing" (*b.Erubin* 14b). This Talmudic case is interesting because it cites the authority from the previous cases dealing with the blessing over the water.

Medieval Jewish legal authorities (*poseqim*) differ as to why customs are authoritative where there is no legislated law. The issue at stake is whether the violation of customs is punishable by the court or not. One school of thought claims that customs are mere laws that were once enacted long ago but are no longer applicable.[1] This position grants custom latent juridical authority. Another school of thought claims customs derive from divine authority (*b.Pesahim* 66a). Concerning secular matters of Jewish law, most scholars claim that customs are authoritative because parties can agree to make

[1] Comments of Mordekhai to Baba Meẓia 366; Responsa of the Rosh 55:10. Mordekhai ben Hillel HaKohen, also known as The Mordekhai or, by some Sephardic scholars, as The Mordechie, was a thirteenth-century German rabbi and poseq. His chief legal commentary on the Talmud, referred to as The Mordekhai, is one of the sources of the Shulḥan Arukh. He was killed in the Rintfleisch massacres in 1298.

transactions according to their own conditions. Thus, in those instances, Jewish law defers to customs, which then become the law.

Three Cases of International Law

Like Jewish law, international law falls back on customary law where certain legal matters may not be defined by codified law. *Jus cogens* includes norms that outlaw slavery, torture, genocide, aggression, or crimes against humanity. Sovereign states are under a legal obligation to comply with customary international law (CIL) norms, even though they have not explicitly consented to these norms. During decolonization after World War II, some states felt they could choose which customary laws they would accept. While some states accepted this view, others abandoned it (Thirlway 2019, 61). Traditionally speaking, the binding criteria for endorsing a custom in the International Law Commission (ILC) conclusions are stipulated within the "two-element theory," requiring both ancient practice and sufficient evidence of *opinio juris* (ibid., 65). Once a general rule of customary law has become established, it is impossible to become a persistent objector, that is, to opt out of the rule for the future. Although changes in customary international law can occur through practice, they take a certain amount of time for dissentient states to disagree. The accumulation of cases against such a rule of law can lead the UN General Assembly to vote against or abstain from relying on customary law. The following cases shed light on how these criteria have played out in the real world.

In 1951, the *Fisheries Case* in the North Sea between the United Kingdom and Norway set a precedent in international law. In 1935, Norwegian authorities set aside an exclusive zone for Norwegian fisheries. In 1951, the UK government presented its case before the ICJ to determine whether such delimitation by the Norwegian government was in accordance with international law. After a careful investigation and a vote of ten to two, the Court found that Norway's 1935 decree was not contrary to international law.

The coastal zone in dispute is a mountainous region exceeding 1,500 kilometers, with islets, reefs, fjords, and bays. Within the coastal zone are shallow banks which have a plethora of fish. Inhabitants of the mainland and of the islands have derived their livelihoods from fishing these waters since time immemorial. The dispute between British and Norwegian fisherman had been taking place for three hundred years. However, British vessels with improved gear reappeared in the Norwegian coastal zone in 1906. Since then, both governments had tried to arrange agreements, but without success. The arrest of British trawlers in 1948 and 1949 prompted the UK government to present its case before the ICJ.[2]

The question in judgment was whether the lines stipulated within the 1935 decree were produced in accordance with international law. Norway argued that the UK relied on its own system of delimitation, contrary to international law. The Court found that the 1935 delimitation decreed by Norway did not violate international law, based on the fact of long usage. The Court found that Norway had relied on the historic title of the Lopphavet, that is, the divergence between the baseline and the land formations, since the seventeenth century.

American law professors analyzed this case in detail to flesh out its underpinnings. A law professor at Vanderbilt University, Jonathan Charney (1942–2002), argued that the majority judgment was silent on the persistent objector rule (Charney 1994). Since some members of the Court held that general international law gave preferential rights to coastal states, recalling the persistent objector rule would be significant in this case. The persistent objector rule is said to provide states with a way out from the otherwise universal binding force of customary international law. It establishes that if a state persistently objects to a newly emerging norm of customary international law during the formation of that norm, then the objecting state is exempt from the norm once it crystallizes into law. Similarly, Northwestern University law professor Anthony D'Amato (1937–2018) argued, "In any event the ten-mile rule would appear to be inapplicable to Norway, inasmuch as she has always opposed any attempt to apply it to the Norwegian coast" (Mendelson 1998, 229) D'Amato suggests that this observation was about a special customary rule. Indeed, Charney and D'Amato agreed that the *Norway-UK Fisheries* case pivoted around customary international law. This case highlights the relationship between the persistent objector rule and customary international law.

According to American Israeli lawyer and judge Theodore Meron, customary law has played and continues to play an important role in the formation of international humanitarian law (Meron 1996). He highlights the *Tadić* case in 1995, dealing with Yugoslavia in 1991. Meron agrees with Judge

[2] For a review of this case, see Teruo J. Kobayashi, *The* Anglo-Norwegian Fisheries *Case of 1951 and the Changing Law of the Territorial Sea* (Gainesville: University of Florida Press, 1965).

George Aldrich (1932–2019) that the conflicts in Yugoslavia were international, thereby falling under the jurisdiction of the International Military Tribunal. Even though several internal wars took place within former Yugoslavia, many violations were made against international humanitarian law. Therefore, when classified as international crimes, Meron asserts, "The clarification of customary law on this subject is the most important normative contribution of the decision" (Meron 1996, 239).

Prior to the *Tadić* case, three cases contributed to the formation of customary international humanitarian law: *Trial of Major War Criminals*,[3] *United States v. von Leeb*,[4] and the *Nicaragua* case.[5] Each of the respective tribunals had to decide how to interpret Articles 1 and 3 from the Geneva Convention.[6] As in *Tadić*, instead of looking into the practice of states, the courts considered the *opinio juris*. So that the Hague Tribunal could lay to rest *ex post facto* challenges to its subject matter jurisdiction, it resorted to customary law, thereby interpreting Article 3 of the Geneva Convention. Consequently, the court relied heavily on *opinion juris* or general principles of humanitarian law. From a methodological standpoint, this approach was

[3] Trial of German Major War Criminals, 1946, CMD. 6964, Misc. No. 12, at 65.

[4] 11 Trials of War Criminals Before the Nuremberg Military Tribunals Under Control Council Law No. 10, at 462, 533–35 (1948).

[5] Military and Paramilitary Activities in and against Nicaragua (*Nicar. v. US*), Merits, ICJ Rep. 14, 114, ¶¶ 218–20 (June 27, 1986).

[6] Article 1: The High Contracting Parties undertake to respect and to ensure respect for the present Convention in all circumstances.

ART. 3: In the case of armed conflict not of an international character occurring in the territory of one of the High Contracting Parties, each Party to the conflict shall be bound to apply, as a minimum, the following provisions:

1) Persons taking no active part in the hostilities, including members of armed forces who have laid down their arms and those placed *hors de combat* by sickness, wounds, detention, or any other cause, shall in all circumstances be treated humanely, without any adverse distinction founded on race, colour, religion or faith, sex, birth or wealth, or any other similar criteria.
   To this end, the following acts are and shall remain prohibited at any time and in any place whatsoever with respect to the above-mentioned persons:
   a) violence to life and person, in particular murder of all kinds, mutilation, cruel treatment and torture;
   b) taking of hostages;
   c) outrages upon personal dignity, in particular humiliating and degrading treatment;
   d) the passing of sentences and the carrying out of executions without previous judgment pronounced by a regularly constituted court, affording all the judicial guarantees which are recognized as indispensable by civilized peoples.
2) The wounded and sick shall be collected and cared for.

An impartial humanitarian body, such as the International Committee of the Red Cross, may offer its services to the Parties to the conflict.

The Parties to the conflict should further endeavor to bring into force, by means of special agreements, all or part of the other provisions of the present Convention.

The application of the preceding provisions shall not affect the legal status of the Parties to the conflict.

more akin to the domain of human rights than to any other field of international law.

The general customary principle in international humanitarian law covers issues such as the protection of civilian populations; distinction or discrimination; necessity and proportionality; proscriptions on the means and methods of warfare, including prohibited weapons; and the extension of the rules and principles of international law to civil wars (Meron 1996, 240). The Hague Tribunal utilized various sources to determine customary law and practice. However, the Tribunal declared that those sources are not always reliable:

> When attempting to ascertain State practice with a view to establishing the existence of a customary rule or a general principle, it is difficult, if not impossible, to pinpoint the actual behaviour of the troops in the field for the purpose of establishing whether they in fact comply with, or disregard, certain standards of behaviour. This examination is rendered extremely difficult by the fact that not only is access to the theatre of military operations normally refused to independent observers (often even to the ICRC) but information on the actual conduct of hostilities is withheld by the parties to the conflict; what is worse, often recourse is had to misinformation with a view to misleading the enemy as well as public opinion and foreign Governments. In appraising the formation of customary rules or general principles one should therefore be aware that, on account of the inherent nature of this subject-matter, reliance must primarily be placed on such elements as official pronouncements of States, military manuals, and judicial decisions. (Rosenne 1985, 614–16; Meron 1996, 240)

This declaration is directly applicable to the conflict in the Middle East between Israel and Hamas, which was triggered by Hamas operatives on October 7, 2023. While misinformation on social media is abundant, none of that is relevant in the court of law. What the Hague tribunal relies on are the aforementioned sources.

A case that is often cited to exemplify customary international law is the *Asylum* case dealing with Colombia and Peru. Colombia claimed that a regional custom existed, entitling a Peruvian political opponent, Haya de la Torre, to safe conduct (ICJ 1950, 266, at 277). As evidence of this claim, Colombia presented various treaties to which Peru was not a party, but which sought and granted diplomatic asylum. The ICJ observed that "[t]he Party which relies on a [regional or local] custom of this kind must prove that this custom is established in such a manner that it has become binding on the other Party" (Mendelson 1998, 250). Since Peru did not accept this custom, the Court rejected Colombia's claims. Indeed, the Court held that there was not a sufficient uniformity of practice regarding diplomatic asylum to warrant the conclusion that there was a rule of Latin American customary law that the country in whose embassy a fugitive had taken refuge could demand a safe conduct out for him (ibid., 228). Overall, as in the *Norway-UK Fisheries* case, the judgment here was based on the persistent objector rule.

In the *Asylum* case, the Court made a few observations in issuing its verdict. The Court added:

> But even if it could be supposed that such a custom existed between certain Latin-American States only, it could not be invoked against Peru which, far from having by its attitude adhered to it, has, on the contrary, repudiated it by refraining from ratifying the Montevideo Conventions of 1933 and 1939, which were the first to include a rule concerning the qualification of the offence in matters of diplomatic asylum. (ICJ 1950, 266, at 277–8)

The Court also observed:

> The facts brought to the knowledge of the Court disclose so much uncertainty and contradiction, so much fluctuation and discrepancy in the exercise of diplomatic asylum and in official views expressed on various occasions, there has been so much inconsistency in the rapid succession of conventions on asylum, ratified by some States and rejected by others, and the practice has been so much influenced by considerations of political expediency in the various cases, that it is not possible to discern in all this any constant and uniform usage, accepted as law, with regard to the alleged rule of unilateral and definitive qualification of the offence. (Mendelson 1998, 213)

One can draw two conclusions from these observations. The first is that the Court was willing to hear Colombia's claim dealing with a custom that only applied in Latin America. Moreover, one learns from the *Asylum* case that "density of practice" is required, that is, a "constant and uniform usage" (ICJ 1950, 266, at 277).

These three cases demonstrate how it takes time to build up constant and uniform usage. In the *Norway-UK Fisheries* case, Norway had established the coastal zone over three hundred years ago. Similarly, in the *Tadić* case, the rules and practices of international humanitarian law go back to the European reworkings of Roman law in the early modern period. The *Asylum* case is interesting because it highlights how the Court relied on *opinion juris* and the persistent objector rule to deny Colombia's claim of safe conduct for a political enemy. The eventual accumulation of cases can also contribute to the notion of *opinio juris*.

Conclusions

A comparative study between Jewish law and international law on the treatment of customary law leads us to various conclusions. Both legal systems lack a living legislator. Jewish law and international law are both nonterritorial. Most important, they both lack enforcing power. As such, they rely on trust in the rule of law. These aspects lead jurists within both legal systems to rely on customary law and practice. We can conclude that when Talmudic rabbis said, "Go and see what the people are doing," they were acting just as jurists of international law do today. The following chapters will explore how Jewish law experts have incorporated foreign legal practices and customs. They also examine how many aspects of international law have been influenced by Jewish law.

After having begun our analysis by exploring the commonalities between international law and Jewish law, Chapter 2 will explain why Jewish law sometimes incorporated local law and other times did not. The chapter offers a detailed history of Jewish law and local legal systems. Sometimes Jewish law incorporated some aspects of foreign legal systems, while at other times it rejected them; this chapter will justify those reasons.

Chapters 3 and 4 explore the areas of law that are inclined to be open to incorporation of international law. They explore when uniformity is important and when unique values of a subcommunity are worth preserving. They will explain why some areas of law are more open to international law and will identify those that are less open to incorporation.

Chapter 5 discusses cases where a detailed Jewish law conversation pivots around international law. This will entail a historical analysis from the sixteenth century until 1948. Chapter 6, examines the incorporation of international law within Jewish law after 1948. The discourse surveys four views: nonexistent or forced, hierarchical, interaction, and comparative law. Overall, this chapter highlights the Israeli rabbinic intellectual history as it relates to international law.

Chapter 7 pivots around interactions between the Jewish tradition and antisemitism in structured legal systems and how the Jewish tradition has responded to those systems. Here, we will distinguish between antisemitic and unfair legal systems. In doing so, we show how the Jewish tradition decides when a legal culture is unethical and incorporation is not possible.

Chapter 8 discusses how international law might process future developments in Jewish law and how Jewish law may interact with international law. The chapter will then reflect on what both legal systems can learn from each other and how they may work together. Finally, we will reflect on what Jewish law can learn from its interactions with international law and vice versa.

Bibliography

Primary Sources

Asylum Case, *Colombia v. Peru*, Judgment, 1950 I.C.J. 266 (Nov. 20).

Babylonian Talmud. Tractate Berachos Schottenstein Edition. Edited by R. Hersh Goldwurm, Yisroel Simcha Schorr, and Chaim Malinowitz. Rahway, NJ: Artscroll Mesorah Publications, 1997.

Jerusalem Talmud. *Pe'ah*. Edited by Jerome Schottenstein. Rahway, NJ: Artscroll Mesorah Publications, 2022.

Jerusalem Talmud. *Ma'aser Sheni*. Edited by Jerome Schottenstein. Rahway, NJ: Artscroll Mesorah Publications, 2022.

Koskenniemi, Martti. "Histories of International Law: Dealing with Eurocentrism." *Rechtsgeschichte* 19, no. 152 (2019): 152–76.

Secondary Sources

Anghie, Antony. *Imperialism, Sovereignty, and the Making of International Law*. Cambridge: Cambridge University Press, 2004.

Becker-Lorca, Arnulf. *Mestizo International Law: A Global Intellectual History, 1842–1933*. Cambridge: Cambridge University Press, 2014.

Brody, Robert. *The Geonim of Babylonia and the Shaping of Medieval Jewish Culture*. New Haven, CT: Yale University Press, 1998.

Broyde, Michael J. "Public and Private International Law from the Perspective of Jewish Law." In *The Oxford Handbook of Judaism and Economics*, edited by Aaron Levine. Oxford: Oxford University Press, 2012.

Charney, Jonathan I. "Progress in International Maritime Boundary Delimitation Law." *American Journal of International Law* 88, no. 2 (1994): 227–56. https://doi.org/10.2307/2204098.

Dorff, Elliot. "Judaism as a Religious Legal System." *Hastings Law Journal* 26, no. 6 (1978): 1331–60.

Elazar-DeMota, Yehonatan. "Nação Legal Consciousness and Its Contribution to the Seventeenth-Century Dutch Republic Debate on Slavery and the Slave Trade." PHD diss., University of Amsterdam, 2021.

International Court of Justice (ICJ). *Reports of Judgments, Advisory Opinions and Orders 1950.* The Hague, The Netherlands: ICJ, 1950.

Israel-Vleeschhouwer, Amos. "The Attitudes of Jewish Law Towards International Law: Analyzing the Jewish Legal Materials and Processes." PhD diss., Tel-Aviv University, 2011.

Kobayashi, Teruo J. *The* Anglo-Norwegian Fisheries *Case of 1951 and the Changing Law of the Territorial Sea.* Gainesville: University of Florida Press, 1965.

Koskenniemi, Martti. *The Politics of International Law.* Oxford: Hart, 2011.

Mendelson, Maurice H. *The Formation of Customary International Law.* Waardenburg, The Netherlands: Martinus Nijhoff, 1998.

Meron, Theodor. "The Continuing Role of Custom in the Formation of International Humanitarian Law." *The American Journal of International Law* 90, no. 2 (1996): 238–49.

Ouaknin, Marc-Alain. *The Burnt Book: Reading the Talmud.* Princeton, NJ: Princeton University Press, 1998.

Paz, Reut Yael. "Making It Whole: Hersch Lauterpacht's Rabbinical Approach to International Law." *Goettingen Journal of International Law* 4, no. 2 (2012): 417–45.

Rosenne, Shabtai. *The Law and Practice of the International Court of Justice.* Dordrecht, The Netherlands: Martinus Nijhoff, 1985.

Thirlway, Hugh. *The Sources of International Law.* Oxford: Oxford University Press, 2019.

Wood, Michael. "Second Report on Identification of Customary International Law." United Nations. https://digitallibrary.un.org/record/774305?ln=en&v=pdf.

Zelcer, Heshey. *A Guide to the Jerusalem Talmud.* Irvine, CA: Universal, 2002.

2

Jewish Law and Incorporation of Local Law: Theories of Why, What, and When

The Application of International Law within Jewish Law

Proposals for international law as a more robust and comprehensive legal system—a law for all peoples and nations—have recurred over the past sixty years, particularly with the creation of the United Nations following World War II. These proposals have gained much currency in recent decades as technological advances in transportation, telecommunications, and media have transformed the global economy, increasing the types of transactions available worldwide as well as the ability of individuals to participate. Many in the legal community now contend that the effects of globalization and the diminishing role of national boundaries require a more expansive system of international law, sometimes referred to as world law. These modern proposals argue not only that nations need to obey international law, but that international law should govern the conduct of each and every transaction, even between individuals, as long as they reside in different nations (Berman 1995).

The State of Israel, created in 1948, achieved secular legitimacy from the resolution passed by the United Nations the previous year calling for the establishment of a Jewish state in Palestine.[1] Despite this legitimacy, however (and with wonderful contemporary exceptions, such as relations with the United States and Canada), the Jewish encounter with secular law has been routinely harsh, leading one to question any unmoderated optimism about an expansive system of world law (Broyde 2002; Witte 2005, 143–85). International law did not serve as a serious obstacle to the Holocaust in

[1] G.A. Res. 181 (November 29, 1947). Indeed, Israel's own Declaration of Independence makes repeated reference to the authority of the UN resolution: "On the 29th November, 1947, the United Nations General Assembly passed a resolution calling for the establishment of a Jewish State in Eretz-Israel. . . . This recognition by the United Nations of the right of the Jewish people to establish their State is irrevocable. . . . Accordingly we . . . by virtue of our natural and historic right and on the strength of the resolution of the United Nations General Assembly, hereby declare the establishment of a Jewish State in Eretz-Israel, to be known as the State of Israel."

Jewish Law and International Law. Michael J. Broyde and Yehonatan Elazar-De Mota, Oxford University Press.
 DOI: 10.1093/9780197805275.003.0002

Europe eighty years ago, and even the most casual observer of international law senses that within the world community, the State of Israel has been a victim of vast discrimination over the past thirty years.

One can suggest that the glaring potential problem of expanded international law is that it might end up being merely another version of legal positivism and majoritarian rule, such that the decisions of the many or the powerful become the standards of the group and are imposed upon all. To borrow a term from US Supreme Court Justice Oliver Wendell Holmes, international law, like national and municipal law in many nations, would revert to being a "game according to the rules,"[2] without justice—both procedural and substantive—as its goal (Hand 1960, 306–7). Confident as one can be that the collective decisions of the global community would produce just results, the remembered Jewish experience of being an ethnoreligious minority in a vast society has hardly been overwhelmingly positive and has rarely inspired the Jewish community to believe that one can successfully put one's faith and trust in the just nature of one's neighbors. Nothing encountered in the past five, ten, or fifty years seems to mitigate such concerns.

This chapter lays the foundation to answer a basic question that reflects on the technical issues related to the applicability of international law proposals within Jewish law. In discussing how halakhah generally incorporates domestic (municipal) law, we can perhaps formulate a Jewish law view of world law. This chapter surveys the long and detailed history of why Jewish law sometimes incorporated local law and other times did not. It presents the four basic competing theories of incorporation used by Jewish law and explains the interesting history of incorporation.

Treaties in Jewish Law

The Jewish tradition maintains that in messianic times, there will *and should be* Gentiles—people who are not members of the Jewish faith (*b.Yebamoth* 24b). The existence of those who are not Jewish is not merely a concession to facts on the ground but part of the Jewish ideal, wherein all—Jew and Gentile

[2] As Judge Learned Hand recalled: "I remember once I was with [Justice Holmes]: it was a Saturday when the Court was to confer. It was before we had a motor car, and we jogged along in an old coupe. When we got down to the Capitol, I wanted to provoke a response, so as he walked off, I said to him: 'Well, sir, goodbye. Do justice!' He turned quite sharply and he said: 'Come here. Come here.' I answered: 'Oh, I know, I know.' He replied: That is not my job. My job is to play the game according to the rules'" (Hand 1960, 306–7).

alike—worship the single God differently and distinctly, each in their own mode of worship. Indeed, the Talmud insists that in messianic times, conversion into Judaism will not exist: Jews and Gentiles will peacefully coexist (ibid.).

Several fundamental insights derive from this formulation of the scope of the Jewish tradition. Especially important is the role of foreign law, particularly insofar as it regulates private international law in the Jewish tradition. Precisely because Jewish tradition does not insist that it be the exclusive source of law governing all of the world's inhabitants, Jewish law embraces doctrines of comity—substantive recognition of the inherent validity of legal rules and systems besides Jewish law—that are encapsulated in the interrelated group of doctrines of *dina demalkhuta dina* (the law of the land is law), *dinim* (law enforcement), and *din melekh* (the law of the monarch).[3] In fact, many rabbinic jurists find some connection between the obligation of Jews to obey *dinim* and the requirement to obey the secular law.[4] This finding is generally driven by liberal conditions doctrines in Jewish commercial law so that even conditions that might violate Jewish law are valid.

As a direct corollary of not thinking that all people ought to be Jewish, halakhah does not require that all people obey it. The rubrics of *dina demalkhuta dina*, *din melekh*, and *dinim* say to adherents of halakhah that there will be times and places—almost always outside ritual law—where Jewish law mandates that Jews obey a legal code besides Jewish law, and that, in certain situations, the external legal code can even supplant native Jewish law. The reason these doctrines are so strong in the Jewish tradition is obvious. If all people do not have to be Jewish and need not obey Jewish law, then other legal systems must then be valid. Consequently, Jews are called upon to respect and obey these legal systems when they correctly operate in their spheres.

Furthermore, and more to the point here, sometimes those other legal systems will regulate Jews and their conduct. For example, Jewish law maintains that secular courts and secular laws are the proper legal framework for

[3] See Maimonides (Rambam), Mishneh Torah, *Gezelah we-Abedah*, chap. 5; *Shulḥan Arukh, Ḥoshen Mishpaṭ*, 225, 369. *Minhag ha-soḥarim* is a distant cousin of these three doctrines and deals with laws as practiced, a related but different concept. Moreover, *minhag ha-soḥarim* is essentially contractual in nature, while these three are deeply structural.

[4] See, for example, Rashi to *Gittin* 9b. R. Meltzer, *Even ha-Azel, Nizke Mamon* 8:5 freely mixes as near synonyms the terms *dina demalkhuta dina, din melekh*, and *bene Noaḥ meṣubbim al ha-dinim* (Noahides are obligated in *dinim*) in a discussion about why a Jew must return property lost by another when such is required by secular law and not halakhah.

resolving disputes between Jews and Gentiles, and secular criminal law is the proper framework for punishing Jewish or Gentile criminals in the general society (Broyde 2007, 122–24). In yet dozens of other such examples, halakhah comfortably and ideally tells adherents that using secular law as the foundation for one's interactions with the general community is proper.

A more complex conversation among Jewish law authorities concerns the type of municipal legislation that may be implemented through *dina demalkhuta dina*. Three theories predominate, identified by the honorific names of the rabbis who proposed them. R. Yosef Karo (Maran) (1488–1575) rules that secular law is halakhically binding only to the extent that it directly affects the government's financial interests. Thus, secular laws imposing taxes or tolls would be valid under Jewish law, but laws for the general health and safety of society would not be (*Shulḥan Arukh, Ḥoshen Mishpaṭ* 369:6, 11). R. Moshe Isserles (Rama) (1530–1572) agrees that secular laws directly affecting the government's financial interests are binding but adds that secular laws that are enacted for the benefit of the people of the community are, as a general matter, effective under Jewish law (ibid.). In this model, all health and safety regulations would also be binding. R. Shabbatai ben Meir HaKohen (Shach) (1621–1662) disagrees with the Rama in one respect. He maintains that even if secular laws are enacted for the benefit of the community, they are not valid under Jewish law if they specifically contradict indigenous halakhic precepts (*Sifte Kohen* on *Shulḥan Arukh, Ḥoshen Mishpaṭ* 73:39).[5] Thus, general health and safety rules would be binding, but, for instance, Jewish law has a rule that rooftop railings must be about a meter high, while a secular law setting a lower height would not be halakhically valid (*Shulḥan Arukh, Ḥoshen Mishpaṭ* 427:1).

There is substantial debate among halakhic authorities as to which approach to follow (*Ḥelqath Ya'akob* 3:160).[6] Nevertheless, most contemporary authorities agree that, at least outside the State of Israel, the Rama's view should be applied, and such is the view of the four twentieth-century Ashkenazi deans of halakhah in the United States: R. Moshe Feinstein (1895–1986),[7] R. Yosef Eliyahu Henkin (1881–1973),[8] R. Joseph Soloveitchik

[5] Thus, for example, according to Shach, secular law can require that one return lost property in a case where halakhah permits but does not mandate that it be returned, while secular law cannot permit one to keep a lost object that the halakhah requires to be returned.

[6] See R. Shmuel Shilo, *Dina deMalkhuta Dina*, at 145–60, who lists authorities adopting the approach of either Shach or Yosef Karo.

[7] *Iggeroth Moshe, Ḥoshen Mishpaṭ* 2:62.

[8] *Teshuboth Ibra* 2:176

(1903–1993),[9] and R. Yoel Teitelbaum (1887–1979).[10] In this view, almost all applications of secular law are valid under Jewish law.[11] Ḥakham [12] José Faur (1934–2020), professor of law and the Talmud, maintained: "The governments serving as the host of the Jewish people are not the supreme legal and political authority of the Jews. The rules and legislations governing the Jewish people are not the fiat of the authority of that country over them, but of negotiations and accords arrived at by two equally autonomous parties" (Faur 1982, 326). In agreement with the Maran, Faur asserts that while Jews are in exile and live in their respective host countries, they nevertheless have political and legal autonomy.

Within the domain of treaty law, Jewish law presents four overarching theories: the Rambam (Moses Maimonides, 1135–1204), the Radbaz (R. David ben Solomon Eben Abi Zimra, 1479–1573),[13] the Ralbag (R. Levi ben Gershon, 1288–1344), and the Radak (R. David Kimhi, 1160–1235). In his *Mishneh Torah*, the Rambam codifies the law of treaties, "It is prohibited to breach treaties" (Maimonides, *Hil. Melakhim* 6:3). The Radbaz comments on this law, "This is learned from the incident of the Gibeonites, since breaking one's treaties is a profanation of God's name" (Abi Zimra 1882; Broyde 2005, 83). This rationale agrees with R. Moshe ben Naḥman's (Ramban or Nachmanides) commentary on the treaty between Jacob and Laban, where he argues that God oversees treaties. In the case between Joshua and the Gibeonites, even if the treaty were entered on false pretenses, violating it would constitute a profanation of God's name. The Egyptian Gaon, exegete, and philosopher Se'adya Al-Fayyumi (882–942) emphasized

[9] This is indicated in *Nefesh ha-Rab* 267–69, and has been confirmed by many other sources as well.

[10] See *Dibere Yoel* 1:147.

[11] See also Shilo, *Dina deMalkhuta Dina*, at 157, who asserts that most halachic authorities adopt the Rama's view and lists many of these authorities. A contemporary, R. Menashe Klein, questions whether *dina demakchuta dina* applies in the United States, and his view would be the same of world law. He states: "[The applicability of the principle of] *dina demalkhuta dina* in our times, when there is no king but rather what is called democracy needs further clarification. As I already explained the position cited in the name of Rivash quoting Rashba, one does not accept *dina demalkhuta dina* except where the law originates with the king" (R. Menashe Klein, *Mishneh Halakhoth* 6:277).

Despite R. Klein's views, it is important to note that most authorities have held that *dina demalkhuta dina* does not apply only to laws issued by a king, as noted by R. Obadia Yosef in *Yeḥaweh Da'ath* 5:64: "Even in a nation not ruled by a king, but rather by a government chosen by its citizens, the general principle of *dina demalkhuta dina* applies." Moreover, a number of preeminent Jewish law authorities have specifically held that *dina demalkhuta dina* applies within the United States, and they have not found any problems caused by the democratic form of government. See references to R. Feinstein, R. Henkin, R. Soloveitchik, and R. Teitelbaum above.

[12] Wise one. Title used among Sephardic Jews for rabbinic scholars.

[13] R. David ben Solomon Eben Abi Zimra, also known as the Radbaz, was born in Spain in 1479 and passed away in Safed, Israel, in 1573.

the oversight of the divine influence when King Saul ordered the assassination of the priests and the Gibeonites at Nob (1 Sam. 22:1–23; Deut. 29:15; Al-Fayyumi 1960). The Israelites broke the treaty after four hundred years of its being in force. Consequently, they experienced famine: "During the reign of David, there was famine for three successive years; so, David sought the face of the Eternal One. The Eternal One said, 'It is on account of Saul and his blood-stained house; it is because he put the Gibeonites to death"' (2 Sam. 21:1). The Ralbag, a French Rabbi and commentator, claimed that the nations of the world would view the breaking of this treaty as evidence that the Jewish nation did not believe in God (Gershon, Josh. 9:5). A Spanish Rabbi and grammarian, the Radak, suggested that lest the nations think that the nation of Israel violates treaties, all treaties should be kept, no matter what (Kimḥi, Josh. 9:5).

In summary, treaties in the Jewish tradition are sacred because God is present; a violation of a treaty is tantamount to causing God's name to be trampled upon.

Whatever the precise basis of the obligation to honor treaties, each of these theories presupposes that treaties are basically binding according to Jewish law, even when they contradict Jewish law.[14] It is only in the case of an obvious breach of treaty by one party that the second party may decline to honor it. Thus, Jewish law accepts that when a war is over, the peace that is agreed to is binding. Indeed, even in a situation where there is some unnoticed fraud in enacting or ratifying a treaty, it is still in force.

Treaties Binding on Non-Jews

Jewish law conceptualizes a universal law for non-Jews through the binding nature of treaties. In essence, Jewish law recognizes seven basic frameworks of universal commandments as part of a universal law code; the final commandment is the obligation to create *dinim* (i.e., law enforcement or a system of justice).[15]

[14] This is also the unstated assumption of the Gemara, *b.Gittin* 45b–46a, which seeks to explain why treaties made in error might still be binding.

[15] The Talmud recounts seven categories of prohibition: idol worship, taking God's name in vain, murder, prohibited sexual activity, theft, eating flesh from a living animal, and the obligation to enforce laws. As is obvious from this list, these seven commandments are generalities which contain within them many specifications. Thus, for example, the single categorical prohibition of sexual promiscuity includes both adultery and the various forms of incest (*b.Sanh.* 56a). According

Medieval rabbinic jurists present two different interpretations of this obligation. The Rambam rules that the obligation to create *dinim* requires only that the enumerated universal laws be enforced in practice and that society need not create a more general universal law (although, presumably, it may). He states:

> How are all obligated to create laws? They must create courts and appoint judges in every province to enforce these six commandments . . . for this reason the inhabitants of Shekhem [the city] were liable to be killed[16] since Shekhem [the person] kidnapped[17] [Dina], and the inhabitants saw and knew this and did nothing.[18]

According to the Rambam, every society bears an obligation to create and enforce the universal precepts of law that halakhah holds to be binding upon non-Jews.

However, the Ramban argues with this formulation and understands the obligations of *dinim* to be much broader. According to his postulation, *dinim* encompass not only the obligations of society to enforce particular regulations of the other six Noahide precepts but it also commands society to create general rules of law governing fraud, overcharging, repayment of debts, and the like.[19] Furthermore, the Ramban presents the dispute as to what substantive laws Noahides are supposed to adopt. In his responsa, the Rama states that according to the Ramban, in those areas of *dinim* where non-Jews are supposed to create laws, they are obligated to incorporate Jewish law into Noahide law unless it is clear contextually that doing so is inappropriate.[20] Most authorities reject this interpretation and accept either the Rambam's ruling or that of the Ramban. Therefore, those rules created under the rubric of *dinim* need only be generally fair and not identical to Jewish law.[21] One cannot find even a single medieval Jewish legal authority

to R. Shmuel b. Ḥofni, thirty specific commandments are included. See generally appendix to *Encyclopedia Talmudith* 3:394–96.

[16] See Gen. 34.

[17] As to why the Rambam uses the word *gazal* (stole) to describe abduction, see *b.Sanh.* 55a and *Ḥatam Sofer, Yoreh Deah* 19.

[18] See Rambam, *Laws of Kings* 9:14.

[19] Commentary of the Ramban to Gen. 34:14.

[20] *Teshuboth ha-Rama* 10. His ruling is also accepted by *Ḥatam Sofer, Ḥoshen Mishpaṭ* 91 (as well as *Likutim* 14) and R. Ya`akov Lorberbaum (of Lissa), *Naḥalaht Ya'aqob (Teshuboth)* 2:3.

[21] See R. Yitzchak Elchanan Spektor, *Naḥal Yiṣḥaq, Ḥoshen Mishpaṭ* 91; R. Avraham Isaiah Karelitz, *Ḥazon Ish* on *Hil. Melakhim* 10:10 and *Baba Qamma* 10:3; R. Isser Zalman Meltzer,

who accepts the ruling of the Rama, but one can find many who explicitly disagree.[22]

In theory, world law would be a fulfillment of this obligation according to most medieval *poseqim* (halakhic decisors), both in the view of the Rambam and in most understandings of the Ramban. Jewish law could well imagine the creation of world law in public international law, grounded in reciprocal treaties and mandated by society to fulfill the obligation to create an ordered and just society. If properly organized and enforced by the world's many nations, treaties to impose international law would be entirely valid within the Jewish legal framework. Rabbinic jurists would agree to such a proposal to universalize justice. Indeed, a claim could be made that such has happened already with regard to the international rules of war, where many *poseqim* rule that international law governs these matters, not Jewish law.[23]

Treaties and Torah

Public international law is essentially a system of treaties and agreements and can be readily analyzed within the Jewish legal framework for international

Eben ha-Azel, Ḥobel wu-Maziq 8:5; R. Yechiel Michel Epstein, *Arukh ha-Shulhan he-Atid, Melakhim* 79:15; R. Naphtali Tzvi Yehuda Berlin, *Ha'ameq She'elah* 2:3; R. Avraham Yitzchak Kook, *Eṣ Hadar* 38, 184; R. Tzvi Pesach Frank, *Har Ṣebi, Oraḥ Ḥayim* vol. II, *Kuntres Mile di-Berakhoth* 2:1; R. Obadia Yosef, *Yeḥaweh Da`ath* 4:65; R. Yitzchak Ya`akov Weiss, *Minḥath Yiṣḥaq* 4:52:3. For a more complete analysis of this issue, see Nahum Rakover, "Jewish Law and the Noahide Obligation to Preserve Social Order," *Cardozo Law* Review 12 (1991): 1073, and app. 1 & 2 at 1098–1118.

22 Most authorities do not accept the Ramban's opinion. See, for example, Rambam, *Hil. Melachim* 10:10; *Teshuboth ha-Ritva*, no. 14 (quoted in *Beth Yosef, Ḥoshen Mishpaṭ* 66:18); Tosaphoth, *b.Erubin* 62a s.v. *ben Noah.* The comments of R. Yosef Albo are also worth citing: "One finds although Torah law and Noahide law differ in the details, the principles used are the same, since they derive from the same source. Moreover, the two systems exist concurrently: while Jews have Torah law, the other peoples abide by the Noahide code" (*Sefer ha-'Iqarim* 1:25).

23 There is quite a literature on the question whether the State of Israel needs to conduct itself merely by international law or also in accordance with halakhah. R. Shaul Yisraeli demonstrates that basic framework for the halakhah of war is not found in Jewish law, but instead in (secular) international law; see R. Shaul Yisraeli, *'Amud ha-Yemini* chap. 16. This view is predicated on the famous comments of the Netziv in *Ha`ameq Dabar*, Bereshith 9:5 and supported by Tosaphoth *Shebu'oth* 35b, s.v. *Katla Ḥad*, as well as R. Avraham Kahana-Shapiro, *Debar Abraham*, 1:11 and R. Menachem Zemba, *Zera Abraham* 24. For a survey of the contemporary *poseqim* on this topic, see R. Ya'acov Blidstein, "The Treatment of Hostile Civilian Populations: The Contemporary Halakhic Discussion In Israel," *Israel Studies* 1, no. 2 (1996): 27–44. His final conclusions are not beyond dispute. This literature, too, represents the incorporation of international law into Jewish law.

agreements (Broyde 2005, 82). The Hebrew Bible is replete with treaties between individuals and groups. The Hebrew equivalent is *berith*, stemming from the Akkadian verb *biritu* (to bind). Establishing treaties within that context required the cutting up of a specific number of animals and then both parties walking through the parts. This act conveyed the idea that anyone who violated a treaty would suffer the same fate as the animals involved in the ritual.

The Torah records the first treaty between two families after Jacob ran away from Laban's home with his family and property. After having cheated Jacob many times, Laban wanted to secure the welfare of his daughters under Jacob's care and protect his interests from potential retaliation. The Ramban, in his commentary on the treaty between Jacob and Laban, explains Laban's words, "And let the covenant be for a witness between us, for he who violates it should be cursed with all the curses of the covenant" (Ramban, Gen. 31:34).[24] The Ramban's rationale recalls the Akkadian cultural idea of violating a treaty, resulting in curses. After swearing an oath and entering a covenant, the parties offered sacrifices and made a great feast. The Ramban comments that perhaps it was customary for the parties involved in a treaty to break bread, as a sign of love and companionship (ibid.). Furthermore, the Ramban comments on why the pillar was called *Miṣpeh*, "The Eternal One will *yiṣeph* [watch]." This formulation indicates that a *berith* invites divine supervision:

> Come, let's make a treaty, you, and me, and let something be our witness. So, Jacob took a stone, set it up as a sacred pillar, and said to his relatives, "Gather stones." So they took stones, made a mound, and ate there near the mound. Laban called it *Jegar-sahadutha,* but Jacob called it *Galeed.* Laban said, "This mound is our witness today," and, therefore, he too named it *Galeed.* He also named it *Miṣpeh*, because he said, "The Lord will observe both of us when we are separated from each other. If you treat my daughters badly and if you marry other women, though we aren't there, know that God observed our witness." Laban said to Jacob, "Here is this mound and here is the sacred pillar that I've set up for us. This mound and the sacred pillar are witnesses that I won't travel beyond this mound and that

[24] Moshe ben Naḥman was born in Girona, Spain, in 1194. He wrote a commentary on the Torah which usually contradicts the Rashi's commentary. After moving to the Holy Land, he passed away in Acre in 1270.

> you won't travel beyond this mound and this pillar to do harm. The God of Abraham and the God of Nahor will keep order between us." So, Jacob gave his word in the name of the awesome one of his father Isaac. (Common English Bible, Gen. 31:43–48)

The monument erected by Jacob and Laban served as a physical reminder of the treaty they established between their respective families. This example parallels how treaties are established within the framework of international law—the respective parties meet, reach an agreement, stipulate the conditions, and ratify the treaty.

Another example of a biblical treaty is between Jacob's family and Shekhem. After Jacob's daughter (Dinah) was raped by Shekhem, Hamor (father of Shekhem) insisted, "Arrange marriages with us: give us your daughters and take our daughters for yourselves. Live with us. The land is available to you: settle down, travel through it, and buy property in it" (Gen. 34:8). The people of Shekhem accepted the terms, including circumcision of all their males. Dinah's brothers were upset with the decision and contrived a plan to assassinate all the males while they were weak from the circumcision. After the brothers carried out their plan, Jacob expressed disdain toward Shimon and Levi, the masterminds behind the assassinations: "You've put me in danger by making me offensive to those who live here in the land, to the Canaanites and the Perizzites. I have only a few men. They may join forces, attack me, and destroy me, me and my household" (Common English Bible, Gen. 34:30). Jacob was worried on two accounts: for violating the treaty and for creating enmity and inviting warfare from his neighbors. The sixteenth-century Italian Jewish commentator R. Obadiah Sforno (c. 1475–1550) explains, "The local population would accuse us of having gone back on our agreement after the people of Shekhem had circumcised themselves" (Sforno, Gen. 34:30). In other words, violating a treaty in the land of Canaan could lead to war.

One of the most important treaties in the Hebrew Bible takes place between the nation of Israel and the Gibeonites. After the Israelite conquest of Canaan, the Gibeonites disguised themselves and came before Joshua to make a treaty. They presented themselves as coming from a faraway nation. "Joshua made peace with them. He made a treaty with them to protect their lives. The leaders of the community made a solemn pledge to them" (Common English Bible, Josh. 9:15–16).

Examples from the Nação

One can find clear instances where local domestic law was incorporated into Jewish law in the eighteenth-century responsa literature of Amsterdam's Portuguese Jewish community, or the Nação. Under the auspices of the *Shulḥan Arukh*, the Nação excelled in international commerce for over two centuries. This legal system, like international law, had no police force but was based solely on trust and goodwill. Nacão merchants and non-Jews conducted international business through the legal mechanisms of power of attorney and notaries. However, business ventures among Nação members were stipulated according to the laws contained within the *Shulḥan Arukh*. Anyone who violated the rules fell under the jurisdiction of the local Jewish tribunal. The Talmud Torah Eẓ Ḥaim Portuguese Jewish community in Amsterdam was granted political-religious autonomy to adjudicate cases by the *parnassim* (trustees) of the Mahamad, under the counsel of the *ḥakhamim* (jurists) of the *beth din*.

All disputes within the community were presented before two or three members of the Mahamad. They would listen to litigants and follow the procedures of the halakhah when hearing cases. When confronted with complex cases, they would consult the *beth din*, which comprised three *ḥakhamim*. The Mahamad would summon the litigants to appear before them. If the defendant did not appear, he or she would be fined six guilders. The defendant would be summoned a second time, after which the Mahamad would issue a ruling (Grausz 2019, 239). These rulings were recorded in *Livro de citaçoes e resoluçoes* (Book of summons and resolutions), covering the period from 1717 to 1816. Cases that were referred to the *beth din* were often assigned to students at the Yesiba Eẓ Ḥaim in the form of legal responsa. These cases were recorded in the fifteen volumes of the *Peri Eẓ Ḥaim She'eloth u-Teshuboth*. An in-depth legal analysis of three cases offers insight into how Nacão jurists from the School of Eẓ Ḥaim and merchants developed private international law by subscribing to halakhah, via the *Shulḥan Arukh*.

The first case deals with a partnership between two members of the community who engage in long-distance trade. This responsum was written in 1731 by Ishac ben Shelomọ Saruco, under the guidance of Ḥakham Ishac Haim Abendana de Brito. Abendana de Brito was the head of the Eẓ Ḥaim Talmudic academy at that time. He helped organize the collection of legal decisions in the *Peri Eẓ Ḥaim* responsa from 1732 to 1733. Abendana de Brito functioned as the *Ab beth din* (chief justice), with judges Ḥakham Solomon Ayllon and Ḥakham David Israel Athias. His student, Ishac Saruco, was born to Shelomo Saruco in Hamburg (1686) and passed away in Amsterdam in 1762.

The case involves Dan and Naftali, generic names used to protect the identities of the real parties. They enter a partnership agreement based on certain stipulations (*tena'im*) and a *shebu'ah* (oath). Jewish law and jurisprudence recognize five types of oaths: false oaths, vain oaths, oaths about deposits, oaths about testimony, and oaths administered by judges. This case refers to *shebu'ah piqadon* (an oath about deposits). Regarding this type of oath, Moses Maimonides (Rambam, 1135–1204) codifies that anyone who has in his possession money belonging to another person, whether a deposit or a loan, or who has robbed or exploited him, or who has found a lost article of his and failed to restore it, should return it when the person demands it (*Mishneh Torah*, *Shebuoth* 1:9). Halakhah further stipulates that in a case of a deliberate default, the defendant must not only return the principal value of the deposit but also an additional one-fourth of the value (*ḥomesh*). This type of oath requires the presence of two trustworthy witnesses and placing one's hand on a holy article, such as a Torah scroll. Indeed, the violation of an oath constitutes the destruction of the divine name of God (Exod. 20:7). When Nacão merchants entered into business agreements, they would go before members of the Mahamad, who would record the oral agreements in their records.[25] Since this business venture involved the use of stipulations, it required the deliberation of the *beth din*.

To decide the case of Dan and Naftali, Ishac ben Shelomo Saruco consults several legal sources, including the Babylonian Talmud and the Ba'ale Tosaphoth (thirteenth-century Franco-German glossators of the Talmud), the Rif (Isaac HaCohen Alfasi 1013–1103), the *Mishneh Torah* (Rambam), the Rosh (Asher ben Yeḥiel 1250–1327), the Tur (Jacob ben Asher c. 1269–c. 1340), the Maharashdam (Samuel de Medina 1505–1589), and the Leḥem Mishneh (Abraham de Boton c. 1560–c. 1605). Saruco consults the Talmud and its commentaries to present the source of law concerning *shebu'ah piqadon*. Implementing the classic Sephardic legal approach, he consults the Rambam first. Thereafter, he consults the medieval and early modern legal

[25] An example of such a case took place in 1723 between Jacob Gomes Costa and Mordehay Abenatar, who went before the Mahamad and entered a business deal involving a ship named Margarita (G.A. Res. 334, at 875).Thanks to Manon Moerman at Maastricht University for providing this source.

commentaries which explain the Rambam's codification of Talmudic law. He bases his conclusions on the majority opinion of the Sephardic jurists.

The question to the case goes as follows:

> Dan and Naftali enter a business relationship, based on an oath with two conditions (according to halakhah) that during the whole time of the partnership, they will not involve anyone else, and that they will not engage in gambling. They sent merchandise to an island and suffered financial loss. After some time, Dan breached one of the conditions of the contract and Naftali heard about it. Naftali requests Dan to pay half of the business debt. Dan refuses, arguing that since he breached the oath, he is not part of the partnership. Naftali argues that Dan only breached one of the conditions, therefore, he must pay half of the debt incurred. What is the law? (Meldola 1767a, 90)[26]

Saruco begins by explaining the question. He identifies two issues that must be resolved, namely, whether the partnership was annulled due to Dan's actions and whether Dan is required to pay full damages due to a breach of contract. Saruco explains that the first issue is simple according to halakhah, as the laws of contractual agreements are very clear: if any of the conditions of the stipulations are not met, the partnership is annulled. He further elucidates that from the moment that Dan breaches the contract, Naftali is no longer bound to the solemnity of the oath. Ultimately, Saruco decides the verdict in favor of Naftali, so that Dan must pay half of the damages incurred as a result of a breach of contract.

Saruco's responsum is an exemplary case involving the intersection of private international law with commercial law, because the partners made their agreements in Amsterdam but engaged in business transactions in another territory. Since they made their contractual agreements according to halakhah, only one jurisdiction and one law governed the activities of Nacão merchants. The jurisdiction lies with the *parnassim* and the *beth din* of the Kahal Kadosh Talmud Torah Eẓ Ḥaim.

This case reveals that the Mahamad could not arbitrate or mediate, requiring a legal decision from the *beth din*. The *beth din* can facilitate a *pesharah* (agreement), offer a *berirah*, or issue a *pesaq* (rabbinical decision). Saruco's explanation of halakhah demonstrates a case of *berirah* (arbitral

[26] Translated by Yehonatan Elazar-DeMota.

sentence) in Jewish jurisprudence. The legal analysis deals with a clarification of halakhah, as opposed to a *pesaq*, which is issued for cases without legal precedents. Overall, the legal mechanisms implemented here afforded the two business partners a way to resolve their conflicts without the need for international arbitration or litigation.

Jewish Law and a Case of Piracy

Our second case deals with international commerce, where one member of the Nação grants another member power of attorney to take care of his merchandise. This responsum was written on the twenty-third day of the month of Nisan, in the year 1760 by Ishac ben Yahacob Henriques Faro, shortly after the passing of the late Ḥakham Ishac Haim Abendana de Brito (1760). At the end of his responsum, Henriques Faro writes many words of praise in honor of his teacher. After Abendana's death, the position of *Ab beth din* remained vacant for about two years. In 1762, Solomon Salem (born at Adrianople 1717–1781) came to Amsterdam from Sofia, presiding as chief justice until his death ("Jewishencyclopedia.com," Amsterdam).

This case uses the generic names Reuben and Shimon to conceal the identity of the litigants. Reuben granted power of attorney to Shimon to take care of his merchandise on an island. This island was probably located in the West Indies, where the Nação had trading posts and communities. Reuben decided to assign Shimon as his agent instead of an insurance company, thereby taking advantage of Shimon's social influence at the location of the business. Most likely, Reuben wanted a trustworthy member of the Nacão to take care of his property, since Jewish ethics requires that a *shaliaḥ* (agent) be a member of the covenant (*b.Meẓia* 71b).[27] The Rambam codifies that a *shaliaḥ* can act as the principal in every sense to fulfill their duties. He also adds that the principal doesn't need to perform a *qinyan* (act of acquisition to transfer ownership) or have two witnesses present; an oral declaration suffices (*Mishneh Torah*, *Sheluḥin wu-Shuttafin* 1:1). This type of legal mechanism assumes that there is trust and goodwill between the parties involved, so that neither a written record nor witnesses are required.

[27] The Sages also derive: "Just as you, . . . who appoint agents, are members of the covenant [Jews], so too, your agents must be members of the covenant."

As Reuben's agent, Shimon was responsible for the merchandise. However, the misfortune of piracy befell the ship, and Shimon lost Reuben's property. When Reuben heard of it, he presented his claim before the *beth din*. Shimon claimed that he was not liable on the grounds of being *anus* (under duress due to *force majeure*). The only reason Reuben may have a claim was because of the issue of intent at the moment of granting a power of attorney. If Shimon assumed total responsibility, including in cases of *force majeure*, then he would be liable to pay damages; otherwise, he would be free. Indeed, this case required deliberation from the *beth din*.

Henriques Faro consults a few legal sources: the Babylonian Talmud and the Rashi (Shelomo Yiṣḥaqi 1040–1105), the Rambam, and the *Beth Yosef* and *Shulḥan Arukh*. Henriques Faro begins his legal analysis by citing a relevant passage in the Babylonian Talmud (*b.Gittin* 73b).[28] The passage in question determines the legal parameters of *onesuth* (cases of *force majeure*) within business transactions. Thus, accidents that are unavoidable and uncommon

[28] 'There was a certain man who sold land to another, and he accepted upon himself the responsibility for any unavoidable accident that might happen to the land. In such a case he would reimburse the buyer for the damage. In the end they diverted a river into it, meaning the government decided to make a new canal through the land that he sold. The buyer came before Rab 'ena to lodge a claim. Rab 'ena said to the seller: Go pacify him, that is, reimburse him, as you accepted upon yourself responsibility for any unavoidable accident that might happen. Rab Aḥa bar Taḥalifa disagreed and said to Rab 'ena: It is an uncommon, unavoidable accident, and the condition of the sale should not apply in such a case. The matter was circulated, as this ruling was never finalized, and it came before Raba. He said to them: It is an uncommon, unavoidable accident, and the seller should not have to pay. Rab 'ena raised an objection to Raba: Isn't it taught that if the husband said: This is your bill of divorce if I am not healed from this illness, and the house collapsed on him or a snake bit him then it is a valid bill of divorce? These cases are both uncommon, unavoidable accidents, yet the bill of divorce is valid. Raba said to him: But you can say an opposite inference from the first clause: If a husband says: This is your bill of divorce from today if I die from this illness, and the house collapsed on him or a snake bit him, then it is not a valid bill of divorce. Apparently, an uncommon, unavoidable accident is not included within his condition. If so, the inference from first clause of the *baraita* contradicts the inference from latter clause and it cannot be used to prove either opinion. Rab Aḥa of Difti said to Rab 'ena: And because there is a difficulty presented by the contradiction between the first clause of the *baraita* and the latter clause, can we no longer raise an objection from it? Seemingly, the challenge raised by Rab 'ena from the latter clause of the *baraita* is still valid. Rab 'ena said to him: Yes, Raba was correct. Since there is a difficulty presented by the contradiction between the first clause of the *baraita* and the latter clause, this *baraita* was never stated in the study hall and it is corrupted. As it is not possible to rely on this *baraita* one must follow reason, and the most reasonable interpretation is that his condition would not include an uncommon and unavoidable accident. It is related that Rab Pappa and Rab Huna, son of Rab Yehoshua, purchased sesame on the bank of the Malka River. They hired sailors to cross them to the other side of the river, and the sailors accepted upon themselves responsibility for any unavoidable accident that might occur. In the end the Malka River was dammed so that the merchandise could not be transported by river. The two Sages said to them: Hire donkeys and release them to us in order to transport the sesame, as you accepted upon yourself responsibility for any unavoidable accident that might arise. The two Sages came to court before Raba and he said to them: You white geese [*kake ḥivare*], referring to their long, white beards, who strip men of their cloaks. You are acting unfairly with the sailors. It is an uncommon, unavoidable accident for the Malka River to be dammed, and the sailors did not accept responsibility for this case.'

fall under this category. Raba (Abba ben Yosef bar Ḥama c. 280–352) rules that in business transactions where such circumstances occur, the seller is not held liable since the circumstances were beyond their control.

Henriques Faro continues his explanation of this passage by citing the Rif, who states that the law is in accordance with the legal opinion of Raba. This is crucial to Sephardic jurisprudence since, many times, the Talmud offers contradictory opinions without clear rulings (Fishman 2018, 131). Next, Henriques Faro cites Rashi's commentary to the Talmud to clarify that if the buyer accepts the condition of buying property or an item, they are liable for those things that are common and expected. Henriques Faro then cites the Rambam, who reinforces what Raba, the Rif, and the Rashi state (*Mishneh Torah, Mekhirah* 19:5). Accordingly, if a seller sold a property under the condition that the buyer would accept whatever might happen to it, even if a non-Jew stole it, the buyer would be responsible for the loss. However, "acts of God" or "acts of nature" are outside human control, thereby exempting the buyer from liabilities resulting from such causes (ibid., 19:6). Finally, Henriques Faro cites the *Beth Yosef* and the *Shulḥan Arukh*, stating that if a person buys movable or immovable property under the condition to accept whatever may happen, they are responsible for the loss, except for "acts of God" (*Shulḥan Arukh, Ḥoshen Mishpaṭ* 225).

All these jurists, spanning a millennium, agree with the legal decision in the Talmud by Raba. The author of our case decides that Shimon accepted the responsibility for anything that would befall the ship, including piracy, even though it was not implicit. Therefore, he must pay Reuben damages.

Piracy was a common occurrence in the early modern period. Pirates were considered such vile criminals that Dutch jurists decided that they should be sold into slavery (Bynkershoek 2008, 21).[29] Dutch jurist Simon van Leeuwen (1625–1682) stipulates in his commentary on Dutch-Roman law that anyone seizing property in the seas is to be punished as thieves (Leeuwen 1820, paras. 8–9). Ishac Henriques Faro alludes to a clause which was added to business agreements by Ḥakham Ishac Haim Abendana de Brito called, *poliza de seguros* [insurance policy], according to the custom of merchants and traders in Amsterdam:

[29] In 1661, the States-General gave orders to their admiral to sell as slaves all the pirates that he should take. The same thing was done in 1664. To the slavery of prisoners succeeded the custom of exchanging them according to their respective grades and ranks and detaining them until redeemed.

> We have accepted the liability for damages which result from crises at sea: fire, wind, storms, hurricanes, tempests, etc., also the captain's or the crew's evil schemes, or their involuntary mishaps, or any kind of accidents and potential loss of properties and merchandise, whether they come to mind or not, whether common occurrences or even uncommon occurrences, there is no difference. (Meldola 1767b, 97)[30]

This contractual agreement considers Dutch maritime law and practice regarding cases of *force majeure*. As such, piracy does not fall under the category of *force majeure* but is a human act that could be anticipated.

The question to the case goes as follows:

> Reuben has a lot of merchandise which he wanted to ship to an island. However, he did not want to send it with an insurance (*seguros*), rather with Shimon, who is wealthy and renowned in mercantile trade. Reuben made a written agreement with Shimon (according to the custom of the rabbis). Shimon accepted all responsibilities dealing with the ship or what may happen at sea. Reuben sent his merchandise with Shimon, and just two days after departing, something bad happened. There was mutiny on the ship and the captain was killed. All the booty was confiscated by the evil group. Reuben heard about it, then went to Shimon to receive his insurance. Shimon told Reuben that upon accepting the responsibilities for his merchandise, he did not have in mind this type of event, and that he is not responsible for it, because it is not included in rabbinic law. He claimed that this is a situation of *force majeure*, and therefore he was not liable for damages incurred. They went before the Jewish court to present the case. Who is the law in favor of in this case? (Meldola 1767b, 97)[31]

This responsum is an exemplary case where halakhah adopts Dutch maritime and trade law, leading the jurists of the Jewish community to draft business documents that reflect the legal conventions of their host country. Whenever the local Jewish community is faced with a situation not discussed in the Talmud or the legal codes, contemporary jurists may implement a *taqanah* (legal enactment) or *gezerah* (legal decree) to safeguard *el alma de*

[30] Translated by Yehonatan Elazar-DeMota. Ishac Henriques Faro states that this clause was translated from Dutch to Hebrew.

[31] Translated by Yehonatan Elazar-DeMota.

la ley (the spirit of the law). A *taqanah* is not permanent but usually lasts until the death of the jurist who enacted it or until the circumstances change (Abrahams 2010, 72–73). Ḥakham Abendana de Brito's formula for the *poliza de seguros* reveals this exercise of authority as chief justice to actualize halakhah according to the social circumstances and legal traditions of the time. Ergo, in eighteenth-century Amsterdam, the *ḥazaqah* (legal presumption) was that piracy was common and within human control to either prevent it or anticipate it.

Jewish Law and Inheritance

Our final case deals with estate and inheritance law, which intersects with private international law. This responsum was written by Moshe ben David Rodrigues Lopes under the guidance of Ḥakham Daniel Cohen de Azevedo on the eve of Sukkoth in the year 1795.[32] Ḥakham Daniel Cohen de Azevedo succeeded his father, Ḥakham David Cohen de Azevedo, in 1792. He passed away in 1823. The author of our responsum was born to David Rodrigues Lopes circa 1780.

Like the previous case, this one uses the generic names Reuben, Shimon, and Levi to conceal the identities of the parties involved. Apparently, Reuben and Shimon entered a business agreement in London. At some point, whether before or after the business venture with Shimon, Reuben married. He then decided to move to Amsterdam, but before doing so, he appointed Levi as a fiduciary of his estates in London. Time elapsed, and Reuben had not paid Shimon the sum stipulated in their contractual agreement. Shimon tried to contact Reuben to collect payment, but Reuben had died in the interim. Both Shimon and Reuben's widow appeared before the *beth din* in London to determine whether Reuben's estate would be used to pay his debt to Shimon or, alternatively, would be used to fulfill the widow's *ketubah* (prenuptial agreement).

Even though the contractual agreement between the litigants was made in London, this case was brought to the attention of the *beth din* of Eẓ Ḥaim in Amsterdam for a *berirah*. This is surprising because in 1705, after a disagreement between the two Nacão communities, the Mahamad of the Shaar

[32] Sukkoth is a holiday when Jews live in booths for seven days as ordained in the Torah, Lev. 23:33–43.

Hashamayim in London resolved never again to resort to the arbitration of the Amsterdam *beth din* or *parnassim* (Shaar Hashamayim, MS 103, 1678–1724, f°53 verso).[33] Prior to 1705, the London community had referred all their cases to Ez̧ Ḥaim. This resolution was probably ignored because the case involves the deliberation of the *beth din* of Ez̧ Ḥaim concerning the death of Reuben.

In Jewish tradition, prenuptial agreements are made between husband and wife through a legal document called the *ketubah*. This document includes the duties and obligations of the husband toward his wife and the dowry, extra gifts, and stipulations added by the father of the bride to protect her interests. The *ketubah* is like a debt that is time-bound, and it can be collected only after the death of the husband or after divorce (*Shulḥan Arukh, Eben-Ha'Ezer* 93:1). Moreover, halakhah stipulates that if the husband travels overseas and word comes that he has died, witnesses must testify before the *beth din* to release the wife from the marriage.[34] Most important, halakhah stipulates that in cases dealing with financial matters, two tribunals in different places can unite testimonies of the witnesses to settle disputes and claims (*Shulḥan Arukh, Ḥoshen Mishpaṭ* 30:11).[35] Even though

[33] Havendo em dias pasados algumas pesoas de nossa Naçaõ que entaõ erao todos nossos yehidim, e agora ainda algums o saõ, sem o conhecimento dos Senhores do Mahamad, pedido ao do Kaal Kados de Amsterdam referise a seu Bet din a doctrina que predicou neste Santo Lugar o senhor Nosso Haham Rabbi David Netto en 23 de kislef 5464, na perasa de Vayeseb Jahacob, se era contraria a a Ley de Deus ou naõ, resolveu ditto Mahamad (comforme as notticias gerais) que seu Bet Din se compuzesse por essa vez em lugar de tres Hahamim que he ordinariamente, de cinco, aos quais lhe preguntarao, se emcargavao sua conciencia em naõ responder a ditta pregunta, lha levarao que a naõ encarregavao. Depois para ca os senhores deste Mahamad levados de seu zello e dezejo de adquerir a paz, como por a petiçaõ de algumas de dittas pesoas, escreverao a ditto Mahamad de Amsterdam, mandandolhes os documentos pertencentes ao ponto tanto pro como contra, suplicandolhes (ao passo que o geral se achava satisfeito de ditta doctrina), sometesem todo a seu bet din para que desem huma sentença difinitiva se era ou naõ contrario a Ley de Deus, para por essa via alcançar o fim dezejado, naõ acharaõ aprepozito o fazelo, antes para dilatado pediraõ couzas imposiveis de alcansar, como selhes representou em reposta a sua carta, reyterando nella nosso dezejo e nova suplica de fazer julgar ditto ponto, pois dependia delles nossa paz, e em falta de otorgalo bolvesem a entregar nossos papeis o que logo fizeraõ, mostrando fazer mais cazo de hums particulares que de toda huma kehila, e assi em resentimento deste trato, resolveraõ os Senhores do Mahamad fazer esta ordem e que se publique neste Sagrado Pulpito, que para o futuro nenhum Mahamad possa, por rezaõ imaginada ou por imaginar, mandar pedir din ou outro julgado ao ditto bet din ou Mahamad de Amsterdam, e havendo cazo urgente que se necessite de hum ou outro ou ambos, se recurra a qualquer outra kehila que parecer ao Mahamad que entaõ servir, e Deus de Israel diriga nossas accoems a seu santo serviço e bendiga a seu povo com paz, amen. Londres a 16 de tamus 5465. Se leu na thebah em sabath 19 de tamus 5465. M de Medina Gabay.

[34] A woman whose husband went overseas and was testified to be dead, even by one witness—even if the witness is a slave or a maidservant or a woman or a relative—is free. Even a witness from the words of a witness, or a woman from the words of a woman, or a slave or a maidservant or a relative, are worthy of this testimony. Shulḥan Arukh, *Eben ha-Ezer* 17:3.

[35] If one testified in this court and the second testified in another court, one court may join with the other court and combine the testimony.

the Shaar Hashamayim community had resolved decades earlier not to hand over their cases to the *beth din* of Ez̤ Ḥaim, this type of collaboration would be allowed and deemed necessary.

Moses Rodrigues Lopes consults several legal sources to answer the question at hand: the Babylonian Talmud the Ba'ale Tosaphoth, the Rosh, the Tur, the Mahariq (Joseph Colon Trabotto 1420–1480), the *Sefer ha-Agudah* (Alexander Zuslin ha-Kohen d. 1348), the Mordekhai (Mordekhai ben Hillel 1250–1298), the Ribash (Isaac ben Sheshet, 1326–1408), the Rashba (Shelomo ben Aderet 1235–1310), the Ran (Nissim of Gerona 1320–1380), the Rif, the Rambam, the *Maggid Mishneh* (Vidal of Tolosa, fifteenth century), and the *Kessef Mishneh* (Yosef Karo).

He begins his legal analysis by stating that, a priori, Shimon has no legal claim from Reuben's estate. He builds his case by citing the legal opinion of the Rosh, "the appraisement of values which have not been given or a gift without an appraised value, is void" (Tur, *Ḥoshen Mishpaṭ* 104:5, 10). Then he cites the Rosh, who states that a creditor cannot request anything from the *beth din* until the judges have determined first that the debtor owes the creditor.[36] Rodrigues Lopes continues his analysis with the Mahariq, who mentions the custom that an agent from the community who wishes to collect a debt in the possession of a third party cannot do so until the claim has been ratified by the authorities.[37] Rodrigues Lopes then analyzes relevant law from the Mishnah, which says that when someone comes to the *beth din* stating a claim against another person and knowing with certainty where the other person's assets are physically located, there is no legal claim until after the *bet din* has determined that a debt is indeed owed. To strengthen this argument, Rodrigues Lopes cites the Mordekhai and the Ba'ale Tosaphoth, who state that even if there is a contract, it must be verified by witnesses before the *beth din*.[38] Relying on these sources, Rodrigues Lopes then makes an inference *argumentum a minori, ad maius: vel a fortiori*—that is, if the minimal requirement to uphold a claim dealing with debts is that the witnesses come before the tribunal, then Shimon has no right to present himself before the judges to demand payment (from Levi).

After explaining the first part of the question on how credits and debts function according to halakhah, Rodrigues Lopes addresses the question of

[36] Responsa *Rosh* 90:1; Responsa *Mahariq* 86.
[37] Responsa *Mahariq* 109.
[38] The law requires that the witnesses are summoned and given thirty days to appear before the judges. *Mishneh Torah, Sanhedrin we-ha'onashim* 7:6.

whom the *beth din* will hand the assets to. He begins by comparing the law in the Babylonian Talmud with the Jerusalem Talmud, where the jurists have opposing opinions (*b.Ketuboth* 84a).[39] The law follows the legal opinion of Rabbi Aqiba, who states that the heirs of a deceased man inherit his movable property. However, if creditors have a legal claim to collect a debt, they are paid before the widow since the fulfillment of a negative precept (theft) takes precedence over the fulfillment of a positive precept (payment of the *ketubah*). This is how medieval jurists decided the law as well. For that matter, medieval Aragonese and Catalonian rabbinic jurists issued a *taqanah* by adding a special stipulation to the *ketubah*, stating that all movable and immovable property was under the possession of widows, not creditors. This convention permitted a widow to handle the estate to pay her deceased husband's creditors and maintain financial security for herself and her children.

This case reveals the flexibility of halakhah in that its jurisdiction is universal for Jews. In theory, any *beth din* could arbitrate civil laws between members of the Nacão. Moreover, tribunals in different locations can combine their efforts to adjudicate cases dealing with financial matters. The legal mechanisms are made possible because of the concept of *berith* (covenantal relationship). According to Jewish tradition, God made an everlasting covenant with the Hebrew people at Mount Sinai. The nation exclaimed, "Everything that the Eternal One has commanded, we will do, then understand" (Common English Bible, Exod. 19:8). Jewish males are inducted into the covenant on the eighth day after birth through the rite of circumcision. This rite is so crucial to the identity and future of the Nacão that Ḥakham Saul Levi Mortera (c. 1596–1660) preached from the pulpit about it on various occasions (Kaplan 2016, 221). Already in the early seventeenth century, the Eẓ Ḥaim community issued a ruling that Iberian *conversos* who delayed the rite of circumcision would be barred from entering the synagogue (GAA 334:10, fol. 60).[40] This exclusion was tantamount to spiritual and cultural death.

[39] Ribi Aqiba states that creditors require the making of an oath before the judges, but that the heirs do not. Therefore, the heirs inherit their father's estates.

[40] So that no unclean person might enter the synagogue at the time when God is judging His people; and if they are not circumcised by that day, we command them not to enter until they have done so. If other men arrive [from Spain or Portugal] during the year, who, for various reasons, did not have occasion to be circumcised, they will be given a grace period of two months, and after that time they will not be permitted to enter the synagogue until they have been circumcised. *Livro de Ascamot do Kahal Kados Bet Israel*, in the Municipal Archives of Amsterdam.

The following question was brought before the *beth din* of Ez̧ Ḥaim:

> Reuben, who resides in Amsterdam, owes Shimon (who lives in London) the sum stipulated in a contract. Reuben's estate was in the hands of Levi (who resides in London). Shimon came to the *beth din* (in London) to demand the payment of the sum from Reuben's possessions, which are in the care of Levi. As the case developed, Reuben passed away. Then Reuben's widow came to the *beth din* to receive the payment of her *ketubah*. Whom do Reuben's possessions belong to? (Meldola 1767c, 57)[41]

One of the most important ideas we learned from this case concerns the *tena'im* (stipulations) on a *ketubah*. Since Jewish law grants the husband the right to handle financial matters within marriage, Jewish brides can protect their wealth and social status through special stipulations in their prenuptial agreements. In cases where the husband has no children, his inheritance would go to his closest kin, while the dowry and bridal gifts would go to his widow. By implementing *tena'im* on the *ketubah*, the husband's wealth could be transferred to the widow. Ultimately, this legal mechanism grants her the agency to deal with her deceased husband's creditors and control his business interests.

Developments after the Eighteenth Century

The three cases just reviewed demonstrate how Portuguese Jews related to private international law and practice. In some instances, Jewish law implemented the legal conventions practiced by various nations. This was possible through the halakhic mechanism *dina demalkhuta dina*, that is, the precept that the law of the land is the law (*b.Nedarim* 28a). As such, many of the verdicts reflect the international legal consensus at the time. The eighteenth-century School of Ez̧ Ḥaim thus functioned in tandem with international law.

After Napoleon's army invaded the Dutch Republic in 1795, the Batavian Republic was founded. A year later, Jews were formally emancipated and received full political and civil rights. This had implications for the identity and future of the Nação, since that community had abided by the same civil

[41] Translated by Yehonatan Elazar-DeMota.

laws as everyone else. Consequently, the political and legal system by which the Nação in Amsterdam had governed itself for almost two centuries became obsolete.

There have been instances in European Jewish communities where the *dayyanim* (judges) and *parnassim* have not agreed to accept the implementation of local domestic law into halakhah. Such was the case with the Jewish community in Metz in the eighteenth century. In 1734, the Metz government legislated that Jews could not be forced to adjudicate their civil disputes by rabbinic courts (Berkovitz 2005, 91). The head judge of the Jewish tribunal of Metz was compelled to translate the main details of *Ḥoshen Mishpaṭ* on behalf of the French civil court; this way, the French magistrates could adjudicate civil cases involving Jewish litigants. The head judge, Jonathan Eibeschütz, objected that Jews should go to Gentile courts, even when both parties were in agreement. As a defensive measure, the local community imposed a *ḥerem*[42] against any member of the community who presented their cases before non-Jewish courts.

Rabbi Moshe Feinstein (1895–1986) was a prominent Orthodox Jewish rabbi, *poseq* (Jewish legal authority), and author. He was one of the leading authorities on Jewish law and tradition in the twentieth century. Born in Makov, Poland (now Ukraine), to a family of rabbis, he studied in the yeshivot of Kelm and Slabodka, where he was influenced by the teachings of Rabbi Eliezer Gordon and Rabbi Aryeh Levine. He later moved to the United States, where he continued his studies at Yeshiva Torah Vodaas in Brooklyn, New York. Rabbi Feinstein served as a rabbi in several congregations in New York City, including the Young Israel of Flatbush and the Shomrei Emunah Synagogue. He was also a prominent member of the Agudath Israel of America, a major Orthodox Jewish organization. R. Feinstein was recognized as one of the leading *poseqim* of his time, along with Rabbi Yaakov Kamenetsky and Rabbi Joseph B. Soloveitchik. His rulings on Jewish law were widely respected and sought after by Jews worldwide.

R. Feinstein was known for his exceptional talent for Talmudic analysis and his ability to clarify complex halakhic issues. His commentaries on the

[42] *Ḥerem* was a rabbinic decree which excommunicated an individual from access to the Jewish community. Until Jews were emancipated, becoming full citizens of their host countries, this decree was tantamount to social death. An excommunicated person could not marry within the Jewish community, or do business with other Jews, or receive a Jewish burial. Today, this is equivalent to being "cancelled."

Talmud, particularly his *Iggeroth Moshe* (Letters of Moshe), are still widely studied today. This collection of responsa includes twentieth-century cases pertaining to Jewish law within an American legal setting.

R. Feinstein deals with issues pertaining to rent control. In one particular case, a tenant rented a house from a landlord, but then the landlord decided to sell the house and demanded that the tenant vacate. The case goes as follows:

> In the matter of a tenant who rented a house from a landlord for a year, and subsequently, the landlord decided to sell the house and demanded that the tenant vacate it in order to sell it. The tenant claimed the full rental period and also wanted the money he had already paid for the rent, arguing that the house for the rental period is his, and the landlord has no right to sell it during this time.
>
> It is clear that the tenant's claim is valid because the house was already rented for the agreed-upon time, and the landlord cannot cancel the lease in the interim to sell the house. This situation is similar to renting an animal from someone, where it is established that renting (for its time) is considered a sale, meaning that it is owned for that time period.
>
> Therefore, if a person rents a house from someone for a year or any period, the landlord cannot evict the tenant in the middle of the term, because the house is considered the tenant's for that rental period. Additionally, the tenant has the right to sublet it to others and remove any occupants therein. (Iggeroth Moshe, *Ḥoshen Mishpaṭ*, Vol. 2:15)

This responsum clearly outlines that a landlord cannot evict a tenant in the middle of a rental period to sell the property. The rental agreement is considered binding, and the tenant has rights to the property for the duration of the lease.

Another rabbinic authority who dealt with the intersection between civil law and Jewish law was Rabbi Yitzchak Elchanan Spektor (1817–1896). He was a prominent rabbinic authority recognized for his scholarly contributions and his leadership in the Jewish community. He was born in Resh, a small town near Grodno, in what is now Belarus. A prodigious student from a young age, he studied under various prominent rabbis, including Rabbi Benjamin Diskin and Rabbi Yitzchak of Volozhin. He held various rabbinic positions, including Nesvizh (Niasvizh, Baresa (Boćki), Novahrudak (Navahrudak, and Kovno [Kaunas]). In 1864, he became chief rabbi in Kovno, a major center of Jewish life and learning, where he remained until his death.

Rabbi Spektor was renowned for his responsa, which addressed a wide range of halakhic issues. In his collection of responsa, *En Yiṣḥaq* (fountain of Isaac), he deals with issues of Jewish law in the context of Russian civil law. One case concerned the inheritance of daughters in Russia, where a father wished to bequeath part of his estate to his daughters in accordance with state laws, which mandated equal inheritance for all children, sons and daughters alike. Rabbi Yitzchak Elchanan addressed the need to comply with state laws while using halachic tools, such as wills and conditional gifts, to uphold Jewish legal principles. He emphasized that these tools allow for adherence to state laws without compromising halachic principles. R. Elchanan dealt with this issue in a responsum in *En Yiṣḥaq*:

> I was asked about the inheritance of daughters, as the principle of *dina demalkhuta dina* in Russia mandates that daughters inherit equally with sons. Can we uphold this civil law without violating Torah law, which states in Jacob's blessing, "And may He give you the blessing of Abraham, to you and your seed with you, to inherit the land of your sojournings, which God gave to Abraham." The Rashi explains that the blessing is for Jacob's descendants to inherit the land. The Rambam rules in Hilkhoth Naḥaloth [Inheritance Laws], Chapter 1, *Halakha* 1, that the double portion inheritance of the firstborn is a matter of tradition, as derived from the *Sifre*: "It is written, 'to give him a double portion in all that he possesses.' There was an incident where two scholars came before Rabban Gamliel the Elder, one of whom was a firstborn and the other an ordinary son. Rabban Gamliel the Elder said to the ordinary son, 'My son, it is you who the Torah says must give a double portion to the firstborn in all that you possess. You have taken the inheritance, and your brother should receive twice as much'" (Sifre Deuteronomy 21:17). Moses instituted inheritance for the daughters of Zelophehad, as the Torah dictated inheritance for them. It is clear that *dina demalkhuta dina* must be upheld in matters pertaining to the kingdom's laws, even though *dina demalkhuta dina* applies broadly, as ruled by the great *poseqim* in the responsa of the Rashba, the Ran, Rabbenu Yonah, Rabbenu Chananel, the Rosh, the Ramban, the Rambam, the Tur, and Shulchan Arukh Choshen Mishpat, Siman 369, and all the *poseqim* cited there, with the Rema's ruling there. However, it appears that *dina demalkhuta dina* does not apply to inheritance matters explicitly stated in

> the Torah: "On the day he bequeaths to his sons what he has, he may not make the son of the beloved the firstborn over the son of the unloved who is the firstborn." This does not fall under *dina demalkhuta dina*. It is common practice for a daughter who wishes to inherit to make a deed on her assets as a gift, which works even for the firstborn son, as stated "He may not make the son of the beloved the firstborn"—this only applies to inheritance, but with a gift, everyone agrees one can give a gift to whomever they wish, including a gift to a woman over the firstborn son.
>
> Therefore, it seems that even though sometimes clever arrangements are made in these matters, it is better to organize it in a manner of a gift that is effective under *dina demalkhuta dina* without violating Torah law. (*En Yiṣḥaq*, vol. 2, *Ḥoshen Mishpaṭ*, Siman 55)

R. Elchanan discusses the compatibility of the Jewish legal principle of *dina demalkhuta* dina with Jewish inheritance laws as described in the Torah. On the question whether a daughter can inherit equally with sons, R. Elchanan's ruling prioritizes compliance with Torah law over the principle of *dina demalkhuta dina,* while still allowing for creative solutions that balance Jewish legal requirements with secular legal frameworks.

Jewish Law and Secular Domestic Law

In general, Jewish legal authorities have been reluctant to implement the domestic law of their host governments in matters pertaining to Jewish ritual law. In the seventeenth century (1656) and eighteenth centuries (1712), the Nação community in Amsterdam rejected certain marriage prohibitions promulgated by the Estates of Holland. For instance, Menasseh ben Israel (1604–1657) stated that marriages between cousins and between uncles and nieces were the most preferable (Trivellato 2009, 134), contrary to the law of the land. The reiteration of bans on these marriages by Dutch authorities suggests noncompliance by the Nação community (ibid.). Moreover, before the 1639 merger between the three Nação synagogues in Amsterdam, the leaders of each one had agreed on banning any Jew who took a fellow Jew to a secular court, except for cases dealing with seizure of property, letters of exchange, insurance matters, or distant courts (Grausz 2019,233). Any Nação member who had been separated from the community because of secular litigation would have to pay a heavy fine (20 florins) to be reintegrated into the community (ibid.). These rulings and practices among the Nação community demonstrate that the leadership did not want to adopt local domestic law within the domain of Jewish ritual law.

We have seen how Jewish law can readily assimilate foreign domestic law within the domain of commercial law. The legal concepts of *dinim, din melekh,* and *dina demalkhuta dina* facilitate this symbiosis. While not all rabbinic legal authorities agree about the extent to which Jewish law can defer to secular domestic law, they do agree with the aforementioned three concepts. Discussions of choice of law and legal pluralism in Jewish law and thought are the pragmatic and theoretical offspring of this recognition (Israel-Vleeschhouwer 2014, 11). In some cases, Jews were forced to adopt the laws of their host countries. In other cases, the *poseqim* decided that it was in the best interest of the community to adopt foreign legal practices. This was the case in maritime law, where the *lex mercatoria* functioned as a self-enforcing institution.[43] On the other hand, we have seen how rabbinic legal authorities were reluctant to apply domestic law within Jewish family law. Many saw this as tantamount to undermining the Jewish tradition.

One can conclude that, for the most part, Jews living in Europe lost political-religious autonomy during the Enlightenment period, especially after Napoleon Bonaparte emancipated the French Jews in 1806. Except for perhaps in the Ottoman and North African territories, Jews elsewhere were compelled to adopt the civil legal systems *in toto* of their host countries. This change challenged the political and legal autonomies Ottoman and North African Jews had enjoyed for centuries. With the development of modern nation-states and international legal consensus, *poseqim* would have to engage with international legal theory and decide which areas of international law can Jewish law accept and which it cannot. This is the subject of the next chapter.

Bibliography

Primary Sources

Abi Zimra, David ben Solomon Ibn. *Yeqar Tif'ereth.* Warsaw: Mordekhai Kalinberg Publishing, 1882.
Albo, Yosef. *Sefer ha-'Iqarim.* Philadelphia: Jewish Publication Society, 1946.
Al-Fayyumi, Se'adya Gaon. *Al Ha-Torah we-Al Nakh,* Vol. 2. Jerusalem, Israel: Mossad HaRav Kook, 1960.

[43] See Francesca Trivellato, *The Familiarity of Strangers: The Sephardic Diaspora, Livorno, and Cross-Cultural Trade in the Early Modern Period* (New Haven, CT: Yale University Press, 2009), 158.

Babylonian Talmud. *Giṭṭin*. Edited by Jerome Schottenstein. Rahway, NJ: Artscroll Mesorah Publications, 1997.

Babylonian Talmud. *Ketuboth*. Edited by Jerome Schottenstein. Rahway, NJ: Artscroll Mesorah Publications, 1997.

Babylonian Talmud. *Nedarim*. Edited by Jerome Schottenstein. Rahway, NJ: Artscroll Mesorah Publications, 1997.

Babylonian Talmud. *Sanhedrin*. Edited by Jerome Schottenstein. Rahway, NJ: Artscroll Mesorah Publications, 1997.

Babylonian Talmud. *Yebamoth*. Edited by Jerome Schottenstein. Rahway, NJ: Artscroll Mesorah Publications, 1997.

Breish, Mordechai Yaakov. *Responsa Ḥelqath Ya'aqob*. Tel Abib, Israel: Mordechai Yaakov Breish, 1992.

Bynkershoek, Cornelius van. *A Treatise on the Law of War. Translated from the original Latin. The First Book of his Quaestiones Juris Publici*. Clark, NJ: The Lawbook Exchange, Ltd., 2008.

Common English Bible. Nashville: Tennessee Christian Resources, 2010.

Feinstein, Moshe. *Iggeroth Moshe*. Brooklyn, NY: Beth Medrash L'Torah V'Horaah, 1986.

Gemeente Archief Amsterdam [GAA], NA.nr. 334, 875, 17 Menahem Ab 5483.

Gemeente Archief Amsterdam 334:10, fol. 60.

Henken, Yosef Eliyahu. *Teshuboth Ibra*. New York: 1981.

Karo, Yosef. *Shulḥan Arukh, Ḥoshen Mishpaṭ*. Jerusalem, Israel: Mossad HaRav Kook, 1975.

Klein, Menashe. *Mishneh Halakhoth*. Jerusalem, Israel: Mekhon Mishneh Halakhoth Gedoloth, 1970.

Leeuwen, Simon van. *Het Rooms-Hollands-Regt*. Boek I. Deel V. Rotterdam, The Netherlands: Hackens, 1664.

London Metropolitan Archives. Archives of the Spanish and Portuguese Congregation, Minutes of the Mahamad of Shaar Hashamayim, MS 103, 1678–1724.

Maimonides, Moses, Yeḥi'el M. Zilber, and Me'ir A. Horoỵits. *Mishneh Torah: Hilkhoth Abadim*. Jerusalem, Israel: Mekhon Moreshet haNesher Hagadol, 2010.

Maimonides, Moses, Yeḥi'el M. Zilber, and Me'ir A. Horoỵits. *Mishneh Torah, Hilkhoth Mekhirah*. Jerusalem, Israel: Mekhon Moreshet haNesher Hagadol, 2010.

Maimonides, Moses, Yeḥi'el M. Zilber, and Me'ir A. Horoỵits. *Mishneh Torah: Hilkhoth Melakhim*. Jerusalem, Israel: Mekhon Moreshet haNesher Hagadol, 2010.

Maimonides, Moses, Yeḥi'el M. Zilber, and Me'ir A. Horoỵits. *Mishneh Torah, Hilkhoth Shebuoth*. Jerusalem, Israel: Mekhon Moreshet haNesher hagadol, 2010.

Maimonides, Moses, Yeḥi'el M. Zilber, and Me'ir A. Horoỵits. *Mishneh Torah: Hilkhoth Sheluḥin wu-Shuttafin*. Jerusalem, Israel: Mekhon Moreshet haNesher hagadol, 2010.

Meldola, David de Raphael. *Responsa Peri Eẓ Ḥaim*, Vols. 1, 3, 11. Amsterdam, 1767.

Nahmanides, Moshe. *Ramban (Nachmanides) Commentary on the Torah*. 5 vols. Lawrence, NY: Judaica Press, 2010.

Sefaria. "Rabbi David Kimḥi." https://www.sefaria.org/Joshua.9.5?lang=en&with=Radak&lang2=en.

Sefaria. "Rabbi Levi ben Gershon." https://www.sefaria.org/Joshua.9.5?lang=en&with=Ralbag&lang2=en.

Sefaria. "Shulḥan Arukh, Eben ha-Ezer 93." https://www.sefaria.org/Shulchan_Arukh%2C_Even_HaEzer.93?lang=bi.

Sefaria. "Shulḥan Arukh, Ḥoshen Mishpaṭ 225." https://www.sefaria.org/Shulchan_Arukh%2C_Choshen_Mishpat.225?lang=bi.

Sforno, Obadia. *Sforno Commentary on the Torah*. 2 vols. New York: Mesorah, 1987.

Shilo, Shemuel. *Dina deMalkhuta Dina*. Jerusalem, Israel: Academic Press, 1974.

Soloveitchik, Yosef. *Nefesh ha-Rab*. Tel Abib, Israel: Zvi Shechter, 1994.

Specktor, Yitchak Elchanan. *'En Yiṣḥaq Responsa*, Vol. 2: *Ḥoshen Mishpaṭ*. Kovno, Russia, 1876.

Teitelbaum, Yoel. *Dibere Yoel*. Jerusalem, Israel: Hotzaat Yerushalayim, 1981."

"Tur, Ḥoshen Mishpat 104:5." Sefaria. https://www.sefaria.org/Tur%2C_Choshen_Mishpat.104.5?lang=bi.

Yisraeli, Shaul. *Amud Hayemini*. Tel Abib, Israel: Moreshet, 1966.
Yosef, Obadia. *Yeḥaweh Da'ath*. Jerusalem, Israel: Hebrewbooks, 1978.

Secondary Sources

Abrahams, Israel. *Jewish Life in the Middle Ages*. London, UK: Routledge, 2010.

Berman, Harold J. "World Law." *Fordham International Law Journal* 18, no. 1617 (1995): 1617–22.

Berkovitz, Jay. "Civil Law and Justice in the Rabbinic Tribunals of Eighteenth Century Metz." In *Iggud: Selected Essays in Jewish Studies*, Vol. 1: *The Bible and Its World, Rabbinic Literature and Jewish Law, and Jewish Thought*, edited by Baruch Schwartz, 87–99. Jerusalem, Israel: World Union of Jewish Studies, 2005.

Blidstein, Ya'acov. "The Treatment of Hostile Civilian Populations: The Contemporary Halakhic Discussion In Israel." *Israel Studies* 1, no. 2 (1996): 27–44.

Broyde, Michael J. "Informing on Others for Violating American Law: A Jewish Law View." *Journal of Halacha and Contemporary Society* 41 (2002): 5–49.

Broyde, Michael J. "A Jewish Law View of World Law." *Emory Law Journal* 54 (2005): 79.

Broyde, Michael J. *The Pursuit of Justice and Jewish Law: Halakhic Perspectives on the Legal Profession*. 2nd ed. New York: Yashar Books, 2007.

Faur, José. "Modern Sephardic Thought: Religious Humanism and Zionism." In *The Sephardi and Oriental Jewish Heritage*, edited by Issachar Ben-Ami, 325–49. Jerusalem, Israel: Magnes Press, Hebrew University, 1982.

Fishman, Talya. "The 'Our Talmud' Tradition and the Predilection for Works of Applied Law in Early Sephardi Rabbinic Culture." In *Regional Identities and Cultures of Medieval Jews*, edited by Javier Castano, Talya Fishman, and Ephraim Kanarfogel, 201–30. Liverpool, UK: The Littman Library of Jewish Civilization, 2018.

Grausz, Evelyne Oliel. "Dispute Resolution and Kahal Kadosh Talmud Torah: Community Forum and Legal Acculturation in Eighteenth-Century Amsterdam." In *Religious Changes and Cultural Transformations in the Early Modern Western Sephardic Communities*, edited by Yosef Kaplan, 228–57. Leiden, The Netherlands: Brill, 2019.

Hand, Learned. *The Spirit of Liberty: Papers and Addresses of Learned Hand*. 3rd ed. New York: Knopf, 1960.

Israel-Vleeschhouwer, Amos. "Systematic, Dynamic and Complex Analyses of the Interaction of Jewish and Other Legal Systems." *Jewish Law Association Studies* 25 (2014): 1–25.

Kaplan, Yosef. "'This Thing Alone Will Preserve Their Nation Forever.' Circumcision and Conversion in the Early Modern Western Sephardic Communities." In *The Conversos and Moriscos in Late Medieval Spain and Beyond*, edited by Kevin Ingram and Juan Ignacio Pulido Serrano, 218–43. Leiden, The Netherlands: Brill, 2016.

Rakover, Nahum. "Jewish Law and the Noahide Obligation to Preserve Social Order." *Cardozo Law* Review 12 (1991): 1073–1118.

Trivellato, Francesca. *The Familiarity of Strangers: The Sephardic Diaspora, Livorno, and Cross-Cultural Trade in the Early Modern Period*. New Haven, CT: Yale University Press, 2009.

Witte, John, Jr. *Religion and the American Constitutional Experiment*. 2nd ed. Boulder, CO: Westview Press, 2005.

3

Areas of Incorporation of International Law: War and Humanitarian Law

The Development of Just War Theory and Jewish Law

In the previous chapter we presented three theories of why and where Jewish law can incorporate foreign legal systems: the Maran, the Rama, and the Shach, each named for the rabbi who proposed it. The Maran ruled that secular law is halakhically binding only to the extent that it directly affects the government's financial interests. The Rama maintained that secular laws directly affecting the government's financial interests are binding but added that secular laws, which were enacted for the benefit of the people of the community, are effective under Jewish law. In disagreement with the Rama, the Shach held that even if secular laws were enacted for the benefit of the community, they are not valid under Jewish law if they contradict elements of Jewish law.

We argue in this book that national legal systems have something to learn from the readiness of Jewish law to incorporate rules generated by alien legal systems. To illustrate the logic and implications of this approach, we begin by analyzing the body of law concerning war.

The laws of war reflect the political and humanitarian aims of global stability and the preservation of life, or at least the mitigation of atrocities. The laws of war have generated difficult jurisdictional problems that require legal systems to reach outside themselves for a broader matrix of rules. The realities of warfare demand meaningful cross-border coordination for any legal regime to be effective. The development of international law in this domain was inevitable. Each state's laws were territorially bounded, but states typically used military force against other states or at least within another sovereign's territory. It was necessary, therefore, to create legal frameworks.

The development of international law in warfare was a crucial step in regulating the use of force across borders. Each state's laws were initially territorially bounded, but the reality of warfare extended beyond those bounds, creating chaos and harming civilians. The lack of a legal framework by which

Jewish Law and International Law. Michael J. Broyde and Yehonatan Elazar-De Mota, Oxford University Press.
 DOI: 10.1093/9780197805275.003.0003

to contain the chaos and protect innocent noncombatants made it difficult to establish clear rules and guidelines for waging war, leading to moral and humanitarian crises. The need for international regulation of warfare was driven by the recognition that relying solely on national laws was insufficient to deal with modern warfare's complexities.

The gradual development of international law in this domain spanned centuries. The first attempts at regulating warfare date back to ancient times, with the development of codes of conduct such as the ancient Greek concept of *jus ad bellum* (the right to go to war) and the Roman concept of *jus in bello* (the right way of waging war). Augustine and Thomas Aquinas elaborated on these concepts and influenced much Western thought about "just war." However, it was not until the nineteenth and twentieth centuries that international law governing the conduct of war began to take shape as a distinct field. The Hague Conferences of 1899 and 1907 established many principles that govern modern international humanitarian law, including the prohibition against targeting civilians and the protection of prisoners of war.

The Problem of Territoriality

As we have seen already, jurists of Jewish law often have faced a conundrum imposed by local legal systems. Although Jewish law, in theory, applies globally, the authority of particular rabbinic courts and figures is restricted to their local spheres of geographical and cultural influence. Under widely accepted principles dating to the medieval era, rabbinic courts could issue binding decrees only within their local jurisdiction, usually a village or perhaps a country. They could not, however, impose rules by fiat on Jews residing in other territories. The problems of boundary-crossing war thus challenged the assumptions of both municipal law and Jewish law and demanded a regulatory solution beyond localized legal regimes.

The need for a body of international law regarding war was not solely a function of jurisdictional niceties, however. The law of war *must* be global if it is to exist at all. In this respect, the invention of international laws of war did not simply fill a gap. It made law from scratch and replaced anarchy with order. Jewish law, as we shall see, recognizes this paradigm.

Surprisingly, after millennia of use, the word "war" has more or less been discarded by international law. Although the preamble of the UN Charter aims "to save succeeding generations from the scourge of war, which twice in our lifetime has brought untold sorrow to mankind," the operative language of the Charter adopts broader terminology designed to transcend the notion of a formally declared war: "the threat or use of force" is prohibited by Article 2(4), whereas "armed attack" may trigger "the inherent right of individual or collective self-defence" under Article 51. What matters is the fact of armed conflict, the boots on the ground—or perhaps the drones in the air. Whether the politicians and diplomats choose to characterize a battle as a true "war" is of minimal import. As a legally significant category, then, war has become just "an empty shell" (Greenwood 1987, 283, 305). But that is largely a matter of semantics. Terminology notwithstanding, a robust cluster of international law encompassing both treaties and customs has grown to regulate virtually all aspects of the initiation and conduct of warfare.

In Hugo Grotius's foundational treatise *On the Laws of War and Peace*, first published in 1625, he explains why he felt the need to organize and articulate the laws of war:

> I observed throughout the Christian World a Licentiousness in regard to War, which even barbarous Nations ought to be ashamed of: a Running to Arms upon very frivolous or rather no Occasions; which being once taken up, there remained no longer any Reverence for Right, either Divine or Human, just as if from that Time Men were authorized and firmly resolved to commit all manner of Crimes without Restraint. (Grotius 1625, ¶ 29)

As this passage suggests, the international laws of war are split in two. The first body of law, *jus ad bellum* in Latin, governs the legality of the initial decision to use force—which must be justified by a proper cause. As a rule, all nonconsensual use of force is unlawful under Article 2(4) of the UN Charter, subject to the limited exceptions for when authorized by the UN Security Council under Chapter VII or in self-defense against an "armed attack" under Article 51. Alongside this law grounded in the UN Charter and other treaties, a body of customary international law also governs the use of force. In the *Nicaragua* case, the International Court of Justice (ICJ) explained that "customary international law continues to exist alongside treaty law," noting for example that Article 51 "does not contain any specific rule whereby self-defence would warrant only measures which are proportional to the armed attack and necessary to respond to it, a rule well established in customary international law." The Court further observed, somewhat puzzlingly, that since Article 51 does not provide a "definition" of the term "armed attack," any such definition "is not part of treaty law."[1] There remain major disagreements regarding the meaning and scope of terms like "armed attack" and the "inherent" right of self-defense, among many other contested issues. Nonetheless, the UN Charter and customary international law have sharply limited the lawful reasons to use force, outlawing the "Running to Arms upon very frivolous or rather no Occasions" that so outraged Grotius.

The second facet of the international law of war regulates the conduct on the battlefield once war has broken out, without regard to whether the use of force was initially justified. This second body of law—known as *jus in bello*, as well as the law of armed conflict (LOAC) and international humanitarian law (IHL)—is further subdivided into laws governing international armed conflicts (IAC) and those governing noninternational armed conflicts (NIAC), such as civil wars. International humanitarian law is today primarily codified in the four Geneva Conventions of 1949 and their three Additional Protocols (which essentially incorporate and expand the earlier Hague Conventions law). These conventions have been almost universally signed and ratified. Summarizing the various treaty obligations, the ICJ has stated:

> The cardinal principles contained in the texts constituting the fabric of humanitarian law are the following. The first is aimed at the protection of the civilian population and civilian objects and establishes the distinction between combatants and non-combatants; States must never make civilians the object of attack. . . . According to the second principle, it is prohibited to cause unnecessary suffering to combatants.[2]

Although these principles are embodied in treaty law, the Court further explained that "these fundamental rules are to be observed by all States whether or not they have ratified the conventions that contain them, because they constitute intransgressible principles of international customary law."[3] Others have generalized that the "four core concepts" of the law of armed conflict are "distinction, military necessity, unnecessary suffering, and proportionality" (Solis 2016). Despite the significant restraints on warfare

[1] Nicaragua v. United States of America, 1986 I.C.J. 14, 176 (June 27).
[2] On the Threat or Use of Nuclear Weapons, Advisory Opinion, 1996 I.C.J., 78 (July 8).
[3] Ibid., 79.

imposed by the law of armed conflict, it also *authorizes* killing and other destruction when the rules are followed. The law shields those soldiers who comply with LOAC from legal consequences for their lawful acts of killing and violence, which, outside the context of an armed conflict, would be serious crimes. "As in a boxing match," explains Theodor Meron, "pummeling the opponent's upper body is fine; hitting below the belt is proscribed" (Meron 2000, 239, 240).

According to Meron—a Holocaust survivor, Israeli scholar, former diplomat, and later a judge on the International Criminal Tribunals for the former Yugoslavia and Rwanda—the origins of the international law of armed conflict lie in the principle of reciprocity. "In a world of armies, each agrees to follow the law for one overriding reason: the expectation that your enemies will follow the same law and give you the same protection that you afford them." He adds that "this version of legality guaranteed a modicum of fair play even during war. As long as the rules of the game were observed by both parties, it was permissible to cause suffering, deprivation of freedom, and death" (ibid.). Yet through instruments like the Geneva Conventions, the principle of reciprocity was eventually surpassed by broader humanitarian obligations that applied universally, even if an enemy state or army did not make a reciprocal commitment.

War in Halakhah

When placing the tenets of war halakhah alongside the UN Partition Plan for Palestine, it appears that the conflict is unreconcilable. Many Israeli *poseqim*, under the influence of Rabbi Abraham Kook (1865–1935), hold that the biblical injunction to "make war with the seven Canaanite nations" is still valid and should be put into force (Rosenak 2014). On the other hand, Resolution 181 recommended the establishment of independent Jewish and Arab states and a Special International Regime for the city of Jerusalem (UN General Assembly Resolution 181, 1947). Most Zionist factions accepted the plan to partition Palestine, while the Arab Higher Committee, the Arab League, and other Arab leaders and governments rejected it. Since the corpus on this matter is vast, we will limit ourselves to the legal opinions of Rabbi Shelomo Goren (1917–1994), Rabbi Shaul Yisraeli (1909–1995), Ḥakham Ben-Ṣion Meir Ḥai Uzziel (1880–1953), Rabbi Yitzhak Roness, Rabbi Moshe Ariel Abel, and Rabbi Shelomo Aviner.

Classical Jewish law recognized a body of law relating to war and the Israelite monarchy—"The Laws of Kings and their Wars," as Maimonides labeled this area of regulation comprising the final section of his monumental twelfth-century code. Of course, Maimonides was writing in Cairo in the 1160s, so his laws pertaining to a Jewish king were purely hypothetical—intended to apply in the messianic era. Nor had there been a Jewish monarch a thousand years earlier, in the days of the rabbis of the Mishnah and the Talmud, from which Maimonides gleaned his principles. In the absence of Jewish sovereignty, the indigenous Jewish laws of war withered or failed to sprout at all.[4] One contemporary scholar noted, with some overstatement, that "the laws of war almost completely disappeared from the corpus and were certainly not part of the active Jewish tradition. There are no relevant rules or traditions of what is permissible and forbidden in times of war, or the legitimate methods and limitations on the use of force" (Edrei 2006, 192). When Jewish sovereignty reemerged in 1948, after nearly two millennia of nothingness, and the new State of Israel promptly found itself plunged into war, the possible applicability of Jewish laws of war quickly became both real and urgent.

Yet to speak of a *Jewish* law of war obscures the fact that beneath or besides the discrete pools of indigenous Jewish law runs a stream of *international* legal norms, to which Jewish law gives effect. On one level, this is due to the skeletal state of the Jewish laws of war. The realities of diplomacy and combat demand legal answers, and if jurists cannot find them in their own law, they will look elsewhere. But the more profound point is that no self-contained national legal system can generate comprehensive and functional laws of war, because war, by its nature, requires legal communication across peoples and cultures, not to mention states and jurisdiction. Without some shared "communicative and normative framework," Yasuaki Onuma has explained, people from different societies "could not even engage in a war, because the war involves a certain exchange of intentions for surrender, a truce, treatment of hostages and other related matters, which could be done

[4] Fragmentary evidence of Jewish laws of war from the first or second centuries BCE is found in the book of Maccabees—which was not accepted into the rabbinic biblical canon, and relates how Jews would not fight on the Sabbath even in self-defense!—as well as in the scrolls found among the Dead Sea sect at Qumran. See Lawrence H. Schiffman, "The Laws of War in the Temple Scroll," *Revue de Qumran* 13 (1988): 299–311; and Steven D. Fraade, "The Torah of the King (Deut. 17:14–20) in the Temple Scroll and Early Rabbinic Law," in *The Dead Sea Scrolls as Background to Postbiblical Judaism and Early Christianity*, ed. James R. Davila, 285–319 (Leiden, The Netherlands: Brill, 2003). See Shlomo M. Brody, *Ethics of Our Fighters* (Jerusalem: Maggid-Koren, 2023).

only through this framework" (Onuma 2000, 8). The Jewish legal system, no less than any other legal system, must transcend itself to govern international conflicts.

An intriguing demonstration of the need for such an international framework—on top of the specifically Jewish legal norms—is found in the biblical episode of Joshua and the Gibeonites, as interpreted by the Jewish legal tradition. The narrative recounts how the Israelites, under the leadership of Joshua, Moses's successor, had entered the promised land and begun conquering cities, including toppling the walls of Jericho. Terrified, a local people from the city of Gibeon devised a ruse to approach the Israelites, claiming to be a distant people, asking for a peace treaty (*berith*). The Israelites were skeptical at first, conscious of the command not to form a pact with any local peoples of Canaan (Num. 23:32)—and, indeed, to wipe them out entirely (Deut. 20:16). But after the Gibeonites made a show of their tattered clothing, worn-out sandals, and cracked wineskins (part of the elaborate deception to prove how far they had traveled), the Israelites acquiesced, and "Joshua made peace with them; he entered into a treaty with them to spare their lives" (Common English Bible, Josh. 9:15). When the truth came out three days later that the Gibeonites were actually locals, the Israelites set out to confront their new neighbors. But after reaching Gibeon and the environs, the Israelites did not attack. When the common folk questioned this dovish approach, the Israelite leaders explained: "We swore to them by the Eternal One, the God of Israel; therefore we cannot touch them" (Common English Bible, Josh. 9:19).

Maimonides discusses this episode in the context of his presentation of the laws of war, in the midst of a section that begins, "We may not wage war against any person in the world until we have offered him peace." He cites Deuteronomy 20:10, which states, "When you approach a city to wage war against it, you shall offer it terms of peace" (Maimonides, *Hil. Melakhim* 6:1). In this context, Maimonides introduces a general rule derived from the story of the Gibeonites, explaining that the king may set various terms for peace, but once he reaches an agreement with the foreign nation, "it is forbidden to lie to them regarding their treaty and deceive them after they have made peace and accepted the seven Noahide commandments." Accepting the Noahide commandments is one of Maimonides's terms of peace.[5]

[5] Maimonides is drawing here on a discussion in the Babylonian Talmud (b.*Gittin* 46a) regarding why the Israelites' oath to the Gibeonites was binding if it was procured by fraud. The Talmud explains that, according to the majority view, the oath was technically void but the

Maimonides then codifies a passage in the Jerusalem Talmud stating that Joshua sent three documents to every people residing in the land of Israel, each one offering a different choice: flee, make peace, or wage war (Maimonides, *Hil. Melakhim* 6:5; *y.Shebi'ith* 6:1).[6] Since Maimonides understands this offer to apply to all the inhabitants of the land of Israel, he asks why the Gibeonites had to resort to trickery rather than simply accepting peace: "If so, why did the inhabitants of Gibeon act deceitfully? Because [Joshua] sent them [the three messages] generally but they did not accept it [at first]; and they did not know the law of Israel, so they believed that we may not offer peace [again]."[7]

The answer is revealing. Maimonides implicitly draws a distinction between the peculiar "law of Israel" (*misphaṭ yisrael*)—that is, the three-letter procedure, along with the precise circumstances under which the Israelites were obliged to make peace or wage war—and the universal law of treaties. The Gibeonites were not familiar with the law of Israel, but they certainly understood the concept of a pact or treaty and fully expected that the Israelites would be bound to honor it, as, in fact, they did. Put differently, the deal between the Gibeonites and the Israelites was possible only because there was an implicit international legal norm that treaties must be obeyed, the bedrock principle of *pacta sunt servanda* (agreements must be kept). According to Maimonides, this principle is not part of the "law of Israel," of which the Gibeonites were ignorant. Rather, it is a rule that belongs to international law that nonetheless finds its way into Jewish law and is codified by Maimonides. In fact, this ruling by Maimonides is cited as the primary proof text of the halakhic obligation not to breach a treaty (Bar-Ilan 2013, 1414, ¶ 289). As

"sanctification of [God's] name" nonetheless required that the Israelites continue to abide by it. Implicit in this passage is that, had the Gibeonites' treaty not been fraudulently obtained, it would have been binding as a matter of law, apart from the extraneous considerations of sanctifying God's name. Importantly, in formulating this general rule Maimonides makes no mention of an oath, but simply refers to a pact (*berith*) or treaty. Others, however, have suggested that the Israelites' concern with breaking the treaty was because of the oath, not out of a general obligation to observe treaties. See Eliezer Waldenberg, *Hilkhot Medina*. This is consistent with the premodern view in which "even positive treaty law was considered to have legal force only because treaties were confirmed by oath, which 'being a "sacrament," subjected the obligation incurred to the jurisdiction of the Church.'" Harold Jongju Koh, "Why Do Nations Obey International Law?," *Yale Law Journal* 106 (1997): 2599, at 2604–5 (quoting Arthur Nussbaum, *A Concise History of the Law of Nations* (New York: Macmillan, 1947)).

6 Although this passage of the Jerusalem Talmud is in Hebrew, it borrows the Greek word *prostagma*, which refers to a written royal order or proclamation. Maimonides uses the more prosaic Hebrew word *ketabim*, meaning documents or letters.

7 Maimonides, *Laws of Kings and Their Wars* 6:5.

one rabbi put it in 1950, "[B]ehold these words of Maimonides, who has taught the nation of Israel to be honest and faithful in any international covenant" (Stern 1950, 163).

Although legal theorists continue to debate the matter, *pacta sunt servanda* is best understood as grounded in natural law. Jewish law, according to many scholars, also understands the rule of *pacta sunt servanda* irrespective of positive law—whether in connection with observing an international treaty, as in Maimonides's discussion of the laws of war, or with respect to the more ordinary obligation to abide by the terms of a commercial contract and to pay one's monetary debts. To demonstrate that the binding nature of a contract arises from reason, independent of positive law, some halakhic jurists in the late nineteenth and early twentieth centuries explained that positive Jewish law is founded upon the covenant made at Mount Sinai to observe the Torah—but what makes the Sinaitic covenant binding, if not for an underlying principle that all covenants must be kept?[8] In effect, these authorities argue, the entire system of Jewish positive law rests on a foundation of natural law. Or, if not natural law, beneath the covenant of Sinai there must be what the influential legal theorist Hans Kelsen called a basic norm (*Grundnorm*) establishing that pacts are binding.[9]

The Universality of a "Scrap of Paper"

World War I forced the world to reckon with the weight of a treaty obligation. The Treaty of London, in 1839, had made Belgium a neutral country, but seventy-five years later, in the summer of 1914, Germany declared war on France and then invaded Belgium to get to the French. This act of aggression triggered Great Britain's treaty obligation to defend Belgian neutrality, so Britain declared war on Germany. In a meeting with the British ambassador to Germany on August 4, 1914, German Chancellor Theobald von Bethmann

[8] See Avnei Nezer, 2 Yoreh De'ah no. 306, cited in J. David Bleich, *The Philosophical Quest: Of Philosophy, Ethics, Law, and Halakhah* (New Milford, CT: Maggid Books, 2013), 86–87 n.6; Elisha Friedman, "Natural Law and Religious Philosophy in R. Shimon Shkop's System," *Tradition* 49, no. 4 (Winter 2016): 53; and Alex S. Ozar, "'These Are Matters Which Shatter Roofs': R. Shimon Shkop on Law and Normativity More Broadly," *Diné Israel* 34 (2020): 111.

[9] Kelsen, a legal positivist, initially proposed that *pacta sunt servanda* was the *Grundnorm* of international law, though he later saw that rule as merely an instance of the broader "norm which countenances custom as a norm-creating fact, and might be formulated as follows: The states ought to behave as they have customarily behaved." See François Rigaux, "Hans Kelsen on International Law," *European Journal of International Law* 9 (1998): 325, at 327–28.

Hollweg "harangue[d]" the ambassador, Edward Goschen, expressing outrage that "just for a word—'neutrality,' a word which in war time had so often been disregarded—just for a scrap of paper Great Britain was going to make war on a kindred nation." Goschen replied that the "solemn compact simply had to be kept, or what confidence could anyone have in engagements given by Great Britain in the future?" (Hull 2014, 43).

The German chancellor's "scrap of paper" remark was widely reported in the press and became a central feature of the Allies' propaganda. It was disastrous for Germany's reputation abroad. It also scandalized some rabbis, who were inclined to view this disregard for treaty obligations through the lens of halakhah. A striking example is R. Chaim Hirschensohn, a native of Palestine who had taken a pulpit in Hoboken, New Jersey. In the preface to his 1926 Hebrew work *Eleh Dibere Ha-Berith* (These are the words of the Covenant) analyzing the concept of a covenant (*berith*) in biblical and postbiblical Jewish literature, Rabbi Hirschensohn states that "the initial provocation" that caused him to write the book was a newspaper article reporting the "scrap of paper" comment—which Rabbi Hirschensohn erroneously remembered being uttered by Kaiser Wilhelm himself:

> The American newspapers stated that he described all international covenants as merely a "scrap of paper" (*pisat niyar*), and my heart then prophesied within me that "those who do all that will not escape" (Ezekiel 17:18), and he will fall in his war with "a sword avenging the vengeance of the covenant" (Leviticus 26:25). For it is a divine law among Israel and the nations that those who breach covenants will become "a horror to all the kingdoms of the earth" (Jeremiah 34:17). It occurred to me then to write a book about the covenants in the Torah [bible]. (Hirschensohn 1926, Introduction, n.p.)[10]

R. Moshe Avigdor Amiel—a rabbi in Antwerp who later became an influential chief rabbi of Tel Abib—was also rankled by Germany's "scrap of paper" dismissal. In a popular book of Hebrew sermons published in Antwerp in 1929, Rabbi Amiel described the wicked biblical nation of

[10] The three verses cited by R. Hirschensohn all refer to divine punishment for violating a covenant, though the quotation of the verse in Ezekiel is slightly imprecise.

'Amaleq—which attacked the Israelites after they had left Egypt—in the following sardonic terms:

> The custom among civilized nations is that, even when they have evil intentions, they nonetheless follow the practice of issuing frequent warnings to their adversary prior to waging war—an ultimatum. . . . But 'Amaleq behaved differently, requiring neither delay nor preparation, and disregarding [the practice of issuing] prior warnings and ultimatums. For why should it bother when all international laws are but a flimsy scrap of paper (*pisat niyar keṭanah*) with which a mighty nation like ['Amaleq] need not engage? (Amiel 1929, 132–33)

Although R. Amiel appears to be invoking customary international law rather than treaty law—since no treaty existed between 'Amaleq and the Israelites, as far as the biblical narrative or postbiblical tradition discloses—the reference to a scrap of paper is unmistakable.

Like Maimonides, R. Hirschensohn and R. Amiel understood the Jewish law of war to encompass a universal, international stratum to which the rule of *pacta sunt servanda* belonged. The point is not only that other nations have a right to hold the Jewish people to account in observing their treaty obligations, as Maimonides states. It is also that Jewish law understands the norm of *pacta sunt servanda* to bind all nations of the world. In other words, that norm is a rule of international law recognized by Jewish law as universally binding. That is why R. Hirschensohn and R. Amiel could invoke halakhah to condemn Germany—or, looking backward, the biblical 'Amaleq—for flouting a basic tenet of international law.

Distinction between Jewish and Universal Applicability

Jewish laws of war contain two distinct strands, one universal and the other particularly Jewish. Any specific law, therefore, could be of one or the other type. Some rules are easy to describe as peculiarly Jewish. For example, an ancient law attributed to R. Natan, the second-century Talmudic sage, requires a Jewish army laying siege to an enemy city not to fully encircle it but rather to leave open "the fourth side so they may flee" (Sifre Bemidbar ¶ 157). According to the thirteenth-century Spanish halakhic authority R. Moses b. Nahman (Nahmanides), this law serves both humanitarian and tactical purposes: "Thus we shall learn to act with mercy even toward our enemies during war, and there is another benefit in leaving them an opening to flee so they will not harden themselves against us."[11] Grotius, citing the English writer John Selden, quotes this opinion in the name of the "Hebrew Expositors," offering as its reason "that they might have less Occasion to shed Blood."[12]

There is little doubt that this law does not reflect—and was never thought to reflect—a universal norm. Because "a city surrounded on three sides is not in fact surrounded," contemporary philosopher Michael Walzer has noted, the "radicalism of the Jewish law is that it pretty much abolishes siege warfare" (Walzer 2006, 163). In fact, Walzer has described this "hopelessly naïve" rule as something that "could only appear in the literature of a people who had neither a State nor an army of their own" (Walzer 1977, 161). For this reason, its application to modern conditions is bitterly contested.

On August 6, 1982, amid the Israeli siege of Beirut, Israel's then chief rabbi, Shlomo Goren, published an article in a newspaper arguing that the Israel Defense Forces were in violation of the law prohibiting a complete siege. Another prominent rabbi, Shaul Yisraeli, penned a rebuttal arguing that this law does not apply to a defensive war (as he characterized the fight against Palestinian Liberation Organization forces in Lebanon)—and would defeat the very purpose of the defensive war by allowing the aggressors to escape.[13]

The Jewish law of three-sided sieges, to whatever extent it applies, belongs to the peculiarly *Jewish* legal corpus of war. Yet, for many other rules discussed in Jewish legal sources, it is less clear whether they derive from the universal, international stratum of law or the particular, national one. We will now demonstrate this point by analyzing some pillars of the Jewish *jus ad bellum* and *jus in bello* as reflected in the classical halakhic sources.

[11] Nahmanides, Commentary on Maimonides' *Sefer Ha-Miṣwoth*, "Fifth Forgotten Positive Commandment."

[12] Grotius, bk. 3, chap. 9, § 14 (citing Selden, bk. 6, end of chap. 15). On the use of Jewish sources in the international law treatises of Selden and Grotius, see Charles Leben, "Hebrew Sources in the Doctrine of the Law of Nature and Nations in Early Modern Europe," *European Journal of International Law* 27 (2016): 79.

[13] See Arye Edrei, "Law, Interpretation, and Ideology: The Renewal of the Jewish Laws of War in the State of Israel," *Cardozo Law Review* 28 (2006): 187, at 222–25. R. Yisraeli, however, noted that only the terrorists must not be allowed to escape, but civilians should be granted free exit. See Shaul Yisraeli, 1 *Hawwath Binyamin* § 14, at 87.

Halakhic Sources of Just War Theory

Regarding the Judeo-Arab conflict, Rabbi Avraham Itzhak HaCohen Kook (1865–1933), the founder of religious Zionism and the first Ashkenazic chief rabbi of British Mandatory Palestine, argued:

> Even a Jewish king . . . would need to consult the High Court before embarking on war, for no war—other than purely defensive—might be pursued against those who observe the Seven Commandments, or Noahide laws, and if the enemy were idolators[14] it would still be necessary for the Court to examine their moral condition before declaring the war justified. (Ravitsky 2006, 1–17)

Rabbi Kook held that preemptive strikes are not sanctioned in Jewish law because they require the approval of the Jewish Senate (Sanhedrin). He referred to wars of expansion of territories (*milḥemeth ha-reshuth*). He maintained that non-Jewish residents who keep the universal principles revealed to Noah by God (the Noahide laws) were not to be considered idolators; Christians and Muslims believe in the God of Abraham and, therefore, are considered Noahides. As such, according to Jewish law, the executive power of Israel cannot declare war against the surrounding peoples to expand territories. Essentially, according to R. Kook's legal reasoning, Israeli military policies to acquire the disputed territories in Judea and Samaria (West Bank) would be considered illegal actions.

Rabbi Moshe Avigdor Amiel (1882–1946) was a Jewish philosopher and leader of the Mizraḥi Movement. Before the establishment of the State of Israel, he said:

> In my opinion, even if we knew for certain that we could bring about the Final Redemption [by killing Arabs] we should reject such a "Redemption" with all our strength and not be redeemed through blood. Moreover, even if we were to apprehend several Arab murderers, if there was the slightest possibility that one of them was innocent, we should not touch them, lest the innocent suffer. (Brekke 2006, 63)

[14] This would exclude Muslims and Christians.

Amiel expressed clearly that the sanctity of human life is above any religious ideology. Thus, he did not view Arabs as the collective "enemy."

Ḥakham Ben-Ṣion Meir Ḥai Uzziel was the Sephardic chief rabbi of Jaffa-Tel Abib from 1912 until 1939 and then the chief Sephardic rabbi of Israel from 1939 until his death in 1953. In a public letter written following the 1947 United Nations Partition Plan, Ḥakham Uzziel addressed a call to the leaders of Islam for Peace and Brotherhood:

> To the Heads of the Islamic Religion in the Land of Israel and throughout the Arab lands near and far, peace and blessing: Brothers, at this hour, as the Jewish people have returned to its Land and State, per the word of God and the prophets in the Holy Scriptures, and in accordance with the decision of the United Nations, we approach you in peace and brotherhood, in the name of God's Torah and the Holy Scriptures, and we say to you, "Please remember the peaceful and friendly relations that existed between us when we lived together in Arab lands and under Islamic Rulers during the Golden Age, when together we developed brilliant intellectual insights of wisdom and science for all of humanity's benefit. Please remember the sacred words of the prophet Malachi, who said, "Have we not all one Father? Did not one God create us? Why do we break faith with one another, profaning the covenant of our ancestors?" (Malachi 2:10). We were brothers, and we shall once again be brothers, working together in cordial and neighbourly relations in this Holy Land, so that we will build it and make it flourish, for the benefit of all of its inhabitants, without discrimination against anyone. We shall do so in faithful and calm collaboration, so that we may all merit God's blessing on His land, from which there shall radiate the light of peace to the entire world." (Public letter by Rabbi Uzziel, 1947)

Ḥakham Uzziel addressed the leaders of the Islamic religion in Arabic to remind them of the glorious past when Jews and Muslims worked together in Al-Andalus and throughout the Arab world, as an appeal to do the same in the Holy Land. He understood very well that religious myth motivated both parties and that it was necessary to promote peace and brotherhood through the common language.

In expressing cosmopolitanism and humanism, Ḥakham Uzziel addressed the Jewish people in the Holy Land:

> Passover teaches us to love all those around us, including our declared enemies, as it is written, "You shall not abhor an Egyptian, for you were

> a stranger in his land" (Deut. 23:8). This means that we do not bear any vengeful grudge towards Egypt or the Egyptians for the suffering and enslavement we endured in their land, rather we only remember that we were strangers in Egypt. We forget all negativity and recall only whatever positive treatment they gave us. We once again reach out to our Arab neighbours in peace, for our sole desire is to live together with you in this Holy Land that is sacred to all nations. Let us engage together in fruitful labour for the sake of peace for all inhabitants of this land. Let us work together, using all of our diversity in religion, beliefs, customs, and languages, so that we can build and assure absolute freedom and equality for all inhabitants in this land. Let us together recognize that only God is the ultimate ruler over the earth, for we are all "strangers in God's world."' (Uzziel 1948)

In this address, Ḥakham Uzziel attempted to tackle the Jewish problem of "othering" Arabs, which only led to constant war and strife. In general, Ḥakham Uzziel opposed coercion as a means of achieving justice and peace (Uzziel 1953, 155–56). Conversely, he viewed the international committee as messengers of humanity and agents of redemption (ibid.).

In comparing the United Nations with the Persian kings Artaxerxes and Cyrus, Ḥakham Uzziel suggests that the state's authority for domestic criminal law derives solely from the authority of the international consensus (Uzziel 1939, 159–82). He constructed his argument based on *dina demalkhuta dina*, comparing international law to an imperial ruler, like the Persian emperors who granted authority to Ezra (Ezr. 7:12–26). As such, he considered the State of Israel a vassal government of the UN (Uzziel 1939, 4:159–82). To protect the spirit of democracy among the worldwide Jewish community as well as in the Holy Land, Ḥakham Uzziel suggested the establishment of global Jewish institutions, separate from the State of Israel and its political leadership (Uzziel 1939, 5:214, 323, 601). To sum up, Ḥakham Uzziel maintained that war halakhah conceded to the dictates of the international legal consensus.

War in Classical Jewish Law

Classical Jewish law recognizes three types of war: *milḥemeth miṣwah* (the biblical injunction to make war with the seven Canaanite nations), *milḥemeth ha-reshuth* (authorized war of expansion of territory), and *milḥemeth ezrath Yisrael miyad ṣar sheba alehem* (a defensive war against an enemy attack). Maimonides defines the halakhic category of these wars:

> The king must first wage only obligatory wars. What is an obligatory war? It is a war against the seven nations, the war against 'Amaleq, and a war to deliver Israel from an enemy who has attacked them. Then he may wage authorized wars, which is a war against others in order to enlarge the borders of Israel and to increase his greatness and prestige. (Maimonides, *Hil. Melakhim* 5:1)

While the first two categories of war can be found explicitly in the Hebrew Bible, the basis for defensive war is not clear.[15] Rabbinic jurists provide different explanations for the source and parameters of a defensive war.

According to classical halakha, a Jewish king may engage in two kinds of legally sanctioned wars: an "obligatory war" (*milḥemet miṣwah*) and a "discretionary war" (*milḥemet reshuth*), alternatively translated as "authorized war." Perhaps the most important legal difference between these two sorts of war is that the king may decide on his own to wage an obligatory war, but the Sanhedrin—the High Court in Jerusalem—must authorize a discretionary war. For this reason, most halakhic authorities consider the concept of a discretionary war inapplicable in contemporary times, given the absence of a formally constituted Sanhedrin. In contrast, the majority view is that an actual king is not strictly necessary for a formal war, but rather, any legitimate government possesses the same war-making powers as a proper monarch.[16]

The division between obligatory and discretionary boils down to different kinds of justifications for war. How to sort out the two categories is debated in the Talmud and is difficult to pin down,[17] but the passage from *Laws of Kings and Their Wars* by Maimonides, quoted above provides the

[15] Instead, you must place these under the ban: Hittites, Amorites, Canaanites, Perizzites, Hivites, and Jebusites—just as the Lord your God commanded you (Deut. 20: 17); So once the Lord your God gives you relief from all the enemies that surround you in the land the Lord your God is giving you as an inheritance to possess, you must wipe out Amaleq's memory from under the heavens (Deut. 25:19).

[16] See, for example, Robert Eisen, *Religious Zionism, Jewish Law, and the Morality of War* (New York: Oxford University Press, 2017), 242–46.

[17] See, for example, ibid., 29–42; Yair Lorberbaum, *Disempowered King: Monarchy in Classical Jewish Literature* (London: Continuum, 2011), 73–79; Michael J. Broyde, Just Wars, Just Battles

authoritative formulation. The first two examples of obligatory wars—referring to the biblical injunctions to annihilate the ancient enemy peoples of Canaan and 'Amaleq—are long defunct since Jewish tradition teaches that those groups are no longer identifiable since King Sennacherib of Assyria "mixed up all the peoples" of the region (Maimonides 2010, *Hil. Melakhim* 5:4; *Hil. Issure Bi'ah* 12:25). That leaves the third type of obligatory war, which is essentially a defensive war. Whether defensive war includes a preemptive strike—and, if so, how imminent the threat must be—is a matter of debate (Bleich 1983, 3).

Scholars have long puzzled at Maimonides's definition of an obligatory war as "the deliverance of Israel from the hand of an aggressor." The Babylonian Talmud says a defensive strike against idolaters is *discretionary*, whereas Maimonides seemingly says the opposite. While some have suggested that Maimonides was drawing upon the Jerusalem Talmud's apparent distinction between repelling an attack and initiating hostilities to deter future attacks, that passage is not fully clear (*b.Sotah* 44b; *y.Sotah* 8:10).[18] Moreover, Maimonides's language is almost poetic, recalling the pairing of "deliverance" (*'ezer*) and "aggressor" (*ṣar*) found in biblical poems (Deut. 33:7, Lamentations 1:7, and Ps. 60:13).

One gets the impression that Maimonides thought it obvious that a defensive war was obligatory, but finding no clear Talmudic source to cite or paraphrase, he leaned on biblical phrases for additional support. Maimonides, a famously crisp writer who prized brevity, did not elaborate on his rationale. Nonetheless, we might speculate that Maimonides did not consider self-defense a particularly Jewish concept but rather part of the universal law of nations. Unlike the wars of Canaan and Amaleq, which belong to the Israelite law (*mishpaṭ yisraeli*) that the inhabitants of Gibeon did not fully grasp, a war of self-defense is one that foreigners would have had no trouble comprehending. Moreover, evidently, Maimonides understood the international legal norm of self-defense as imposing a *duty* on the king to defend his people, not merely a right. The verse in I Samuel implies as much, since the

and Just Conduct in Jewish Law: Jewish Law Is Not a Suicide Pact!, in *War and Peace in the Jewish Tradition*, ed. Lawrence Schiffman and Joel B. Wolowelsky (New York: KTAV, 2004), 12–17; Yitzchak Kaufman, *Ha- Ṣaba Ka-Halakhah: Hilkhoth Milḥamah We- Ṣaba* (1994), chap. 1; and Reuven Kimelman, "The Ethics of National Power: Government and War from the Sources of Judaism," in *Authority, Power, and Leadership in the Jewish Polity*, ed. Daniel J. Elazar (Lanham, MD: University Press of America, 1991), 265–67.

[18] See Waldenberg, *Hilkhoth Medina*.

Israelites demanded that the prophet appoint "a king over us; that we also may be *like all the nations*; and that our king may judge us, and go out before us, and fight *our battles*" (8:19–20). Though Maimonides does not cite it, this verse may well have led him to believe that internationally accepted norms require the king to fight in defense of his people—that's the king's raison d'être, after all—so such a war must be halakhically obligatory.

What of the discretionary wars, which Maimonides characterizes as wars fought for territorial gain or political benefit? Those motives smack of the sort of frivolous grounds for war that Grotius abhorred and are obviously prohibited by the UN Charter. Some rabbis were troubled by the apparent halakhic sanction for expansionist wars. For example, writing in Germany in 1738, Rabbi Samuel b. Elkanah Ashkenazi raised a spirited objection that recalls Grotius:

> How could it be that all the wars from Joshua onward are considered completely "discretionary" and in no way commanded? How could Saul dare to battle the Philistines, and David with all his wars of profit and to expand the borders of Israel, and various other wars—who gave them the right to endanger thousands of lives in Israel for a completely discretionary matter that is not a commandment [*reshuth le-gamre we-eno miṣwah kelal*]? (Ashkenazi 1738, 18)

R. Samuel's solution was to reinterpret the word "discretionary" (*reshuth*) as a term of art—even suggesting that the Hebrew is better translated as "authorized" on account of the need for the Sanhedrin to authorize such a war. He reconceptualized a discretionary war as a quasi-commandment, implicitly rejecting the idea that wars could be fought legally for frivolous reasons. Although discretionary war is obsolete due to the lack of a properly constituted Sanhedrin, many prominent rabbis who wrestled with the problem in the twentieth century drew upon R. Samuel's creative thinking.[19]

In a similar vein, R. Joseph B. Soloveitchik, a leading figure of American Orthodox Jewry in the twentieth century, reinterpreted the Talmudic passages that appear to say that economic considerations can justify a discretionary war. Against the plain meaning of the Talmud and Maimonides, R. Soloveitchik posited that even a discretionary war must be justified on

[19] See ibid.; Moshe Tzvi Neriya, *Milḥamoth Shabbath* (1959).

essentially defensive grounds, though it is not obligatory because the threat is remote (Schachter 1994, 97).[20]

Ḥakham José Faur, a prominent Sephardic rabbi, scholar, and author, offered a nuanced view on defensive wars in Jewish law. He emphasized the importance of self-defense within Jewish legal tradition but also stressed the necessity of adhering to ethical principles even in times of conflict. Faur's perspective reflects traditional Jewish teachings that permit defensive warfare when the Jewish community is under threat. However, he also highlighted the ethical constraints outlined in Jewish law, such as the obligation to minimize civilian casualties and to pursue peace whenever possible. Overall, Faur asserts, "Jews are instructed to protect the nation's security as a precursor for the reestablishment of a Jewish autonomous polity therein." Essentially, his approach to defensive wars in halakhah seems to prioritize preserving life and protecting the Jewish community while remaining cognizant of the ethical responsibilities inherent in armed conflict (Faur 1976).

War, Halakhah, and International Law

A second way of approaching the problem of discretionary wars explicitly invokes international law. R. Shaul Yisraeli, an influential halakhic authority of the last century in Israel, pioneered this view. Born in 1909 in Slutsk, in the Russian Empire, Rabbi Shaul Yisraeli studied under Rabbi Isser Zalman Meltzer and Rabbi Yehezkel Abramsky. He escaped Russia in 1933 through Poland, but after he was caught by the Polish authorities, Israeli Chief Rabbi Avraham Itzhak HaCohen Kook petitioned on his behalf. For the next five years, R. Yisraeli studied at *Mercaz Ha-Rab Yeshibah*. After serving as community rabbi for over thirty years, he was appointed judge in the Supreme Rabbinical Court in Jerusalem in 1965. He passed away in 1995 and was buried in the Sanhedria cemetery.

[20] Tzvi (Hershel) Schachter, Nefesh Ha-Rab 97 (1994). See also Aviezer Ravitzky, "Prohibited Wars," in *Law, Politics, and Morality in Judaism*, ed. Michael Walzer (Princeton, NJ: Princeteon University Press, 2006), 171–73. In the early eighteenth century, the illustrious Turkish authority R. Efraim Navon described the war of Amaleq against the Israelites as illegal because it was "a time of peace"—apparently alluding to its aggressive character. Efraim Navon, *Mahane Efraim, Hilkhoth Abadim* § 3 (1738). Similarly, in his commentary on the book of Judges, the nineteenth-century scholar R. Meir Leibush ben Yehiel Michel Wisser ("Malbim") explained the intriguing debate between the Israelite and Amonite leadership as whether the Amonite attack was "contrary to the laws of kings and the norms of states." Malbim, *Commentary on Judges*, 11:27.

More than any other rabbinic decisor, R. Yisraeli developed and discussed the relationship between halakhah and international law. Concerning *jus ad bellum* and *jus in bello*, he maintained that international law overrides Jewish law. Essentially, the international legal consensus can prohibit what the Bible permits and permit what the Bible prohibits. As others before him, he based his premise on the rabbinic principle *dina demalkhuta dina*. Contrary to R. Kook who held that *milḥemeth miṣwah* was still in full force, R. Yisraeli posited that it was exempted from the domain of international law (Fuchs and Hollander 2014, 308).[21]

R. Yisraeli documented the various jurists who based the war of defense on the *milḥemeth miṣwah*, since soldiers engage in war on the premise that they will fulfill the biblical precept "Do not do anything that endangers your neighbor's life" (Roness 2010, 186; Lev. 19:16). However, R. Yisraeli challenged this explanation because it supposes that one must endanger oneself in order to save other lives (Yisraeli 1966, 184). He proposed that a defensive war was legitimate due to the divine mandate to exact revenge on Israel's enemies or to sanctify the Divine Name (Roness 2010, 186).

In *Amud Ha-Yemin* he explains that reprisals may also be justified as a discretionary war. He invokes the Talmudic rule of *dina demalkhuta dina*, or "the law of the land is the law," which gives halakhic force to secular law (Last Stone 2008).[22] R. Yisraeli's breakthrough was to apply this principle to *international law* in addition to ordinary municipal law:

> We can thus say that *dina demalkhuta* [the law of the land] among the states also derives from the consent of the citizens, and that consent is effectual even in matters of life and death. That is the foundation of the legality of war. In fact, if all the nations were to reach an agreement to prohibit war, such that it will cease to be a law practiced among the nations, then neither war nor conquest would be legal, and any nation that initiates war will be judged under the laws of murder and bloodshed. But so long as the practice of war is accepted among the nations, the law does not prohibit war either, and for that reason Israel is also allowed to wage a discretionary war. . . . In war, one need not precisely distinguish between the righteous and the wicked because that is the nature of war—such distinctions are impossible.

[21] For the definition of compulsory versus noncompulsory wars, see Yitzchak Avi Roness, "Halakha, Ideology and Interpretation: R. Shaul Yisraeli on the Status of Defensive War," *Jewish Law Association Studies* 20 (2010): 184–95.

[22] See Shmuel Shillo, *Dina DeMalkhuta Dina* (1975) (Hebrew).

> And even so war has been permitted, so long as it is accepted among the nations.[23]

Remarkably, R. Yisraeli propounds a sweeping incorporation of international law into Jewish law through the vehicle of *dina demalkhuta dina*. R. Yisraeli's essay proved to be profoundly influential.[24] Although he ultimately did not rely on the grounds of discretionary war—which virtually all halakhic authorities hold cannot be waged without a Sanhedrin—his view that the international laws of war are binding as a matter of Jewish law became the standard view with respect to *jus in bello*, as we shall discuss.

Let us first pause for a moment on the question of *jus ad bellum*. Instead of reinterpreting the category of discretionary war as a quasi-commandment, R. Yisraeli understands it to be fully discretionary. In this portion of his essay, R. Yisraeli understood reprisal as a discretionary war because, while fundamentally a defensive act designed to deter future attacks, it is not a defense against an imminent threat. The license to use force in discretionary wars derives from international law, not the authorization of the Sanhedrin or any other source internal to Jewish law. But international law also constrains the ability to use force. Reprisals were once considered lawful, but over the past several decades a near-universal opinion has crystallized forbidding reprisals. For example, the UN General Assembly's "Declaration on Friendly Relations" expressly prohibits reprisals, as does Security Council Resolution 188, passed in 1964, in relation to England's use of force in Yemen.[25] Does this mean that R. Yisraeli would now agree that a reprisal is forbidden? Not necessarily. Scholars have generally explained that R. Yisraeli's view gives weight to the law and custom *as practiced*, not as professed by the states.[26]

Here he parts ways with the mainstream interpretation of international law. Courts and international lawyers tend to reason, somewhat paradoxically,

[23] Yisraeli, *Amud Ha-Yemini*, 137.

[24] On this essay and on R. Yisraeli's views of the laws of war more broadly, see Robert Eisen, *Religious Zionism, Jewish Law, and the Morality of War* (Oxford: Oxford University Press, 2017), 129–66; Roness, "Halakha, Ideology, and Interpretation," 186; Michael J. Broyde, "Public and Private International Law from the Perspective of Jewish Law," in *The Oxford Handbook of Judaism and Economics* (Online ed.) (Oxford: Oxford Academic, 2010); Arye Edrei, "Law, Interpretation, and Ideology: The Renewal of the Jewish Laws of War in the State of Israel," *Cardozo Law Review* 28 (2006): 187; Nerya Gutel, "Lehima Be-Shetah Ravuy Uchlusiya Ezrahit," *Tehumin* 23 (2003): 28, at 40.

[25] See Christine D. Gray, *International Law and the Use of Force*, 4th ed. (Oxford: Oxford University Press, 2018), 205. For a broader treatment and a dissenting view, see generally Yishai Beer, "Regulating Armed Reprisals: Revisiting the Scope of Lawful Self-Defense," *Columbia Journal of Transnational Law* 59 (2020): 117.

[26] Gutel, "Lehima Be-Shetah Ravuy Uchlusiya Ezrahit."

that even violations of international law can be evidence of a prevailing norm when the violation is accompanied by some rationalization. For example, in a landmark case regarding the ability to bring suits under international law in US courts, the US Court of Appeals for the Second Circuit stated that the "fact that the prohibition of torture is often honored in the breach does not diminish its binding effect as a norm of international law."[27] R. Yisraeli, it seems, grants authority to international norms actually observed by states but not those "honored in the breach."[28]

In response to a series of terror attacks, the Israeli government sent commandos across the Jordanian border into the village of Qibya in October 1953 for a reprisal raid. It was a massacre. Sixty-nine people were killed, among them many women and children. Soon afterward, R. Yisraeli penned a defense of the reprisal that focused on the legality of launching attacks against terrorists despite the inevitability of incidentally killing civilians. But R. Yisraeli also treats the reprisal as a question of *jus ad bellum*, offering several reasons why the use of force was justified. He eventually decides that the reprisal is best justified as an obligatory war as a matter of self-defense, which he somewhat confusingly labels a war of "vengeance," borrowing from a biblical passage.

Regarding the deaths of innocent lives taken in warfare, R. Yisraeli expressed:

> And we do not find the obligation in war to distinguish between blood and blood [=between soldiers and civilians] . . . in the course of war, when laying siege to a city and the like, there is no obligation, nor is it truly possible, to be punctilious in this regard. (Yisraeli 1966, 183)

Robert Eisen understands that R. Yisraeli makes this justification on the notion of eliminating the *rodef* (pursuer) (Eisen 2017, 144). So, if Arab civilians threaten Jewish lives by encouraging and supporting terrorism, then they are considered *pursuers*. However, this only includes enemy civilians who

[27] *Filartiga v. Pena-Irala*, 630 F.2d 876, 884 n.15 (2d Cir. 1980). See also Military and Paramilitary Activities in and Against Nicaragua *(Nicar. v. U.S.)*, Judgment, 1986 I.C.J. 14, ¶ 186 ("If a State acts in a way prima facie incompatible with a recognized rule, but defends its conduct by appealing to exceptions or justifications contained within the rule itself, then whether or not the State's conduct is in fact justifiable on that basis, the significance of that attitude is to confirm rather than to weaken the rule.").

[28] See Gray, *International Law and the Use of Force*, 25: "[T]he insistence that breaches may be seen as strengthening rather than negating rules cannot be taken too far without losing plausibility."

are adults. R. Yisraeli justified the Qibya reprisal as a preemptive strike, motivated by the notion of saving lives from a real and imminent threat (Yisraeli 1966, 184, 196). He sourced the defensive war with the biblical account of the injunction given to Moses to declare a war of revenge on the Midianites: "Go after the Midianites and destroy them because they went after you by the deception they devised for you" (Num. 25:17). Indeed, in interpreting this verse as a legal precedent for the third normative category of sanctioned war, then it must be understood as a war of vengeance, and not simply a war to save lives:

> There is room to conduct reprisals and to avenge Israel's enemies, and such a mission is included in the category of a commanded war, and as for any tragedy or harm that may befall the marauders and their comrades—they bear full responsibility, and will bear their sin. There is no obligation whatsoever to refrain from reprisal attacks out of fear that innocents may be harmed, for we are not the cause of any such harm. Rather they themselves are the cause—and we are clean from any sin. (Yisraeli 1966, 198–99)

> Overall, R. Yisraeli reinterpreted this category of war as a "radically militant religious worldview." (Roness 2010, 189)

Moreover, when Jews are attacked for being Jews, a halakhic obligation exists to frustrate the attack. R. Yisraeli argued that this constituted the sanctification of the Divine Name, "When all Jews go out together as one to fight the murderer's intent on harming Jews, the Divine Name is sanctified" (Yisraeli 1966, 131). Interpreting the Rashi's commentary on the account of war with the Midianites, R. Yisraeli understood that "if one stands against Israel, it is as if he stood against the Almighty" (Rashi on Num. 31:3). R. Yitzchak Roness disagrees with R. Yisraeli's halakhic argument: "Nowhere in the halakhic literature do we find this biblical account transformed into a normative precedent for such wars in the future" (Roness 2010, 192).

Translating International Law into Halakhic Language

R. Shelomo Goren (1917–1994) was a leading rabbinic decisor within religious Zionist circles. He was born in Poland and emigrated to Israel in 1925 with his family. He was Israel's first chief rabbi of the military. Many questions he dealt with had no legal precedents within Jewish law. The newly formed Israeli army presented him with many challenges in translating the language of international law into halakhic language (Goren 1959, 8–11). In the long run, he addressed the moral standpoints of international law from a Jewish legal perspective for contemporary society. Although R. Goren criticized doctrines of international law which put the State of Israel at risk, he did incorporate some elements of humanitarian law (*jus in bello*) in his halakhic responsa (Fuchs and Hollander 2014, 301).

R. Goren was forced to find ways to reconcile the idea of democracy, the rights of minorities, and criminal law with Jewish law (Cohen 1998). Even though the Talmud deals with the laws of penal crimes,[29] R. Goren ruled that the death penalty should be annulled for the sake of demonstrating the *standard of civilization* of sovereign nations: "The halakhah regulating the death penalty of non-Jews has been discussed in the Talmud and in some of the *Rishonim* [medieval Talmudic authorities], but for constitutional and practical reasons we shall have to annul *halachically* all death penalties in the Jewish State, as do most of the advanced nations" (Cohen 1998, 155–56). Not only did R. Goren consider the State of Israel to be Jewish, but he also sought to annul the death penalty as a sign of moral advancement.

Regarding the issue of territories acquired by Israel in the 1967 war, R. Goren agreed that Israeli presence in Judea, Samaria, and the Gaza Strip was not an occupation but was valid according to Jewish tradition. At the ICJ, in the advisory on the Western Sahara, it was agreed that only those territories considered *terra nullius* can be acquired through occupation (ICJ Rep. 12, ¶ 80 (1975)). This requires that those territories be devoid of sovereign control. As such, territories inhabited by a population possessing social and political order do not fall under this status. R. Goren maintained:

> Jewish sovereignty over the Land of Israel is not merely an issue of national values. It is a basis for all of the Torah, Torah values, commandments, and prohibitions, as we observe the first commandment of God to Abraham—already in Haran, before he came to the Land of Israel—did not relate to any other commandment besides to go and live in the Land, to take possession of the Land and to settle the Land of Israel, for himself and for his descendants.... The first commandment was to go to the Land of Israel, to take possession thereof, and to settle there. (Goren 1999, 68)

[29] See Mishnah to tractates *Sanhedrin* and *Makkoth*.

On the issue of sovereignty R. Goren asserts, "If we had intended to take possession of Judea and Samaria in the Six-Day War . . . all the liberated area would have automatically become part of the State of Israel, under Jewish sovereignty" (Goren 1999, 281). Even though R. Goren argued that the State of Israel must adhere to the decisions of the international legal consensus as a religious duty; nonetheless, this duty cannot undermine Jewish sovereignty (ibid., 283). Ultimately, Rabbi Goren did not accept the abrogation of *milḥemeth miṣwah* by international law.

During an interview, R. Moshe Ariel Abel—an Israeli citizen and military chaplain in the British armed forces—raised interesting points regarding *jus ad bellum* as it relates to war halakhah. "Essentially," he asked, "to what extent is Arab a term halakhically synonymous with enemy? That would impact greatly upon the premise for deciding halakhically what limits there should be to what happens in those areas. And whether the halakhah follows international law, democratic will or military necessity."[30]

He clearly identifies the issue at stake, namely, that if Arabs are the *enemy*, then it is incumbent upon the Jewish people to eliminate them as threats against the establishment of a Jewish state. Apparently, this would be the only justification for contemporary wars of defense or revenge from a halakhic perspective. R. Abel presents the inherent conflict between international law and war halakhah:

> Finally, whether what requires Sanhedrin approval refers limitedly to what is expropriated for financial gain only (Israel conquering Arab lands for oil wells) or whether it also refers to land annexation resulting from what was taken during a time of war. (War declared on Israel or a war of attrition). Well, I certainly can't agree with that. And the *halakhic* standpoint is incredibly variegated in my view. What halakhah was David carrying out when he put to death the children of Riṣpah bat Ayyah? The halakhah indeed relies upon authority, but to say that an extinct body such as the Sanhedrin must resurge before anything else happens on a regional stage including militarily gained land is peculiar. To resort to saying that if it can't be the Sanhedrin then it can't be *halakhic* is to be too quick, jurisprudentially.[31]

[30] Moshe Ariel Abel, interview with the author on the State of Israel, the Halakhah, and international law, February 23, 2019.

[31] Moshe Ariel Abel, interview with the author on the State of Israel, the Halakhah, and international law, February 23, 2019.

R. Abel holds that a Jewish Senate is not needed for many things within the context of war because the contemporary nonexistence of the Senate would lead to legal and political stagnation.

His analysis presents a complex scenario, where Jewish law is not clear and cannot be applied with blanket statements. His question about what halakhah David carried out in putting to death the children of Riṣpah bat Ayyah refers to a story in the book of Joshua. During the conquest of Canaan, Joshua, son of Nun, made an oath with the Gibeonites, wherein they would not be killed but would serve the Israelites forever (Josh. 9:16–27). King Saul, however, broke this oath, leading to a three-year famine during David's subsequent rule. When David asked the Gibeonites what Israel should do to remedy Saul's violation of the oath, they requested the death of seven of Saul's sons. Riṣpah, daughter of Ayyah was one of King Saul's concubines, and the mother of two of Saul's sons whom David slew (Josh. 21:1–22). R. Abel asks on what grounds David acted.

The introduction of this case supposes that there are legal precedents where extralegal matters are left to the discretion of the monarchy (or the government). He concludes by cautioning against saying that "if it can't be the Sanhedrin then it can't be halakhic." In his view, then, the Israeli government has the right to make political-legal decisions without the approval of the Senate.

In a somewhat different approach, R. Shelomo Aviner asserts that during times of peace, international law should be upheld. However, during times of unrest, all trust is broken, and the Israeli military is obligated to be victorious to prevent the destruction of Jewish lives. During a lecture in 1989 on the status of international agreements and what binds the State of Israel during a time of war, R. Aviner took the stance that all offensive wars are prohibited, but defensive wars are permitted. This would include the right to prevent an enemy attack (Aviner 2000). R. Aviner takes this stance due to the unenforceable nature of international law to prevent wars:

> No one can order to show kindness and to be considerate towards the enemy, not to shoot a paratrooper in the air, out of an excess of humanity and decency. The prohibition of "Thou shalt not kill" is known and should not be violated. But when you are busy saving lives, there is no room for kindness. The lives of the people are in danger; therefore, we must do whatever is necessary in order to save them and be victorious, use all weapons and not be overwhelmed. (Aviner 2000, 164)

In sum, R. Aviner argues that the Israeli army must put humanity and kindness aside during war. This position converges with that of R. Abel, who says that during war, not only are the Geneva Conventions null, but so are Torah laws, such as prohibitions against lying and stealing.

R. Aviner argues that while all treaties between nations must be honored a priori, their abrogation becomes the legal basis for *jus ad bellum*. As such, "we are subject to international agreements, both written and customary, but during war, the rules change" (Aviner 2000, 169). When it comes to peace, R. Aviner identifies three tiers: forced peace, ideal peace, and eternal peace (ibid., 77). If at all, international law secures the first two, whereas the latter will ensue when the long-awaited Messiah rules a Jewish government in the Holy Land:

> When the change of the world state comes, private national pride will diminish, not because of force . . . but due to the elevation of the foundation of God's influence and the recognition of Israel's superiority and righteousness over all the nations of the globe. Then the time of peace will come, when the sword will be broken . . . world peace will come in years or generations. We don't know how many! It will come when Israel itself rises to the highest level, having the power to subdue all the peoples of the earth. Then Israel will take its weapon in hand and execute righteous judgment on the nations. . . . At that time will come the inauguration of the third tier, eternal peace, which is the name of the Almighty. (Aviner 2000, 246–49)

R. Aviner envisions the Messianic era as one that will develop gradually as nationalism decreases in the world and the divine influence is felt among the nations. He also imagines the Jewish state executing righteous judgment on the nations. This vision supposes that the tribunal then in power will have international enforcing authority. Overall, this vision will come to fruition as the people of Israel elevate themselves materially and spiritually.

Halakhah and Humanitarian Law

The consensus among the *poseqim* is that the rules of *jus ad bellum* are determined by international law. The biblical injunction to make war with the seven Canaanite nations and 'Amaleq is superseded by international law. However, opinions regarding *jus in bello* are numerous. Some *poseqim* maintain that the Israeli military must set an example for the nations and not desecrate the Holy Name through its actions. In contrast, others posit that Israel's army may do whatever it takes to defend its citizens. Despite these differences, all Jewish jurists agree that Israel has the right to defend itself from enemy attacks. Whether Israel can attack preemptively or not is the issue at stake in reconciling war halakhah with humanitarian law.

As in international law, it is widely accepted that Jewish law prohibits the targeting of civilians in warfare.[32] This is so despite the numerous biblical passages that seem to endorse slaying entire enemy populations, or at least all adult males. Indeed, Maimonides codifies the law as it would appear from Deuteronomy: When a city refuses to accept the offer of "peace," the Jewish army should "wage war and kill all the adult males, and claim all their property and children, but [they] do not kill the women and children."[33] Perhaps the dominant contemporary view is articulated by R. Eliezer Melamed, an Israeli author of a popular treatise on Jewish law. R. Melamed first justifies the biblical practices on the grounds that, given the then-prevalent barbarism, any lesser acts of slaughter would have exposed the Israelites to further attacks. But he quickly adds: "Thank God, today it is no longer acceptable to kill every [adult] male, and generally [armies] try not to harm the civilian population; consequently, it is forbidden to do so."[34]

Some halakhic authorities have interpreted the command in Deuteronomy 20:13 to "slay every male thereof with the edge of the sword" as referring only to male combatants. This was evidently the view of Se'adya Gaon, the towering tenth-century Babylonian commentator and philosopher. According to Se'adya, the victorious Jewish army should "kill the combatants [*al-muharibin*] and let the rest live."[35] Likewise, writing in Tsarist Russia in the nineteenth century, R. Naftali Zvi Yehuda Berlin

[32] See Amos Israel-Vleeschhouwer, "Endangering Soldiers and Protecting Innocents in Battle: An Analysis of Jewish Legal Attitudes and a Process Oriented View," *Mishpaṭ We-Asaqim* (Law and Business) 17 (2014): 605 (Hebrew]).

[33] Maimonides, *Laws of Kings and Their Wars* 6:4.

[34] Elizer Melamed, *Penine Halakha, Ha-Am we-Ha'Areṣ* 4:14, at 103 (2nd ed., 2005) (Hebrew).

[35] Sefer Ha-Miṣwoth [Kitab Al-Sharia] Le-Rab Se'adya Gaon § 24:5, ed. Nissim Sabato (2019) [Arabic and Hebrew]; see also Moshe Zucker, "*Keta'im Ḥadashim Mi-Sefer Ha-* Miṣwoth *Le-Rab Hefeṣ ben Yaṣliaḥ,*" *Proceedings of the American Academy for Jewish Research* 29 (1960–1962): 52 n.32. This interpretation is questioned (and attributed to the *Kitab Al-Sharia*) by the anonymous interlocutor of Maimonides's son, Abraham, in Teshuboth Rabbenu Abraham ben Ha-Rambam § 64 (A. H. Freimann ed., S. D. Gottein trans. 1937) (Arabic and Hebrew). R. Abraham b. Maimonides replied that he did not know of a source supporting this view. It is noteworthy that, to our knowledge, this view of Se'adya Gaon has not been cited in the literature regarding the Jewish law of protecting civilians in war.

(known by the acronym "Netziv") interpreted the Deuteronomic word for males (*zekhura*) as "combatants" (*lohamim*).[36] Likewise, R. Joseph Soloveitchik understood Maimonides's statement that one should kill the "adult males" as referring strictly to enemy soldiers, not civilians.[37] To the extent that these authorities interpret the biblical command, they may rely on a particularly Jewish norm, not one of international law. Similarly, commenting on the biblical atrocity committed by the evil King Menahem after conquering the city of Tiphsah—"all the women therein that were with child he ripped up"—the prodigious nineteenth-century European scholar R. Meir Leibush ben Yehiel Michel Wisser ("Malbim") explained that this brutal act was "against the laws of war and against the Jewish religion" (*neged ḥuqe ha-milḥama we-neged ha-dat ha-yehudith*), implying that these categories are not identical.[38]

However, R. Soloveitchik describes the principle of not targeting civilians as the accepted custom of nations at the time. This was precisely the wickedness of the nation of Amaleq, he suggests, in that they broke from the customary norm by waging a war of extermination against the Jewish people, targeting even women and children.[39] Similarly, R. Joseph Rosen—a famous halakhic savant from Latvia who died in 1936—wrote that Maimonides's rule against killing enemy women and children derived from the "custom of war" (*nimus milḥama*) among all nations, and that is what startled King Ahasuerus regarding Haman's genocidal plan against the Jewish people in the book of Esther.[40]

Certainly, there is little historical evidence for assertions that massacring women and children violated the customary law of nations in ancient times. Even Grotius was forced to say that the practice was not strictly unlawful and, therefore, could not be punished, though he found it barbaric and morally wrong.[41] Historical accuracy aside, however, the significance of these rabbinic views lies in their understanding of the halakhic prohibition of

[36] See Naftali Tzvi Yehuda Berlin, *Ha'ameq Dabar*, Deut. 20:13. This comment did not appear in the first edition of *Ha'ameq Dabar*, published in 1879, but rather was among the glosses made by the Netziv to his personal copy of the first edition, which were eventually inserted into the next edition published by his son in 1938. See Shemaria Gershuni, *Al Ketivat 'Ha'amek Davar' ve-al Perush 'Hasidekha', Ha-Ma'ayan* 202 (2012): 50, at 52.

[37] Zvi (Hershel) Schacther, Nefesh Ha-Rab 89–90 (1994).

[38] Malbim, II Kings 15:16.

[39] Ibid.

[40] Joseph Rosen, Zaphenath Paneah: Exodus, commentary on Esther 7:5, at 189 (ed. Menahem M. Kasher, 1969).

[41] Grotius, *Laws of War and Peace*, bk. 3, chap. 4, sec. 9.

slaughtering women and children—and noncombatants more generally, according to some—as reflecting a binding *universal* norm, not a particularistic Jewish one.

In addition to these piecemeal acknowledgments of individual binding norms under the law of nations, another halakhic approach categorically imbues the corpus of international law with the force of law. This view is associated with R. Shaul Yisraeli, who, as we saw above with respect to *jus ad bellum*, incorporates the international laws of war into Jewish law wholesale. Since R. Yisraeli invoked international norms only with respect to discretionary wars, there is some debate as to whether he would apply the international law of armed conflict to an obligatory war as well.[42] But the more sensible view is, as expressed by R. Yisraeli's student and son-in-law R. Avraham Sharir, that

> according to R. Yisraeli, there is not *and cannot be* any conflict between the Torah commandment and the custom among nations [in war]. The obligation of the commandment "to deliver Israel from the hand of an aggressor" is a law derived from the Torah, but its contours—based on *dina demalkhuta dina* [the law of the land is the law]—must follow the accepted norms among the nations.[43]

Challenges and Complexities with Legal Symbiosis

After exploring a limited corpus on the legal opinions of some contemporary Jewish authorities, we can conclude that incorporating international humanitarian law into Jewish law is a complex and challenging task. The main difficulties arise from the differences in the underlying principles, sources, and methodologies of the two legal systems. Jewish law, rooted in the Torah and centuries of rabbinic tradition, is a distinct and autonomous system that has evolved. On the other hand, international humanitarian law is a modern and evolving set of rules that aim to regulate the conduct of warfare and protect human rights. Furthermore, Jewish law employs a deductive approach, relying on textual interpretation and analogical reasoning, whereas

[42] See Israel-Vleeschhouwer, "Endangering Soldiers and Protecting Innocents in Battle" (Hebrew).

[43] Avraham Yisrael Sharir, "Al Qiddush Ha-Shem Be-Milḥemeth Miṣwah," *Tzohar* 31 (2008), http://asif.co.il/wpfb-file/zhr-31-7-pdf/ (Hebrew).

international humanitarian law uses a more inductive approach, relying on empirical observation and statutory construction. The incorporation of international humanitarian law may thus lead to conflicts with existing Jewish law and tradition, particularly in areas such as just war theory, self-defense, and the treatment of noncombatants. Thus, there is a need for nuanced interpretation and contextual understanding to avoid unintended consequences or conflicts with existing Jewish law. Ultimately, the successful incorporation of international humanitarian law into Jewish law will depend on careful consideration of these challenges and a willingness to engage in constructive dialogue between scholars and practitioners from both legal traditions.

Bibliography

Primary Sources

Amil, Moshe Avigdor. *Derashoth El Ami,* Vol. 3. Jerusalem, Israel: 1929.

Ashkenazi, Samuel b. Elkanah. *Maqom Shemuel,* no. 18. Altona, Hamburg: HaSefer, 1738.

Aviner, Shelomo. *Meḥayil el Ḥayil: Tuqaf Haskamim Benleumim Be-itot Milḥama.* Jerusalem, Israel: 2000.

Bar-Ilan, Naftali. *Mishtar wu-Medina Be-Yisrael Al Pi Ha-Torah.* 2nd ed. Jerusalem, Israel: Ereṣ Ḥemda, 2013.

Cohen, Asher. *Ha-Ṭalet We-Hadegel: Ha-Ṣiyunut Ha-Datit We-Ḥazon Medinath Ha-Tora Beshnoth Ha-Medina Ha-Rishonoth.* Jerusalem, Israel: 1998.

Goren, Shlomo. Ba'ayot Ha-Medina Le-Or Ha-Halakha. *Or Ha-Mizraḥ* Jerusalem, Israel: 1959.

Goren, Shlomo. *Torath Ha-Medinah: Mehkar Hilkhati Histori Banoṣim Ha-'Omdim Be-Rumah Shel Medinath Yisrael Me'az Tekumatah.* Jerusalem, Israel: 1999.

Grotius, Hugo. *Prolegomena.* Whitefish, MT: Literary Licensing, 2011 [1625].

Hirschensohn, Chayim. *Eleh Dibere Ha-Berith.* London, UK: Ha-Me'orer, 1926.

Kaufman, Yitzchak. *Ha-Ṣaba Ka-Halakhah: Hilkhoth Milḥamah We-Ṣaba.* Jerusalem, Israel: Qol Mebaser, 1994.

Maimonides, Moses, Yeḥi'el M. Zilber, and Me'ir A. Horoyits. *Mishneh Torah: Hilkhoth Issure Bi'ah.* Jerusalem, Israel: Mekhon Moreshet haNesher Hagadol, 2010.

Maimonides, Moses, Yeḥi'el M. Zilber, and Me'ir A. Horoyits. *Mishneh Torah: Hilkhoth Melakhim.* Jerusalem, Israel: Mekhon Moreshet haNesher Hagadol, 2010.

Melamed, Elizer. *Penine Halakha, Ha-Am we-Ha'Areṣ.* Jerusalem, Israel: Toby Press, 2017.

Schachter, Tzvi (Hershel). *Nefesh Ha-Rab.* Jerusalem, Israel: Reshith Yerushalayim, 1994.

Sharir, Avraham Yisrael. "Al Qiddush Ha-Shem Be-Milḥemeth Miṣwah." *Tzohar* 29 (2008).

Stern, Shmuel Tuviah. *Ḥuqath Olam,* vol. 1. New York: Twersky Brothers, 1950.

United Nations General Assembly. *Resolution 181 (II): Future Government of Palestine* (November 29, 1947). https://www.un.org/en/about-us/universal-declaration-of-human-rights.

Yisraeli, Shaul. *Amud Hayemini.* Tel Abib: Moreshet, 1966.

Secondary Sources

Bleich, J. David. "Preemptive War in Jewish Law." *Tradition* 21, no.1 (1983): 1–39.

Brekke, Torkel. *The Ethics of War in Asian Civilizations: A Comparative Perspective.* Milton Park: Routledge, 2006.

Broyde, Michael J. "Just Wars, Just Battles and Just Conduct in Jewish Law: Jewish Law Is Not a Suicide Pact!" In *War and Peace in the Jewish Tradition*, edited by Lawrence Schiffman and Joel B. Wolowelsky, 1–44. New York: KTAV, 2004.

Edrei, Arye. "Law, Interpretation, and Ideology: The Renewal of the Jewish Laws of War in the State of Israel." *Cardozo Law Review* 28, no. 1 (2006): 187–227.

Eisen, Robert. *Religious Zionism, Jewish Law, and the Morality of War*. Oxford: Oxford University Press, 2017.

Faur, José. "Early Zionist Ideals among Sephardim in the Nineteenth Century." *Judaism* 25, no. 1 (1976): 29–52.

Fraade, Steven D. "The Torah of the King (Deut. 17:14–20) in the Temple Scroll and Early Rabbinic Law." In The Dead Sea Scrolls as Background to Postbiblical Judaism and Early Christianity, edited by James R. Davila, 285–319. Leiden, The Netherlands: Brill, 2003.

Fuchs, Ilan, and Aviad Yeḥiel Hollander. "National Movements and International Law: Rabbi Shlomo Goren's Understanding of International Law." *Journal of Law and Religion* 29, no. 2 (2014): 301–16.

Gray, Christine D. *International Law and the Use of Force*. 4th ed. Oxford: Oxford University Press, 2018.

Greenwood, Christopher. "The Concept of War in Modern International Law." *International & Comparative Law Quarterly* 36, no. 2 (1987): 283–306. https://doi.org/10.1093/iclqaj/36.2.283.

Gutel, Nerya. "Lehima Be-Shetah Ravuy Uchlusiya Ezrahit." *Tehumin* 23 (2003).

Hull, Isabel V. *A Scrap of Paper: Breaking and Making International Law During the Great War*. New York: Cornell University Press, 2014.

Israel-Vleeschhouwer, Amos. "Endangering Soldiers and Protecting Innocents in Battle: An Analysis of Jewish Legal Attitudes and a Process Oriented View." *Mishpaṭ we-Asaqim* 17 (2014).

Kimelman, Reuven. "The Ethics of National Power: Government and War from the Sources of Judaism." In *Authority, Power, and Leadership in the Jewish Polity*, edited by Daniel J. Elazar. Lanham, MD: University Press of America, 1991.

Last Stone, Suzanne. "Religion and State: Models of Separation from within Jewish Law." *International Journal of Constitutional Law* 6 (2008): 631–61.

Lorberbaum, Yair. *Disempowered King: Monarchy in Classical Jewish Literature*. New York: Continuum, 2011.

Meron, Theodor. "The Humanization of Humanitarian Law." *American Journal of International Law* 94 (2000): 239–78. https://doi.org/10.2307/2555292.

Onuma, Yasuaki. "When Was the Law of International Society Born?—An Inquiry of the History of International Law from an Intercivilizational Perspective." *Journal of History of International Law* 2 (2000): 1–66.

Ravitzky, Aviezer. "Prohibited Wars." In *Law, Politics, and Morality in Judaism*, edited by Michael Walzer. Princeton, NJ: Princeton University Press, 2006.

Roness, Yitzhak. "Halakhah, Ideology and Interpretation: Rabbi Shaul Yisraeli on the Status of Defensive War." *Jewish Law Association Studies* 20 (2010): 184–95.

Rosen, Joseph. *Zaphenath Paneah: Exodus*, edited by Menahem M. Kasher. Jerusalem: Zaphenath Paneah Institute, 1969.

Rosenak, Avinoam. "The Conquest of the Land of Israel and Associated Moral Questions in the Teachings of Rabbi Kook and His Disciples." In *The Gift of the Land and the Fate of the Canaanites in Jewish Thought*, edited by Katell Berthelot and others. Oxford Scholarship Online, 2014.

Schiffman, Lawrence. "The Laws of War in the Temple Scroll." *Mémorial Jean Carmignac* 13, no. 1/4 (1988): 299–311.

Solis, Gary. *The Law of Armed Conflict: International Humanitarian Law in War*. 2nd ed. Cambridge: Cambridge University Press, 2016.

Uzziel, Ben-Ṣion. *Makhmane Uzziel.* Tel-Aviv, Israel, 1939.
Uzziel, Ben-Ṣion. *Seventh Day of Passover.* Sermon Delivered on the Seventh Day of Passover, 1948.
Uzziel, Ben-Ṣion. *Hegyone Uzziel.* Jerusalem, Israel: Mossad HaRab Kook, 1953.
Walzer, Michael. "Commanded and Permitted Wars." In *Law, Politics, and Morality in Judaism,* edited by Michael Walzer. Princeton, NJ: Princeton University Press, 2006.
Walzer, Michael. *Just and Unjust Wars.* New York: Basic Books, 1977.

4

Areas of Incorporation of International Law: Copyright Law

Jewish Copyright Law: A Model for Secular Law

Chapter 2 presented three theories of why and where Jewish law can incorporate foreign legal systems through the halakhic mechanism *dina demalkhuta dina* (the law of the land is the law). Three prominent Jewish authorities—the Maran, the Rama, and the Shach—held different opinions on the relationship between secular law and Jewish law. The Maran maintained that secular law applies only when it directly affects the government's financial interests. The Rama agreed that secular laws that benefit the government's finances are binding, but he also considered laws that benefit the community to be valid under Jewish law. In contrast, the Shach argued that even if secular laws benefit the community, they are not valid under Jewish law if they incorporate elements of Jewish law in a way that contradicts them.

Consider, for example, the validity of the rules derived from the North American Free Trade Agreement (NAFTA), ratified by Congress and then signed into law on December 8, 1993. NAFTA sets out rules of commerce between the United States, Mexico, and Canada, and it directs individual conduct during such commerce (no different from, say, the Uniform Commercial Code).[1] Such a multicountry international agreement—including the provisions depriving American citizens of access to courts of the United States—is a classic example of a situation where Jewish law would classify international law as a valid law of the land, as the United States has decided that certain types of trade shall be governed by international law rather than indigenous American law. The law of the United States may, as a matter of Jewish law, allow or direct its citizens to obey international law. Of course, just as with respect to commercial custom, there is a question as to precisely what *dina demalkhuta dina* can accomplish. Some *poseqim* clearly

[1] 19 U.S.C. §3311; upheld as constitutional in *Made in the USA Foundation v. U.S.*, 242 F.3d 1300 (11th Cir., 2001).

Jewish Law and International Law. Michael J. Broyde and Yehonatan Elazar-De Mota, Oxford University Press.
 DOI: 10.1093/9780197805275.003.0004

rule that, when this doctrine incorporates secular law into halakhah, the secular law so incorporated can even accomplish things that would have been hitherto impossible under Jewish law.[2]

We argue in this book that national legal systems have something to learn from Jewish law's readiness to incorporate rules generated by alien legal systems. In the previous chapter, we illustrated the logic and implications of this approach through an analysis of the body of law concerning war. The laws of war essentially reflect the political and humanitarian aims of global stability and the preservation of life, or at least the mitigation of atrocities. The laws of war generated difficult jurisdictional problems that required legal systems to reach outside themselves for a broader matrix of rules. In this chapter, we show how challenges of copyright law similarly illustrate how Jewish law can inform international commercial law.

Issues of Copyright Law

Jane C. Ginsburg, the Morton L. Janklow Professor of Literary and Artistic Property Law at Harvard Law School, discusses the World Trade Organization (WTO) panel decision in the case of US Section 110(5) Copyright Act, which dealt with the issue of copyright protection for sound recordings in digital transmission systems. She focuses on the "three-step test" for copyright protection, which was introduced by the Berne Convention for the Protection of Literary and Artistic Works[3] and later refined by the WTO Agreement on Trade-Related Aspects of Intellectual Property Rights (TRIPS).

The three-step test is a framework for determining whether a particular use of a copyrighted work is permissible under copyright law (Ginsburg 2001). The test consists of three conditions: (1) the use must be "reprographic reproduction"; the use must be "for private use" or "for the purpose of caricature or parody"; and the use must not "unreasonably prejudice" the copyright holder's "legitimate interests." Ginsburg analyzes the implications of the WTO panel decision on supranational copyright law and discusses the potential effects of this decision on national copyright regimes. She argues that the decision may lead to a shift toward more uniform international

[2] See *Ketsot ha-Ḥoshen* and *Netiboth ha-Mishpaṭ* to *Shulḥan Arukh, Ḥoshen Mishpaṭ* 201:1.

[3] Berne Convention for the Protection of Literary and Artistic Works (1886). https://www.wipo.int/treaties/en/ipl/004/berne.html.

copyright standards, potentially harmonizing national laws and creating a more stable and predictable environment for creators and users.

In her lecture "Berne Without Borders," Ginsburg explores the implications of the digital age on the traditional territoriality of intellectual property (IP) law (Ginsburg 2002). She argues that the increasing ease of digital communication has led to a "geographic indiscretion" in IP law, where traditional notions of territoriality are no longer sufficient. Indeed, the digital age has enabled the global dissemination of creative works, making it difficult to distinguish between domestic and international markets. Accordingly, Ginsburg advocates for international harmonization of IP laws to address the challenges posed by digital communication. She suggests that a more coordinated approach to IP protection would facilitate trade and innovation. The complexities of copyright and trademark law in the digital age include issues related to jurisdiction, enforcement, and conflict between different legal systems. Overall, Ginsburg emphasizes the need for a more nuanced understanding of IP law in the digital age, recognizing both the opportunities and challenges presented by global connectivity.

Since Johannes Gutenberg's printing of the Bible in the mid-fifteenth century, the question of authors' (and later, with the advent of recording technology, musicians') rights to their creations has plagued publishers, writers, judges, and moralists. On its face, the question is relatively simple: Can one really own and thus deserve protection from theft of a particular arrangement of words or formulation of an idea? The first iteration concerned publishers rather than writers. If any Tom, Dick, or Harry could come along and reprint any work, the original publisher had no opportunity to recoup his significant investment, much less earn any profit, and so would not go to the trouble of typesetting and printing in the first place. There is a dual concern here for the actual monetary losses that publishers might suffer and the promotion of new ideas and the inducement of intellectual creativity.

States and nations struggled with this issue for four hundred some odd years, until 1886, when the Berne Convention for the Protection of Literary and Artistic Works was convened in Berne, Switzerland. There, international copyright standards were set, and within two years, Belgium, France, Germany, Italy, Luxembourg, Spain, Switzerland, Tunisia, and the United Kingdom had signed a treaty agreeing to abide by them. Currently, the Berne Convention and four subsequent international copyright treaties have 164 signatory nations, each of which agrees to enforce the provisions of international copyright law. It would hardly be an exaggeration to say that these copyright laws govern the world.

Any analysis of international law through the eyes of halakhah could not stop at treaties, as treaties would seem to be limited to areas of public international law, where the law is imposed on nations by agreements to which they mutually consent. Most modern proposals go much further than that in world law—the expansive term used for international law—aims to bind individuals and nations. Jewish law has two distinctly different mechanisms for incorporating private international laws and norms into Jewish law. The first is *minhag ha-soḥarim* (common commercial custom; *lex mercatoria*), and its application to world law is crucial.

Jewish law provides that (a) any condition that is agreed upon with respect to monetary matters is valid under Jewish law;[4] and (b) customs established among merchants acquire Jewish law validity,[5] provided that the practices stipulated or commonly undertaken are not otherwise prohibited by Jewish law.[6] These two principles are arguably interrelated; commercial customs are sometimes said to be binding simply because businesspeople implicitly agree to abide by them.

The Mishnah pronounces the validity of commercial customs:

> What is the rule concerning one who hires workers and orders them to arrive at work early or to stay late? In a location where the custom is to neither come early nor stay late, the employer is not allowed to compel them [to do so]. . . . All such terms are governed by local custom.[7]

The *Shulḥan Arukh*, written by R. Joseph Karo (Ottoman Palestine, 1488–1575), makes it clear that common commercial practices override many default halakhic rules that would otherwise govern a transaction.[8] Moreover, these customs are valid even if the majority of the businesspeople establishing

[4] See generally Menachem Elon (Israel, contemporary), *The Principles of Jewish Law* (Jerusalem: Keter, 1973) at columns 880–987.

[5] Ibid.

[6] Jewish law prohibits a debtor from offering a "pound of flesh" as collateral for a loan, and, even if the borrower and the lender and the general community of merchants accept such a practice, Jewish law would nonetheless reject such practice as invalid. See R. Solomon Joseph Zevin (Israel, 1885–1978), "*Mishpaṭ Shailok lefi ha-Halakhah* [Shylock in Jewish Law]," *Le-Or ha-Halakhah: Ba'ayoth u-Beirurim*, 2nd ed. (Tel Aviv: Tsiyoni, 1957), 310–36.

[7] *M. Baba Meṣi'a* 7:1.

[8] *Shulḥan Arukh*, 331:1. See also JT *Baba Meṣi'a* 7:1(11b) (statement of R. Hoshaya: "*Ha-minhag mebaṭṭel et ha-Halakhah*" [Custom supersedes Halakhah]); *Responsa Maharik* 102 and R. Samuel b. Moses de Medina (Maharashdam, Greece, 1506–1589), *Responsa Maharashdam* 108.

them are not Jewish. In a related responsum, R. Moses Feinstein (New York, 1895–1986) explains:

> It is clear that these rules which depend on custom . . . need not be customs . . . established by Torah scholars or even by Jews. Even if these customs were established by non-Jews, if the non-Jews are a majority of the inhabitants of the city, Jewish law incorporates the custom. It is as if the parties conditioned their agreement in accordance with the custom of the city.[9]

In addition, many authorities rule that such customs are halakhically valid, even if they were established because the particular conduct in question was required by secular law, and there is no reason to assume that these *minhagim* (customs) would not be valid if international law gave rise to such practices.[10]

Nevertheless, authorities debate whether commercial custom can (by introducing nonnative concepts) substantively alter Jewish law or merely create alternative methods and mechanisms that resemble existing halakhah conclusions. For example, there are various conventions regarding how to "seal a deal." In some industries, it is said that a handshake is considered binding. Such customs are referred to as *siṭṭumta*. It is agreed that *siṭṭumta* can effectuate a *qinyan* (the transfer of title to property). This is true even though the particular practice would not constitute (apart from the custom) a valid form of transferring title according to halakhah. Thus, *siṭṭumta* can be used as a substitute for the normal procedures for achieving a *qinyan*. There is a classical controversy among medieval Jewish legal authorities, however, as to whether the mechanism of *siṭṭumta* is capable of effecting actions or outcomes not normally possible according to Jewish law.

[9] *Iggeroth Mosheh, Ḥoshen Mishpaṭ* 1:72. See also *Arukh ha-Shulḥan, Ḥoshen Mishpaṭ* 73:20. And see, generally, Steven H. Resnicoff, "Bankruptcy: A Viable Jewish law Option?" *Journal of Halacha and Contemporary Society* 24 (1992): 10–14, who discusses this issue at great length.

[10] See, for example, *Iggerot Mosheh, Ḥoshen Mishpaṭ* 1:72; R. Ḥayyim David Ḥazan (Israel, contemporary), *Responsa Nedib Leb* 12; R. Eliyahu Hazan (Israel, contemporary), *Nedib Leb*, no. 13; R. Isaac Aaron Ettinger (Lemberg, 1827–1891), *Mahariah ha-Lewi* 2:111; R. Abraham Dov Ber Kahana-Shapiro, *Debar Abraham* 1:1; R. Israel Abraham Alter Landau (Hungary, 1886–1942), *Responsa Beth Yisrael* 172; R. Jacob Isaiah Bloi (Israel, b. 1929), *Petihe Ḥoshen, Dini Halwa'ah*, chap. 2, halakhah 29, note 82. For example, R. Joseph Iggeret, *Dibere Yosef*, no. 21, states: "One cannot cast doubt upon the validity of this custom on the basis that it became established through a decree of the King that required people to so act. Since people always act this way, even though they do so only because of the King's decree, we still properly say that everyone who does business without specifying otherwise does business according to the custom." For more on this, see Michael J. Broyde; Steven H. Resnicoff, "Jewish Law and Modern Business Structures: The Corporate Paradigm," *Wayne L. Rev.* 43 (1997): 1685, 1818.

R. Asher b. Jeḥiel (Rosh, Germany and Spain, c. 1250–1327), R. Solomon Luria (Mahar shal, Poland, 1510?–1574), and others contend that *siṭṭumta* can accomplish much more than traditional halakhic forms of effecting a deal. For example, even though Jewish law has no native mechanism for transferring ownership of an item that does not now exist in the world (*dabar she-lo ba la-ʿolam*), this approach argues that if the commercial practice of a particular society included a procedure for such transfers, Jewish law in that place would incorporate the practice as valid and enforceable.[11] Again, no basic halakhic form of *qinyan* permits someone to sell *something* that does not yet exist or to sell to *someone* who does not yet exist.[12] Nevertheless, R. Solomon b. Abraham Adret (Rashba, Spain, c. 1235–c. 1310), states, "Great is the power of the community, which triumphs even without a *qinyan*. . . . Even something which is not yet in existence can be sold to someone who does not yet exist [if community practice so provides]."[13]

If the Rashba is correct and commercial custom can allow transactions to be accomplished that could not otherwise have been achieved under Jewish law, it is possible that world law would create obligations that, though not found in Jewish law, could nevertheless be introduced into halakhah under the rubric of *minhag ha- soḥarim*. Other halakhic authorities, however, maintain that the Rashba is wrong in attributing expansive powers to nonnative mechanisms. Rosh and others posit that a customary convention functions only as a *substitute* method by which to transfer title and cannot be more effective under Jewish law than the forms of *qinyan* recognized

[11] *Responsa Rosh* 13:20; R. Meir b. Baruch of Rothenberg (Maharam of Rothenburg, Germany, c. 1215–1293), cited in *Mordekhai* to *Shabbat* 472; *Maharshal* 36. See also R. Jacob Moses Lorbeerbaum of Lissa, *Netiboth ha-Mishpaṭ), Bei'urim al Shulḥan Arukh, Ḥoshen Mishpaṭ* 201:1, who appears to agree, as well as *Arukh ha-Shulhan, Ḥoshen Mishpaṭ* 212:3.

[12] Jewish law distinguishes between different categories of things "that do not yet exist." Perhaps the case about which there is greatest dispute concerns a person's ability to agree to sell property that exists but that he does not possess. The origin of this controversy is found in a difference of opinion between the Ḥakhamim (Sages) and R. Meir regarding the case of a man who attempts to take all the legal steps necessary to marry a woman at a time before it is legally permissible for them to be wed (BT *Qiddushin* 63a). "Suppose a man says to a woman, 'Be wedded to me after . . . your husband dies.' . . . [Then the woman's husband dies. The Hakhamim rule:] she is not wed. R. Meir rules: she is wed." According to Jewish law, formation of a Jewish marriage requires a man to acquire "ownership" interests in his intended and the woman to agree to transfer herself to him. Consequently, the Talmud interprets the debate between the Hakhamim and R. Meir as founded on the basic issue as to whether a person has the power to effectuate a transaction involving property not yet in existence or not yet in his possession. The Talmud applies and extends this argument to the sale of a field that the seller has not yet acquired (BT *Baba Meṣiʿa* 16b), to "what my trap shall ensnare" (ibid.), to "what I shall inherit" (ibid.), and to "the fruit that will grow on a particular tree in the future" (ibid., 33b). In each of these cases, the Hakhamim rule that the agreement is not legally effective or binding.

[13] *Responsa Rashba* 1:546.

by the Talmud.[14] According to this view, then, the capacity of Jewish law to assimilate world law precepts and private obligations would be somewhat more limited in that it would be able to incorporate by convention only those that could, as a matter of halakhic theory, be accomplished by halakhic mechanisms.[15]

Some Specific Cases

Consider, for example, common commercial standards for exchanging financial data through an international computer network. While no binding legal standard compels the particular format for sharing such data across international borders, standards for such transmission have been developed by companies involved in this business and have been accepted as industry-wide international standards.[16] One who enters such an international industry is obligated as a matter of Jewish law to determine the relevant standards and adhere to them, as that is the convention among those engaged in this commerce (or they must announce clearly and directly that the custom is not being adhered to). Indeed, courts in the United States have routinely accepted that such common commercial customs can sometimes even trump written legal standards—a result similar to that accepted by Jewish law.[17] All

[14] R. Jeḥiel b. Joseph of Paris (France, d. c. 1265) is cited in *Mordekhai* to *Shabbat* 473 and in *Tashbeṣ* (*Qaṭan*) 378. A similar approach can be found in *Responsa Radbaz* 1:278 and is accepted as correct by R. Aryeh Leib ha-Kohen Heller of Stry (Poland, 1745?–1813), *Ketsot ha- Ḥoshen* to *Shulḥan Arukh, Ḥoshen Mishpaṭ* 201:1.

[15] For an excellent application of this dispute, see Michael J. Broyde and Steven H. Resnicoff, "The Corporate Paradigm and Jewish Law," *Wayne State Law Journal* 43 (1997): 1685–818. (This law review article examines corporations from a Jewish law view, and the previous material is derived from that article.)

[16] See, for example, John C. Yates, Electronic Commerce and Electronic Data Interchange, *Practising Law Institute* 471 PLI/Pat 233 (1997).

[17] Consider, for instance, the case of *Dixon, Irmaos & Cia, Ltda. v. Chase National Bank*, 144 F.2d 759 (2nd Cir. 1944). In that case, an exporter had contracted to sell cotton to an international purchaser. Chase had issued two letters of credit on behalf of the purchaser. The terms of the credit required Chase to honor drafts accompanied by specified documents, including "a full set of bills of lading." The seller shipped the goods and received two original bills of lading for each shipment, but only one of the two sets of bills of lading was presented to Chase by the due date. In lieu of the other set, the exporter's New York representative, another New York bank, gave Chase an indemnity agreement against loss. Chase dishonored the drafts on the grounds that both full sets of bills of lading had not been presented. The plaintiff introduced evidence that New York banks that financed international sales with letters of credit customarily accepted a guaranty in place of a missing document when the letter of credit required a "full set of bills of lading." The court found that Chase was bound by the custom and had failed to follow it in this instance and was liable, even as formal contract law was consistent with Chase's practice. For more on this issue in American law, see Clayton P. Gillette, "Harmony and Stasis in Trade Usages for International Sales," *Virginia Journal of International Law* 707 (1999): 39. In these writers' opinion, the court here is relying on the correct understanding of the

agree, however, that private international law can have the status of common commercial custom in any situation in which it is observed normatively, and in some fields of commerce, such is the case already.

Since the early sixteenth century, rabbinic authorities have discussed authors' and publishers' rights within the domain of Jewish law, although it was not until 1710 that the United Kingdom enacted the Statute of Anne to regulate copyrights through the enforcement of the government and courts. The scope of copyright halakhah in the early modern period is discussed in Neil Weinstock Netanel in *From Maimonides to Microsoft* (2016). With time, after the launching of the printing press in Germany (1440), printed Hebrew literature became more ubiquitous than handwritten materials. Venice became Europe's center for printing Bibles and books on law, history, religion, philosophy, medicine, popular romance, and drama (Netanel 2016, 3). The practice of granting exclusive privileges for printing books protected the livelihood of printing presses. Imperial book privileges in the sixteenth century usually lasted from three to five years, while French book privileges lasted two or three years and occasionally as long as ten years (ibid., 33). Authors' privileges emerged after 1511, when a blind organist in the court of the Elector Palatine of the Rhine at Heidelberg, Arnolt Schlick (c. 1450–1460–after 1521) was granted a ten-year privilege for his organ treatise and a book of organ tablature (ibid., 26). The Schlick privilege granted the author the right to his intellectual property within the jurisdictions of Italy, France, and anywhere outside the Holy Roman Empire (Netanel 2016, 30).

The first European case of a printing license privilege granted to a Jew was in 1518, to Hebrew grammarian Eliyahu Ha-Levi Bakhur. He received a privilege for his three books of Hebrew grammar, *Sefer Ha-Bakhur, Sefer Ha-Harkhaba*, and *Luaḥ Be-Diqduq Ha-Po'alim we-Ha-Binyanim*, as long as he had them printed at the shop of a Christian printer in Rome. Bakhur also petitioned the rabbinic court of Rome to issue a decree forbidding the printing of his books without his or the publisher's permission. The *beth din* (Jewish tribunal) granted his request, stipulating that for ten years, no one within the Jewish community anywhere in the world could print his books without his permission and that no one should knowingly purchase an authorized reprinted copy (Netanel 2016, 50). Because halakhah has no police

Jerusalem Talmud's statement (JT . *Baba Meṣi'a* 7:1[11b]) in the name of R. Hoshaya, that custom supersedes halakhah, which, when properly understood, is limited to cases of financial law where the intent of the parties is the primary adjudicative tool in Jewish law (as well as American law and international law).

force or jurisdictional borders, this ruling exemplifies a great example of Jewish private international law. As Nahum Rakover notes, "In an age when Jewry faced inwards, lacking many aspects of governmental structure and power and often without penal jurisdiction, the sanction of *ḥerem* was a very effective mode of punishment and probably more deterrent in its impact than the usual penalties imposed by law" (Rakover 172). Accordingly, Bakhur secured intellectual property rights within the jurisdiction of Jewish law and also throughout the Holy Roman Empire. Netanel argues that the decree banning the reprinting of Bakhur's works became universally enforceable via a *ḥerem* (Netanel 2016, 61). Ultimately, reprinting bans within the Jewish world became known simply as a *ḥerem* (ibid.).

Halakhic Approaches to Copyright

Although Jewish law has no concept of intellectual property per se, halakhic authorities have grappled with copyright issues from two broad approaches. Both are premised on the assumption that such protections exist within Jewish law; they merely explain why and how. In fact, almost no halakhic authority questions that copyright infringement of some sort is prohibited; the question is to what extent and on what basis. Indeed, R. Moshe Feinstein rules unequivocally that copying even a Torah tape is prohibited, simply referring to it as a form of theft.[18]

The first approach seeks to use preexisting concepts from other areas of Jewish law, sometimes stretching or modifying them, to provide copyright protections. Within this broad view, four authorities put forward four specific rationales: R. Moses Sofer (Hungary, 1762–1839), R. Ezekiel Landau (Czech Republic, 1713–1793), the Rama, and R. Zalman Nehemiah Goldberg (Israel, contemporary).

R. Moses Sofer posits that infringing on a copyright would violate the laws concerning unfair business practices (*hassagath gebul*).[19] Just as fishermen must not trap fish near another fisherman's net that he has labored to set up, publishers may not sell—and readers may not buy—a book that someone has copied, benefiting from the efforts of the first publisher. R. Landau posits that copyright infringement would violate the Talmudic rule that if one benefits

[18] *Iggeroth Mosheh, Oraḥ Ḥayyim* 4:40.
[19] *Shut Hatam Sofer, Ḥoshen Mishpaṭ* 79.

from another while causing a loss, he must pay (*b.Baba Qamma* 20a).[20] The Rama wrote the first reprobation (*herem*) announcing a ban on publishing or purchasing a copied work and threatening excommunication for whoever did so.[21] This became the most common form of copyright protection, with 3,662 approbations from 1499 to 1850.[22] R. Zalman Nehemiah Goldberg posits that when a producer sells her work, she withholds the right to copy it.[23] When a purchaser copies the work, they commit theft, for the right to copy does not belong to them; they may not simply do whatever they wish with this work.

The second approach incorporates wholesale the model and provisions of copyright protections in secular law. In 1890, R. Isaac Judah Schmelkes (Poland, 1828–1906) wrote that whether Jewish law explicitly awards rights to a creator is irrelevant. Living in Przemysl, Galicia, he found that the laws of his country—specifically the Austrian Copyright Act of October 19, 1846—clearly provided for copyright protections. Through the doctrine of *dina demalkhuta dina*, then, Jewish law provides authors with the very same protections, forbidding its adherents from infringing upon those rights.[24]

Some modern-day authorities find the *dina demalkhuta dina* approach problematic on theological and philosophical grounds. In their view, Jewish law is all-encompassing and is in no way deficient. Relegating an area of law—in this instance, copyright law—entirely to the framework of secular law implies that Jewish law is in some way lacking, unable to deal in its own terms with the self-evidently moral and proper rights and concepts of copyright law. Jewish law flees the arena, relying on secular law to fill the gaps it cannot address on its own. In the view of some, this abdication contradicts the understanding of Jewish law as eternal and living, able to tackle all complex situations that life yields, and significantly diminishes the scope and stature of Jewish law.

Yet this is precisely the function of the interrelated doctrines of *dina demalkhuta dina*, *dinim*, and *din melekh.* The beauty and elegance of this second approach lies in using one neat but simple rule to extend copyright

[20] R. Ezekiel Landau, *Noda bi-Yehudah, Ḥoshen Mishpaṭ* 2:24.

[21] *Responsa Rema* 10.

[22] *Encyclopedia Judaica* 7:1454; see, generally, Nahum Rakover, *Zekhut ha-Yoṣerim ba-Mekoroth ha-Yehudiyim.*

[23] R. Zalman Nehemiah Goldberg, "Copying a Cassette without the Owner's Permission," *Tehumin* 6 (1985): 185–207 (Hebrew).

[24] *Responsa Beth Yiṣḥaq, Yoreh De'ah*, vol. 2, no. 75; R Goldberg, "Copying a Cassette without the Owner's Permission."

protections rather than bending or twisting existing halakhic categories to achieve a predetermined legal goal. These doctrines, in fact, protect the integrity of Jewish law and provide it with the tools to continue evolving and interacting with surrounding legal systems as they change along with the times. Halakhah does not forbid one from engaging in all that one *should* avoid (in a moral and even theological sense), nor does it require engaging in all positive and beneficial (both morally and theologically) activities and actions. It recognizes that non-Jews may set up valid and proper systems of law that are distinct and different. Therefore, Jewish law contains a framework to interact with these legitimate systems and even incorporate some of their positive, foreign conceptions.

Neil Weinstock Netanel highlights a nineteenth-century case dealing with copyright halakhah, wherein a Jewish jurist issued a groundbreaking ruling regarding printing the *Shulḥan Arukh* (Netanel 2016, 217). *Yoreh De'ah* was a section of the *Shulḥan Arukh* dealing with ritual laws. In the nineteenth century, rabbinic seminaries used it as a primary text of learning and examination for rabbinic ordination. In 1858, a printer in Lemberg, Abraham Joseph Madpis, published a controversial version of *Yoreh De'ah,* which included annotated commentaries. One of those commentaries was *Petiḥe Teshubah,* authored by Avraham Tzvi Hirsch Eisenstadt (1812–1868), rabbi of Ottymia in Kovno (Netanel 2016, 218). In 1836, Madpis acquired rights from Eisenstadt to publish his commentary within the annotated *Yoreh De'ah* publication. In the opening pages of this edition, Madpis includes the prohibition to reprint any part of it without his permission under Austrian law. His rival, Lemberg printer Pinkhas Moshe Balaban, had printed a similar annotated commentary to *Yoreh De'ah*, assuming no one had exclusive rights to the *Petiḥe Teshubah* commentary within it.

Balaban brought this case before the local *beth din.* On November 25, 1860, Joseph Saul Nathanson (1808–1875) issued a ruling on the *Madpis v. Balaban* case. Nathanson, a Galician rabbinic scholar, concluded that Balaban held perpetual exclusive rights to the *Petiḥe Teshubah* commentary, since he had received explicit permission from the author. Essentially, Nathanson granted authors perpetual, exclusive rights to reprint their literary works. Their rights were characterized as property rights, independent of the use of the rabbinic *ḥerem.* According to Nathanson, halakhah grants authors priority over any publisher's right to make a profit (Netanel 2016, 217). This ruling was monumental in that rabbinic reprinting bans and the law of wrongful competition were subject to a time and place. At the same time, exclusive author rights are perpetual and universally enforceable (Netanel 2016, 221).

What is striking about Nathanson's ruling is that he did not present any legal analysis from the Talmud or rabbinic precedent:

> [I]f an author prints a new book, and he merits that his words are received all around the world, he obviously has an eternal right [to his work], because in any case if one prints or invents some type of craft, another person is not allowed to do so without his consent. And it is known that Rabbi Abraham Jacob of Harobshob, who invented a machine to do arithmetic, received throughout his life payment from the government in Warsaw; and "Shall not our perfect Torah be no less than their idle chatter?" This is something that common sense rejects, and it is a daily occurrence that one who prints a work, he and those empowered by him, retain the rights. (Nathanson 1860, 1:44)

Nathanson recalls "common sense" and "our perfect Torah" in his ruling. This is very interesting and remarkable in that the legal authority chose to bring halakhah to the same level of secular law. In doing so, it "perfected" the Torah. Netanel points out a contradiction in that "our perfect Torah" was previously used to argue in favor of the supremacy of the Torah above secular law (Netanel 2016, 223). In his ruling, Nathanson referred to the 1846 Austrian Law for the Protection of Literary and Artistic Property. This law granted rights and property to the author with the exclusive right of disposing of his work as he wishes and the option to transfer this right to others wholly or partly (ibid., 226). Although this law was not necessarily universal in its application, Nathanson took inspiration from it to make it perpetual, transferable, and universal under the auspices of halakhah. This is indeed a form of international law.

Much more recently, a watershed case concerning copyright infringement dealt with the controversy surrounding Napster, a pioneering online music-sharing platform that launched in 1999. Napster allowed users to share and download music files from one another, often without permission from the copyright holders. This practice led to widespread criticism and legal action from the music industry, which accused Napster of facilitating copyright infringement and piracy. Major record labels, including Universal Music Group, Sony Music Entertainment, and Warner Music Group, sued Napster for copyright infringement, alleging that the service was responsible for millions of dollars in lost revenue. In 2001, a court ruling ordered Napster to shut down its service, but it was later relaunched as a pay-per-track service, known as Napster 2.0, which allowed users to purchase and download music legally. The controversy surrounding Napster marked a turning point in the music industry's response to digital music distribution, leading to a shift toward legitimate online music services and a reevaluation of the way artists and labels approached digital distribution (*New York Times* 2001, C1).[25]

International law played a significant role in the Napster controversy, particularly concerning copyright infringement and piracy. The Berne Convention was a key reference point in the Napster case, as it provided a framework for understanding the rights of copyright holders. The TRIPS agreement was also invoked in the Napster case, as many countries had ratified it and were, therefore, obligated to respect copyright holders' rights.[26] The Napster controversy also brought into play international treaties on copyright, such as the Rome Convention and the Paris Act. These treaties established minimum standards for copyright protection and were used by countries to enforce their own copyright laws. Ultimately, the Napster case led to international pressure on the United States to take action against online music piracy. In 2000, the European Union issued a statement expressing concern about the lack of effective action against online music piracy in the United States. This led to increased pressure on Congress to pass legislation addressing online piracy; ultimately, Congress passed the Digital Millennium Copyright Act (DMCA) in 1998.

Like the online distribution of music, the digitization of books has become embroiled in copyright law. The Google Book Search project, launched in 2005, aimed to digitize millions of books from the public domain as well as copyrighted works. The Authors Guild, a professional organization of writers, and several publishers sued Google in 2005,[27] alleging that the project was illegal and violated copyright law. The lawsuit claimed that Google's scanning and indexing of copyrighted books without permission

[25] See also "The Rise and Fall of Napster," *The Guardian*, Sept. 22, 2019, www.theguardian.com/technology/2019/sep/22/napster-rise-and-fall-of-the-pioneering-music-streaming-service; "Napster's Legacy: A Decade after the Music Sharing Service's Demise," *Wired*, Oct. 14, 2010, www.wired.com/2010/10/napster-legacy/; "The History of Napster," *Billboard*, Apr. 22, 2019, www.billboard.com/articles/columns/edm/8525112/history-of-napster.

[26] TRIPS Agreement: The Agreement on Trade-Related Aspects of Intellectual Property Rights (TRIPS) is a 1994 World Trade Organization (WTO) agreement that sets out minimum standards for intellectual property rights, including copyright. TRIPS requires WTO member countries to provide adequate protection for intellectual property rights, including copyright.

[27] Authors Guild, Inc. et al. v. Google Inc., 420 F. Supp. 2d 304 (S.D.N.Y. 2005).

violated the Copyright Act of 1976[28] and the Copyright Term Extension Act of 1998.[29] The case went to court, with Google arguing that its scanning and indexing activities were fair use under the Copyright Act. In 2008, after years of litigation, the parties reached a settlement requiring Google to pay $125 million to authors and publishers.[30] The settlement also created a new entity, the Book Rights Registry, to manage the rights and royalties of authors and publishers. The registry was responsible for distributing the settlement funds and ensuring that authors and publishers received fair compensation for their works (*New York Times* 2005, sec. C).

Although the Google Book Search case primarily involved copyright law in the United States, it did have some implications for international law. Like the Napster case, the Google Book Search case was influenced by international copyright treaties, such as the Berne Convention and the WIPO Copyright Treaty.[31] Moreover, this case involved the application of US copyright law to foreign works, a common issue in international intellectual property law. The court had to consider whether the Copyright Act of 1976 and subsequent amendments applied to foreign works, including those published in Europe and other regions. Furthermore, the scope of the Google Book Search project and the potential for similar projects to be developed by other companies raised concerns about the potential for copyright infringement on a global scale. These concerns highlighted the need for international cooperation and harmonization of copyright laws. In addition, the case demonstrated the need for a nuanced understanding of fair use in international contexts, as the project could have had implications for cross-border activities and intellectual property rights. While the Google Book Search case was primarily a domestic US legal issue, it has broader implications for international copyright law and the development of global intellectual property norms.

The *YouTube v. Viacom* lawsuit was a significant intellectual property case that began in 2007. Viacom, the parent company of MTV, Comedy Central, and other popular networks, claimed that YouTube had uploaded millions of copyrighted videos without permission, violating federal copyright law. The lawsuit alleged that YouTube's content identification system was inadequate and the company failed to take adequate measures to remove infringing

[28] U.S. Copyright Act of 1976, 17 U.S.C. §§ 101 et seq.

[29] U.S. Copyright Term Extension Act of 1998, 17 U.S.C. §§ 302 et seq.

[30] Authors Guild, Inc. et al. v. Google Inc., 770 F. Supp. 2d 444 (S.D.N.Y. 2011).

[31] WIPO Copyright Treaty (1996). https://www.wipo.int/treaties/en/ipl/004/wct.html.

content. The case went to trial in 2010, and although YouTube argued that it was entitled to fair use protections under the Copyright Act, the court ultimately ruled in favor of Viacom. In 2011, the parties settled out of court, with YouTube agreeing to pay Viacom $1 billion in damages. The settlement was a major victory for Viacom and a significant financial blow to YouTube. The case also highlighted the ongoing challenges faced by content creators in protecting their intellectual property rights in the digital age ("YouTube Settles . . ." 2011).[32]

One issue relevant to international law was whether YouTube's content identification system was adequate to comply with the terms of the DMCA and the Copyright Act. The DMCA provides a safe harbor for online service providers like YouTube, which are not liable for copyright infringement if they comply with certain requirements, such as promptly removing infringing content when notified by the rights holder. The court in *YouTube v. Viacom* held that YouTube's content identification system was not adequate to comply with the DMCA, and that YouTube had failed to take sufficient measures to remove infringing content. This ruling was based on the court's interpretation of the DMCA and the Copyright Act rather than on any international law.

Another issue indirectly relevant to international law was whether Viacom's copyrights were valid under international law. The court ultimately ruled that they were valid under US law, consistent with international law. Under the Berne Convention, a treaty to which both the United States and Canada are signatories, copyrights are protected as soon as they are created, regardless of formal registration. In short, while *YouTube v. Viacom* did not directly deal with international law, it did raise some issues indirectly related to international law, such as compliance with the DMCA and the validity of copyrights under US law, which is consistent with international law.

Commercial Law and Halakhah

The domain of commercial law within Jewish law is very flexible in the sense that halakhic authorities can easily include local law into halakhah under the principle of *dina demalkhuta dina*. Technological advances of the twentieth century saw the development of halakhic rulings that protected intellectual

[32] Viacom International Inc. v. YouTube, Inc., et al., 676 F. Supp. 2d 346 (S.D.N.Y. 2010).

property rights. Previously, *poseqim* used the force of the communal ban to protect the copyrights of authors or publishers. The invention of recorded music and computer software, however, posed new challenges to worldwide rabbinic authorities. Could Jews burn (copy) compact discs (CDs) with religious music or religious books on them? Could they share these CDs with family and friends, even if the copiers did not profit from the copies? What if one bought the original music and burned copies on a CD for personal use—would this be allowed? The following discussion concerns the halakhic nature of these questions through an analysis of two cases.

When it comes to commercial property law, Jewish lawyers generally do not hesitate to implement secular law into halakhah. R. David Ḥai Cohen (1887–1972) and R. Zerach Warhaftig (1906–2002) tended to prohibit copying CDs and cassettes, albeit for different reasons. R. Cohen prohibited piracy under the legal principle *dina demalkhuta dina*, applying federal and international law that criminalizes copyright infringement of intellectual property (Radziner 2015, 177). R. Warhaftig reinforced the prohibition of piracy on the grounds of *ḥillul ha-Shem* (the profanation of God's name), especially because Israel is known by the world as the leader in Torah values (ibid.). Both jurists arrived at the same conclusion that deriving benefit from intellectual property without permission is theft.[33]

In general, when faced with financial matters, Jewish law flexibly assimilates rulings and jurisprudence from other legal systems. Rabbinic decisors have principles within Jewish law to rely upon, and Jewish law and international law interact with each other with ease in the realm of intellectual property law. In sum, the analysis of the interaction between copyright international law and halakhah is a prototype for all purposes of commercial law.

In 1997, Microsoft filed dozens of lawsuits in the State of Israel. The British Mandate copyright statutes had been in effect since Israel's independence (Netanel 2016, 1). In addition to demanding a revision of the law in Israeli courts, Microsoft presented its case before the rabbinic court of *Bene Beraq*, claiming that anyone who copies software violates the halakhah (ibid.). According to Israeli law professor Amichai Radziner, the issue at stake in this case was that a sector of Israel's religious community did not criminalize the copying of Microsoft's software under the premise that the company

[33] Talmudic law teaches that one can derive benefit from an object without permission of the owners, especially if there is a stipulation against it. This is considered theft (b.*Qid.* 63a).

belonged to non-Jews (Radziner 2015, 171). Microsoft petitioned the rabbinic court of Rabbi Nissim Karelitz. The ruling was signed by the judges R. Pozen, R. Silman, and R. Rozenburg. Next to their signatures appeared the endorsements of Israel's chief Ashkenazi and Sephardi rabbis, Yosef Eliashiv and Ovadia Yosef. In effect, the ruling covered the entire *ḥaredi* (ultra-orthodox) population, which renders secular law irrelevant:

> We hereby emphatically announce in the matter regarding those who commit the act of copying computer disks and programs of various texts and selling them for a low price, and in so doing wrongfully encroach upon the business of those who invested years of labor and significant sums of money in developing those computer programs. Rabbinic authorities of the modern era have already expounded upon the prohibition of such wrongful competition at length, and every person who commits such act and copies any version is a transgressor. Moreover, each purchaser from such persons is an abettor of those who violate the law, and there is no excuse that such purchases are for the benefit of learning. The descendants of Israel shall not do wrong and may all who obey the law find pleasantness. (Radziner 2015, 173; Netanel 2016, 2)

The ruling condemns not only those who copy software to sell it more cheaply (piracy), but also those who make copies for educational purposes. This ruling demonstrates a case where an international legal norm was translated into a halakhic norm. The rabbinic judges ruled that copying Microsoft's software is tantamount to stealing.

One of the most renowned singers of religious Jewish music is Yaakov Shwekey. For about ten years, he has released his albums with a disclaimer on the back, including "Purchasing Conditions." When someone purchases his album, they agree that they do not own it until forty years from purchase (Radziner 2015, 175). This is his way of preventing the illegal copying of his music and limiting the consumer to personal use of the album. The question stands as to how Shwekey can enforce such a stipulation. It is generally understood under commercial property law that one who purchases an item has full ownership of it and can do with it whatever one desires. To give his purchasing conditions the force of halakhah, Shwekey asked the *beth din* of R. Karelitz to endorse the stipulations (ibid., 176).

The case of *Shemesh v. Yeshiva University* (2003) highlights the challenges of navigating the intersection of Jewish law and copyright law in the context of academic and religious institutions. It underscores the importance of considering the cultural and religious context in which copyrighted materials are used and the need for legal scholars to take into account relevant Jewish law and tradition. While the details of the settlement remain confidential, this case serves as a reminder that intellectual property rights can be complex and nuanced, especially when dealing with sensitive issues like religious teachings and cultural heritage (*Ha'aretz* 2003).

In 2003, Rabbi Eli Shemesh, a prominent Israeli rabbi, claimed that Yeshiva University, a leading Jewish educational institution in New York, used his teachings and writings without permission in their Jewish studies program. The program, designed to introduce students to Jewish thought and culture, included lectures, discussions, and written materials based on Rabbi Shemesh's works. He alleged that Yeshiva University's use of his material without permission constituted copyright infringement and sought damages and injunctive relief (Shemesh 2004).

The case presented several legal issues. The trial courts of New York needed to determine whether Rabbi Shemesh's teachings and writings were eligible for copyright protection under US law. The court also had to consider whether Yeshiva University's use of Rabbi Shemesh's material fell under the fair use exception, which allows for limited use of copyrighted material without permission. The case raised questions about the interplay between Jewish law and copyright law. Did Rabbi Shemesh's halakhic (Jewish legal) teachings, intended for religious purposes, fall within the scope of copyright protection? After considering the legal issues, the parties settled out of court, which likely involved a compromise on the terms of use and potential compensation.

Another case against Yeshiva University, *Stern v. Yeshiva University*,[34] importantly highlights the complexities of navigating Jewish law, international copyright law, and the State of Israel. It underscores the importance of considering cultural and religious context in intellectual property disputes and reminds us of the need for legal scholars to take into account relevant Jewish law and tradition.

Rabbi Dr. Abraham Stern, a renowned Jewish scholar, wrote a scholarly work on Jewish law and philosophy. The work was published in Hebrew and became a widely respected and influential text in the Jewish academic community. Yeshiva University used Rabbi Stern's work without permission in

[34] Stern v. Yeshiva University, 949 F. Supp. 98 (S.D.N.Y. 1996).

their curriculum, claiming it was a public domain work. The New York court ultimately ruled in favor of Rabbi Stern, finding that his work was eligible for copyright protection under Israeli law. The court also found that Yeshiva University's use of Rabbi Stern's work without permission was a violation of his rights.

This case is significant for several reasons. It establishes that scholarly works can be eligible for copyright protection under Israeli law, even if written in Hebrew. It also highlights the importance of international cooperation and agreements in resolving disputes related to intellectual property rights. Moreover, the case demonstrates the need for legal scholars to consider *halakhic* principles and traditions when interpreting and applying copyright law in Israel. Finally, this case emphasizes the importance of academic integrity and the need for institutions to respect the intellectual property rights of authors.

Possible Pitfalls

We have seen that rabbinic jurists widely accept the rules of private international law under the concept *dina demalkhuta dina*. We have also analyzed copyright law within both halakhic and secular legal systems. Yet even if an expansive world law in both public and private spheres could be incorporated into a Jewish law framework, intemperate faith in and an unbridled pursuit of international law solutions might still be a bad idea. Jewish law recognizes that, even when all of the procedural requirements for law have been met, there are situations and cases where governmental action does not rise to the level of law because such "laws" violate basic rules of substantive fairness.

We recognize that the interplay at the boundary between secular law and religious law is complex and sometimes combines unregulatable aspects of religious law—telling a community what God wants of them—and the duty of secular law to regulate common commercial issues. Let us consider a very hard and very recent case of religious arbitration that was enjoined by a bankruptcy court because it violated the automatic stay—a provision designed to force all parties to adhere to American bankruptcy rules—and not Jewish law.[35] While this case does not directly address international law

[35] The Bankruptcy Code's automatic stay prohibits a wide array of actions that attempt to collect prepetition claims or that otherwise interfere with property of the estate. See 11 U.S.C. § 362.

and Jewish law, it illustrates how the ritual and religious parts of Jewish law are sometimes in tension with secular commercial law (and even some parts of Jewish commercial law), and it highlights the tensions that will take place in the international law arena as well.

In *In re Congregation Birchos Yosef*,[36] an Orthodox Jewish creditor sought to have an Orthodox Jewish debtor summoned to an Orthodox Jewish religious tribunal (*beth din*) to adjudicate the propriety (and even perhaps the validity) of the debtor's bankruptcy filing as a matter of Jewish law. In the absence of the debtor's agreeing to appear before the rabbinical court for such adjudication, the creditor wished the rabbinical court to issue a writ of contempt against the debtor as being in violation of Jewish law. The debtor filed a motion in bankruptcy court seeking to enjoin the creditor and the rabbinical court in question from considering whether bankruptcy is a valid option under Jewish law, whether the creditor owed the debtor money, and whether the rabbinical court may issue a contempt citation under Jewish law. The bankruptcy court held that the automatic stay applies to the proceedings of the rabbinical court no differently than to any other court. It stated simply:

> The automatic stay is clearly neutral on its face and is also neutral and generally applicable, as far as religious exercise is concerned, in practice. It applies to anyone who falls within the ambit of 11 U.S.C. § 362(a) (here, to anyone who commences a proceeding or takes another action covered by either 11 U.S.C. § 362(a)(1) or (3)). It prohibits the invocation of all covered proceedings, whether in state or federal court, a foreign court, *or a beis din [sic. Beth din].* (emphasis added)[37]

It is worth understanding what was *not* under consideration in this case. All parties agreed to the following:

> The rabbinical court cannot issue a legally binding order, even with an arbitration agreement signed by both parties, if it contradicts the directive of the bankruptcy court.
>
> The debtor's assets cannot be used to repay the debt upon the directive of the rabbinical court, since the assets are under the control of the bankruptcy court.

[36] *In re* Congregation Birchos Yosef, 535 B.R. 629 (Bankr. S.D.N.Y. 2015).
[37] Ibid., at 637.

By noting that the automatic stay applies directly to the rabbinical court, the bankruptcy court not only precluded the creditor and debtor from submitting to rabbinic court arbitration (which is an easy matter to preclude under bankruptcy law), but also used its authority to stay the rabbinical court's religious pronouncements concerning the correctness under Jewish law of the debtor's decision to file bankruptcy to begin with. Even if it could not have reached any meaningful decision on the merits of the case itself, the rabbinical court here may have wished to issue the *sheṭar serub,* or writ of contempt, against the debtor in order to signal to both the parties and the wider Jewish community that the debtor had violated Jewish religious law by filing for bankruptcy in order to avoid paying his debts.[38]

While such religious pronouncements lack any real legal authority or implications, they are important from a religious perspective. The bankruptcy court, however, made it clear that such religious pronouncements must cease.[39] This would be just as true in an international bankruptcy as a uniquely American one. Tension between religious and civil aspects of law are part of a complex dialogue in Jewish law, and part of its conversation with international law as well. This is even more true if local law is tainted with antisemitism, as we show in Chapter 7. Furthermore, this chapter shows that the exact boundary between Jewish law and local law or international law will always be gray in some applications.

Authority alone does not in the Jewish tradition create law; law must rest on pillars of justice and fairness as well as basic right and wrong. Though the medieval rabbinic decisors tended to point to arbitrary taxation—a procedural violation of due process—as emblematic of unjust regimes,[40] in fact the pursuit of justice entails a much broader obligation: Before law can be truly valid, there must be *both* procedural and substantive fairness in the legal system. Absent that, the Jewish tradition coined a phrase—"the theft of the

[38] For more on this, see Michael J. Broyde, "Forming Religious Communities and Respecting Dissenters' Rights," in *Human Rights in Judaism: Cultural, Religious, and Political Perspectives*, ed. Michael J. Broyde and John Witte, Jr. (Northvale, NJ: J. Aronson, 1998), 35.

[39] The bankruptcy court states directly: "Based on the record of the hearing, while the full extent of the effect of a *sirov*, if issued, is somewhat unclear, the mere threat of the issuance of a *sirov*, and, in fact, the commencement of the *beis din* proceeding itself, has already adversely affected the Debtor, through its principals, and made it more difficult to conduct this case by exerting significant pressure to cease pursuing the Debtor's claims against those who invoked the *beis din*." *In re Congregation Birchos Yosef*, 535 B.R. at 631–32.

[40] See R. Jacob b. Asher (Spain, 1269–1343), *Tur*, *Ḥoshen Mishpaṭ* 128; *Responsa Maharashdam,Ḥoshen Mishpaṭ* 135, 389; and R. Elijah b. Hayyim (Maharanah, Greece, 1530?–1610?), *Responsa Mayim Amukim*, vol. 2, no. 95.

government"—which is definitively not the law,[41] and insisted that no person could bear an obligation to obey unjust regimes.

Bibliography

Primary Sources

"Copyright and Jewish Law: *The Shemesh v. Yeshiva University* Case." *Ha'aretz*, September 10, 2003.

"Google Book Search Sued by Authors and Publishers." *New York Times*, October 20, 2005, sec. C.

"Napster Co-Founder to Pay $1.5 Million in Ruling." *New York Times*, March 14, 2001, C1.

"Napster Ordered to Pay $1.5 Billion in Damages." *USA Today*, March 15, 2001, 10A.

"YouTube Settles Viacom Suit for $1 Billion." 2011. *New York Times*, March 18. https://www.nytimes.com/2011/03/19/technology/19youtube.html.

Secondary Sources

Broyde, Michael J. *Sharia Tribunals, Rabbinical Courts, and Christian Panels: Religious Arbitration in America and the West.* Oxford: Oxford University Press, 2017.

Ginsburg, Jane C. "Berne without Borders: Geographic Indiscretion and Digital Communications." Stephen Stewart Memorial Lecture, Intellectual Property Institute, London, 2001. Reprinted in *Intellectual Property Quarterly* (2002): 111.

Ginsburg, Jane C. "Toward Supranational Copyright Law? The WTO Panel Decision and the 'Three-Step Test' for Copyright." *Revue Internationale du Droit d'Auteur* 187 (January 2001): 3–24.

Nathanson, Joseph Saul, *Sho'el U-Meshib*, part 1, no. 44. Lvov, Ukraine: 1860.

Netanel, Neil Weinstock. *From Maimonides to Microsoft: The Jewish Law of Copyright Since the Birth of Print.* New York: Oxford University Press, 2016.

Radziner, Amichai. "The Intellectual Ambivalence: Contemporary Halakhah and the Question of Copyright Defenses." In *Interdisciplinary Studies*, edited by Miriam Markovitz-Bitton and Lior Zamar, 169–214. Tel-Aviv, Israel: Nebo, 2015.

Radziner, Amichai. "Yeḥasu shel hagri'a Herzog la-Mishpat ha-Shawa'ti." In *Masuah Le-Yitzchak*, edited by Yitzhak Herzog, 506–32. Jerusalem, Israel: Rambi Publications, 2009.

Rakover, Nahum. "The Protection of Privacy in Jewish Law." *Israel Yearbook on Human Rights* 5 (1975): 169–80.

Shemesh, Eli. "Rabbi Shemesh's Copyright Claim Against Yeshiva University: A Study of the Interplay between Jewish Law and Copyright Law." *Israel Law Review* 38, no. 2 (2004): 265–84.

[41] *Hamsanuta de-malketa*; see *Entsiklopedyah Talmudith.*

5

Jewish Law and International Law: The Past

Legal Discrimination

In the early modern period, there were Jewish centers of learning throughout Europe, the West Indies, North Africa, the Middle East, and the Ottoman Empire. With the facility of the printing press, intellectual communication became easier throughout the Jewish Diaspora. The Babylonian Talmud, prayer books, and various treatises on ethics were disseminated among the entire Jewish population. The Jewish Diaspora was characterized by fragmented ethnic groups: Sephardi, Ashkenazi, Provençal, French, Byzantine, Italian, North African (Maghreb), Yemenite, Kurdish, Portuguese, and Musta'arab in the region of Bilad a-Sham. After the forced conversions of Jews in Spain and Portugal (1492–1497), Iberian "New Christians" established a worldwide trading network that linked coreligionists and kinships in major port cities. At that time, Yosef Karo, a leading rabbi and Sephardic exile, composed two major Jewish codes of law—the *Beth Yosef* and its abridged version, *Shulḥan Arukh*. This legal project encompassed the legal understandings of Sephardi and Ashkenazi legal scholars. Its aim was to coalesce the Jewish people under one legal consciousness and religious tradition.

Roni Weinstein advances the thesis that the changing role of legality within Jewish life during the early modern period indicated an overall radical transformation, which was truly global, in response to the power emerging in the states of Europe (and their overseas colonies) and in the Islamic empires. Minority groups and stateless peoples, such as the Jews, did not have a voice within the political and legal framework established by the Peace of Westphalia in 1648. Thus, the *Shulḥan Arukh* redefined the role of law and legal codification in forging state power and community identities (Weinstein 2018, 1–18).

Until recently, the history and theory of international law has been Eurocentric while claiming to be an *international* project. This chapter

Jewish Law and International Law. Michael J. Broyde and Yehonatan Elazar-De Mota, Oxford University Press.
 DOI: 10.1093/9780197805275.003.0005

explores the various fields and cases in which a detailed Jewish law conversation focuses on international law. The corpus includes academic articles, rabbinic responsa, philosophical treatises, rabbinic letters, sermons, halakhic codes, Jewish communal records, and municipal records. Most of these discussions were written in Hebrew and a few in Spanish, Portuguese, German, Yiddish, or English, from the sixteenth century until the establishment of the State of Israel. This period covers the intellectual history related to natural law, the law of nations, just war, slavery, sovereignty, treaties, maritime law, trade law, human rights, arbitration, and jurisdiction of courts.

Early Jewish Perspectives on Natural Law

In the early to mid-seventeenth century, Jewish communities throughout Western Europe regulated the book trade through small committees, with the assistance of the *beth din*. This practice limited the exclusive and arbitrary right of the *beth din* to issue a *ḥerem*. For instance, the Mahamad (board of directors) regulated the printing of books within the Sephardic Jewish communities in Venice and Amsterdam. It was usual and customary within these two communities to dedicate a Jewish literary work to the members of the Mahamad after the title page. The following page usually included the *ascamah* (seal of approval). Indeed, in Amsterdam, one could not print any Jewish material without an *ascamah*, under penalty of ostracism. Menasseh ben Israel's *Conciliator* caused much upheaval within the Portuguese community in Amsterdam, such that the community leaders reconfirmed the "pre-censorship established in May 1632 over publications by Jews" (Katchen 1984, 106). According to Aaron Katchen, this was part of a larger scheme to protect the Nação from possible threats to its safety (ibid.).

In his *Nacão Legal Consciousness*, Yehonatan Elazar-DeMota (2021) highlights this legal culture by analyzing the language and intellectual history of the Spanish and Portuguese works of Menasseh ben Israel (1604–1657), Ishac Athias (1585–d.?), Ishac Aboab da Fonseca (1605–1693), Immanuel Aboab (c. 1555–1628), Ishac Cardoso (1603–1683), Saul Levi Mortera (1596–1660), and Abraham Pereyra (1606–1674). These authors mobilized the language of *a lei da natureza, la ley natural, la ley de naturaleza,* and *la ley de humanidad* to construct justifications in favor of the institution of slavery and the slave trade. Equating slavery with part of the seven Noahide laws, they argued that it was part of *la ley natural* (natural law).[1]

According to the legal consciousness of the Nacão, *la ley natural* includes a positive precept to establish courts to exact judgment (*denim*). In his *Tratado da Verdade da Lei de Moisés* (1659), Mortera expounds his natural law theory (*a lei da natureza*) by analyzing the biblical story about the war between Abraham and five Canaanite kings (418). Abraham rescued his nephew, Lot, who had been enslaved as a war captive. Afterward, Abraham appeared before Melchizedek, the king of Salem (Genesis 14). Mortera posits that Melchizedek administered righteous rulings according to the precepts of *a lei da natureza* and virtue that existed then. Thus, Melchizedek had the power to punish and demand righteousness from the inhabitants of Salem. Mortera then concludes that if humans kept the Noahide laws as a form of natural law, then enslavement was possible as the result of a just war (Elazar-DeMota 2021, 234).

Another jurist from the School of Eẓ Ḥaim who contributed to the conception of the Noahide laws as a form of universal natural law was Immanuel Aboab. In his *Nomologia o Discursos Legales* (1629), he suggests that these precepts were revealed to God and Noah and were transmitted orally. His conception of la *ley de naturaleza* was divine law. Aboab posits that *la ley de naturaleza* is rational, eternal, and simultaneously natural and positive. He arrives at this conclusion by arguing that God taught Adam (the first human) all the details and procedures for the application of homicide law (49). This is a crucial difference from the influential School of Salamanca jurists Francisco de Victoria (1483–1546) and Francisco Suárez (1548–1617), who separated natural law from divine law. While de Victoria and Suárez agreed that slavery could result from a violation of natural law, they did not justify this claim as a divine mandate (de Victoria 1963, 1, ¶ 318; Suárez 2018, tr. VII, I.6, c. 2, n. 20, Vol. 15, 394; tr. VII, I.2, c. 12, n.17, Vol. 15, 173). Like Mortera, Aboab held that a war captive could be enslaved for violating the precepts of the Noahide laws.

Isaac Cardoso, a physician and philosopher of the Eẓ Ḥaim community, also conceived of a universal and divine form of natural law, calling it *la ley natural*. Contrary to Christian doctrine, in his *Excelencia de los Hebreos*

[1] The seven Noahide precepts are: not to commit idolatry, not to commit adultery, not to kill, not to steal, not to blaspheme God's name, not to eat a limb of a live animal, and to institute judges and tribunals. See Maimonides, *Laws of Kings and Their Wars*, chap. 9, 1.

(1679) Cardoso argues that non-Jews can obtain salvation by keeping the precepts of *la ley natural*, and if they want a greater reward in the world to come, they should join the Children of Israel by becoming proselytes (9). He asserts that after the biblical account of the Flood, humans did not follow Adam's righteous example of repentance but gave themselves over to idolatry, pride, and lordship. Therefore, Cardoso agreed that human enslavement was a result of sin and tyranny. Spanish jurists Bartolomé de las Casas (1484–1566) and Domingo de Soto (1494–1560) agreed that slavery was a consequence of human desire and avarice (Jiménez Fonseca 2017, 141; Davis 1999, 202).

Lawyers and thinkers at the School of Eẓ Ḥaim also mobilized the language of *ius gentium* in their literary works. Menasseh ben Israel conceived of *la ley de humanidad* based on Roman law (Elazar-DeMota 2021, 187). In *Thesouro dos dinim* (1647), he cites Roman jurists such as Gaius and Cicero to argue the relation of slavery to the law of nations (181). In a detailed account of the halakhah of slavery, Menasseh mentions two types of slaves: one who undergoes ritual immersion and one who does not. The ritual crucially gives the one who undergoes it a quasi-Jewish status; otherwise, he would lack legal personality before Jewish courts (Maimonides 2010, Hilkhoth Abadim 5:8). For that matter, Menasseh exhorted Jewish slave owners to remember the dictates of *la ley de humanidad* (ibid.). *Ius gentium*, under the tenets of Roman law, provided numerous protections for slaves from harsh treatment (Shumway 1901, 636–53). In essence, Menasseh exhorted Portuguese Jewish slave owners to uphold a higher standard of law than halakhah.

In contrast to Menasseh ben Israel's conception of *la ley de humanidad*, Abraham Pererya, a philosopher of the Portuguese Jewish community in Amsterdam, distinguishes between natural law and the law of nations in his *Espejo de la Vanidad del Mundo* (1671). Juxtaposing the natural instincts of animals and the human intellect, Pererya wondered why humans, who possess *la ley de humanidad*, obey God less than animals do their masters (78).[2]

[2] "Si los irracionales brutos, que tienen solo el instinto natural, conque reconcer el beneficio, sirven, agradecen, y acompañan a sus bienhechores; el hombre, que tiene tanto mayor lumber, para reconocer el bien que recibe, como es possible, que viva tan olvidado, de quien tanto bien le haze? Come se dexa vencer de las bestias, en Ley de humanidad, lealtad, y agradecimiento?" [If the irrational brutes, who possess natural instinct to recognize what is beneficial, serve, thank, and accompany their benefactors, how is it possible for man, who has so much more strength to recognize the good he receives, to live so oblivious of the one who does him so much good? How does he allow himself to be surpassed by the beasts, in the law of humanity, loyalty, and gratitude?].

Agreeing with Spanish scholastics, Pereyra argued that brute beasts are born with natural instinct, knowing what harms them, but that humans must be taught (253). Natural instincts in humans are not enough to make them virtuous, but knowledge of the divine law of God is necessary. Elazar-DeMota infers that Pererya equated revealed positive law (divine law of God) with *la ley de humanidad* (Elazar-DeMota 2021, 250). Therefore, the Law of Moses contains elements of the law of nations.

Elazar-DeMota contextualizes these discussions within the broader debate in the universities of Évora, Coimbra, Alcalá de Henares, and Salamanca. In the seventeenth century, a significant question for scholars at these universities was whether the law of nations was partly natural or completely positive. This question gave birth to the conception of primary and secondary natural law, and primary and secondary law of nations. Annabel Brett calls the primary law of nations the *naturalized law of nations*, which is simultaneously natural and positive. This convention allowed for the institution of slavery to be related to both natural law and the law of nations. In this sense, the seven Noahide laws are a form of *ius naturae et gentium*.

While some jurists and philosophers of the School of Eẓ Ḥaim held that the seven Noahide laws were mainly universal natural law, Baruh Espinosa [Spinoza] (1632–1677) vehemently disagreed. Disagreements with his teacher, Saul Levi Mortera, led to his excommunication from the community. Mortera espoused Maimonides's view that a person is considered pious, having a share in the world to come, when they accept the Noahide laws as being revealed and commanded by God. Although Espinosa accepted the equivalence between the seven precepts and natural law, he rejected the idea that Judaism alone knew these laws. Noahide's precept to not eat a limb from a live animal requires interpretation from the text in Genesis. According to Maimonides, not every interpretation is acceptable, but only that which was handed down to the prophets of Israel and recorded in the Talmud. This is what Espinosa denied. Instead, he favored the freedom and universal access to divine knowledge which the Gospels celebrated. In other words, he criticized Maimonidean hermeneutics as an attempt to covertly establish the authority of reason in politics by installing a "new type of priest," a philosopher skilled at presenting rational truths in imaginative language (Frankel 2005, 86). Essentially, he argued that the Maimonidean approach to establishing universal law was "harmful, useless, and absurd" (Spinoza 2014, 100).

In distancing himself from the rhetoric of natural law, Espinosa divorced morality from international law, such that states were not bound to contracts that had lost their utility (Spinoza 2015, 3, 14). In the third chapter of his *Tractatus Politicus* (1677), Espinosa advanced his theories of international relations and law. According to legal scholar Gökhan Güneysu, one group of scholars portrays Espinosa as rejecting natural law and international law altogether (Güneysu 2017, 174). This view of Espinosa holds that he equated the state of nature with a society lacking a government that controlled its consciences through fear. Thus, Espinosa argued that it was not possible to interpret natural law as a law because natural law is incapable of establishing obligations (Menzel 1907, 18; Spinoza 2015, 2:23). On the contrary, he viewed commonwealths as natural enemies of each other unless they were willing to help each other mutually. Espinosa wrote:

> The more commonwealths there are, that have contracted a joint treaty of peace, the less each of them by itself is an object of fear to the remainder, or the less it has the authority to make war. But it is so much the more bound to observe the conditions of peace; that is, the less independent, and the more bound to accommodate itself to the general will of the contracting parties. (Spinoza 2015, 3:16)

Espinosa's conception of international law was that humans were not bound to each other because of halakhah (i.e., the seven Noahide laws). Rather, his theory of international law was based on consensus and useful agreements.

Nineteenth-Century Developments

The nineteenth century saw the advent of two critical issues within the realm of halakhah and international law, namely, the concept of sovereignty and the standard of civilization. Legal scholar David Kennedy argues:

> From the mid-nineteenth century, as "law" came to be associated with national sovereignty, "international law" became an act of imagination and argument by analogy. A scholarly profession developed rapidly to undertake

> and promote that imaginative construction, developing theories—arguments, really—for the existence, scope, and content of international law in a world of national sovereigns. (Kennedy 2016, 223)

As nation-states were forming, rabbinic scholars also imagined a sovereign nation in the Holy Land for themselves, through the mobilization of international law. This section discusses some of the discourse concerning international law and Jewish sovereignty.

According to the *The Oxford Handbook of the Sources of International Law*, "The principle of sovereignty, i.e., of supreme authority within a territory, is a pivotal principle of modern international law. What counts as sovereignty depends on the nature and structure of the international legal order and vice-versa" (Besson 2011, 380). With the formation of European nation-states in the modern period, Jews living in Europe and the Ottoman Empire envisioned a sovereign state for themselves within the borders of their ancestral homeland. In the nineteenth century, the Holy Land was under the jurisdiction of the Ottoman Empire. At that time the region was divided into *vilayets* (first-level administrative division) and *sanjaks* (districts). Messianic fervor motivated large numbers of Eastern European Jews to migrate to Ereẓ Yisrael. Modern Zionism emerged during this political and social context.

While a great number of Jewish jurists in the nineteenth century gave their opinions regarding the establishment of a Jewish state in the Holy Land, a few of them expressed their views regarding international law. The issue was how to interpret the Talmudic discussion on the oath of Jews to not forcefully establish sovereignty in their ancestral land by rebelling against the nations of the world (*b.Ketuboth 110b–111a*). While there were many contradictory opinions and interpretations regarding this Talmudic passage, here we explore the concept of sovereignty through the lens of Judah ben Solomon Hai Alkalai (1798–1878) and Sabato Morais (1823–1897).

Judah ben Solomon Ḥai Alkalai, a Sephardic jurist and kabbalist, was a prominent figure in nineteenth-century Zionism. He was born in Sarajevo, under Ottoman rule, and died in Jerusalem. Alkalai was trained in Jewish law in Jerusalem, after which he became the rabbi of the Jewish community in Semlin (Serbia). He authored two important works, in which he presented his international law theory: *Goral l'Adonay* (Lot for the Lord, Vienna 1857) and *Mebaser Ṭob* (Harbinger of good tidings, London 1857).

At the heart of Alkalai's thinking is the Jewish understanding of redemption, which implies Jewish sovereignty in the Holy Land. This sovereignty will come in two stages, first under the Messiah son of Joseph, and second under the Messiah son of David. In the first stage, Messiah son of Joseph will come from a European country and gather the exiles of Israel in the Holy Land. He will stir the nation to rebuild the Temple. Then will follow Messiah son of David, who will usher in a spiritual awakening among the people of Israel and, by extension, all the inhabitants of the world.

Yehudah Alkalai envisioned the kings of the world assisting the Israelite nation to accomplish these goals. In *Goral l'Adonay,* he cites various prophets from the Hebrew Bible and medieval commentators to support his international law theory (Isa. 44, 61; Zech. 1; Hos. 1, 2, 3, 11; Jer. 50). He did not see it possible for the Jewish people to regain sovereignty in the Holy Land without the help of the sovereigns of the world. He cites the famous passage of the Talmud on the three oaths, "not to build a wall against us" (*b.Ketuboth* 111a).[3] Alkalai urged the Jewish communal leaders of his day to gather in London to speak about returning to the Holy Land and appointing a leader as their Messiah, son of Joseph (Alkalai "Mebaser Tob," 4). In his vision of international law, Alkalai posited that the sovereigns would approve this leader of all the nations. Furthermore, he asserts that while the Second Temple was built with the approval of Cyrus, king of Persia, the final Temple will be rebuilt with the approval of all the kings of the Earth. Alkalai held that the Messiah, the son of Joseph, would present the Jewish people's request before the international legal consensus and that God would stir up their hearts to grant the petition of the Jews. He concludes with the words of the prophet, "It is not by might, nor sword, but by my will" (Common English Bible, Zech.

[3] The three oaths reflect significant themes in Jewish thought, such as exile, redemption, and the relationship of Jews with their homeland and the broader world. They are often discussed in relation to topics of Jewish sovereignty, national identity, and the eschatological hopes of the Jewish people, which are outlined in the Talmud:

1. The Oath of the Jewish People—This oath binds the Jewish people not to ascend to the land of Israel forcibly or in rebellion against the nations that inhabit it. It emphasizes a sense of restraint and patience regarding the return to their homeland.
2. The Oath of the Nations—This oath requires the nations of the world not to oppress the Jewish people excessively during their exile. It recognizes the suffering and challenges faced by Jews in diaspora but serves as a reminder of the responsibility of nations toward them.
3. The Oath of God— This divine oath guarantees that God will not abandon the Jewish people despite their trials and tribulations throughout history. It reassures Jews of God's continual presence and support, facilitating hope for redemption.

4:6. In essence, Alkalai resolved the controversy surrounding the Talmudic passage on the "three oaths" by including international law in his halakhic understanding.

On the opposing side of the debate with Judah Alkalai was Sabato Morais. He was trained in Livorno and served as a spiritual leader in the Spanish and Portuguese Jews' congregation in London and then in Philadelphia. He taught Bible and biblical literature at Maimonides College in 1867 (Davis 1947, 55–93) and later helped to establish the Jewish Theological Seminary in New York City (1886).

During the messianic fervor of the nineteenth century, Morais published an English translation of Moses Maimonides's *Letter to the Jews of Yemen*, a twelfth-century work that dealt with false messianic agitation. In the letter, Maimonides warns the Jewish community in southern Arabia against setting dates for the commencement of the messianic era and the emergence of a messianic figure (Morais 1935). This warning was the reason why Morais translated Maimonides's treatise. He worried that an attempt to reestablish Jewish sovereignty under Ottoman rule would lead to the secular overturning of traditional religious beliefs of messianic passivity.

Morais called political Zionism "utopian" and unrealistic. In his opinion, God, not Jews, would initiate a messianic restoration (Kiron 1996, 155–88). He opposed the Zionist movement because he firmly believed in the biblical promises of the restoration of Israel:

> [Is it] indeed in such an issue that the hopes, cherished during ages of suffering, meekly borne for a grand ideal, will find their realization? The very thought is an offense to the memory of the immortal seers in [whose] illumined vision Israel stood purified seven-fold as the embodiment of a humanizing belief [and] as the acknowledged educator of mankind. . . . [It is not] the mere possession of a patch of ground guaranteed by protocols [that constitutes] the aspiration of pious hearts among the remnant of the tribes. . . . Efforts to create a state would prove worse than a chimera. It would be an absolute evil. (Morais 1877, 102)

Morais feared that a mass migration to an impoverished land would create upheaval within the sphere of imperial politics and would depend on the goodwill of the Ottoman caliphate or some other foreign power. Apparently, he was not optimistic about an international consensus facilitating Jewish sovereignty in the Holy Land. On the contrary, Morais viewed the restoration of Jewish sovereignty in Ereẓ Yisrael as emerging through divine authority and timing. For him, international law or human intervention would not play any role in the reestablishment of a third and final Jewish commonwealth.

We have surveyed the attitudes toward international law of two important Jewish jurists of the nineteenth century, Judah Alkalai and Sabato Morais. While Alkalai included international law within his scope of halakhah and Jewish sovereignty in the Holy Land, Morais opposed such an idea. Alkalai envisioned the establishment of Jewish sovereignty through human intervention, while Morais looked strictly for divine volition. With the dissolution of the Ottoman Empire in the early twentieth century, these two opposing views became more engraved in the legal-political consciousness of worldwide Jewry.

Twentieth-Century Developments

In the early to mid-twentieth century, a few Jewish jurists either expressed halakhah in the language of international law or dealt with it within their halakhic responsa. Among these few were Ḥayyim Hirschensohn (1857–1935), Moshe Chalfon Hacohen (1874–1950), Isaac Breuer (1883–1946), and Hersch Lauterpacht (1897–1960). Their legal writings cover various topics of international law, including universal values and justice, sovereignty, human rights, arbitration, and humanitarian law.

Rabbi Ḥayyim Hirschensohn was a proponent not only of Jewish sovereignty in tandem with international law but also of human rights.[4] He was born in Safed, in Galilee, and trained in rabbinic studies in Jerusalem and Russia. Hirschensohn published Torah and scientific articles while in Hungary and Germany in 1884. Ten years later, he served as head rabbi of the Jewish community in Hoboken, New Jersey. He expressed his international law theories in conjunction with halakhah mainly in two works: *Malki ba-Qodesh* (1919–1928) and *Musage Shaw we-ha-'Emeth* (1908–1919).

In the introduction of his collection of responsa, he begins: "There is nothing in biblical law and halakha which contradicts in any way progress or common sense. The objective of my research is to show that halakha does

[4] Israeli scholars Amos Israel-Vleeshhouwer (2011) and Yeshayahu Rothberg (2008) have written excellent PhD dissertations which detail the political and legal ideas of Rabbi Ḥayyim Hirschensohn. These documents were written in Hebrew and are extensive. For more information, one should consult them.

not pose any obstacle to the development of private life or the life of an entire nation" (Hirschensohn 1919).

Without a doubt, he maintained that a Jewish state should abide by international law agreements and the consensus of the nations of the world (Hirschensohn 1926, *Eleh Dibere*, 1:37–38).

Hirschensohn held that all humans were bound to each other because of the *berith* (covenant) between themselves and God. This *berith* served as the foundation of all international law and relations. Like other Jewish jurists in the early modern period, he equated the seven Noahide laws with natural law, focusing on *dinim* (ibid., 1:6). This implies that all universal values, justice, and respect for national laws were within the scope of the Noahide laws (Hirschensohn 1889–1890). Hirschensohn argued that some of the precepts of the Noahide laws were rational, while others were relative to time and place (Hirschensohn 1926, *Eleh Dibere*, 1:187). He posited that God revealed the Torah at Mount Sinai to benefit all humans, to specify and add to some laws that could not be derived by reason alone. Therefore, after the revelation of the Torah, all humans were held accountable to natural law as expressed in the Torah: the children of Noah having seven precepts, and Israelites having six-hundred and thirteen precepts (Hirschensohn 1926, *Eleh Dibere*, 1:187). At the foundation of his international legal theory was the will of the people and treaties: "Just as the individual possesses independence, so the state has independence. And just as individuals make agreements between themselves, so does humanity make agreements in the form of statutes and laws, by which one will do and live by them" (Hirschensohn 1932, 30:71).

Rabbi Hirschensohn was one of the few who mapped out what a modern Jewish commonwealth would look like. He developed a political theology known as "halakhic democracy" (Brown 2022, 442). Hirschensohn envisioned a Jewish state that would follow the dictates of international law (Zohar 2005). He held that as time passed, international agreements embodied higher standards of justice, ever approaching God's will and thereby obligating Israel to respect them. Thus, he argued that it was forbidden for Israel to violate international law even if it contradicted Jewish law (Hirschensohn 1926, *Eleh Dibre*, 1:69). Indeed, he posited that keeping agreements and treaties overrides halakhah. This implies that the leaders of a Jewish state should put aside the biblical precept of exterminating the seven Canaanite nations to avoid genocide (Deut. 7:1). Accordingly, he asserted that a Jewish state in the Holy Land should be democratic, granting equality to Jews and non-Jews, and to men and women.

Another important Jewish jurist who expressed his views on international law was Rabbi Moshe Chalfon Ha-Cohen. Born in Djerba, Tunisia, he was educated in Jewish law by his father and Rabbi Joseph Barbi. In 1917, he became a member of the rabbinical court in Djerba, which regulated Jewish life there. Ha-Cohen published over eighty works and is best known for *Responsa Shoel VeNishal*, a collection of more than three thousand responsa in eight volumes, and his *Berith Kehuna*, an organization of the customs of the Jewish community in Djerba. One can find his attitudes toward international norms and institutions throughout his sermons and works published between 1907 and 1939.

R. Chalfon Ha-Cohen based his jurisprudence on three pillars: recognition of the positive aspects of modernity and their internalization and assimilation; awareness of history and the events of the period as a fulfillment of divine will; and the historiosophy of redemption.

Regarding the first pillar, he held that the European Enlightenment and the values of the French Revolution agreed with God's will and an expressed revelation on behalf of the individual and all of humanity:

> In our time, the order of the Redemption has changed completely, and in some kingdoms, it has been agreed that there should be liberty and freedom for Israel as well, with equal rights as known. And every nation and language that did not agree to this is now considered by almost everyone as an animal and wild beast and savage man. For the Eternal One has raised the spirit of Enlightenment from his holy abode, liberty and freedom in the hearts of all human beings. (Chalfon Ha-Cohen 1977, 45; Zohar 2002)

Moreover, Chalfon Ha-Cohen asserted that as the days of the Redemption drew near, the Almighty would influence the speech of the sovereigns of the world to speak about granting liberty and freedom to all of humanity, and to permit the dispersed children of Israel to live in peace and tranquility (Chalfon Ha-Cohen 1926, 52). In general, he affirmed that cultural and religious tolerance, human rights, and equality were an expression of divine will (Chalfon Ha-Cohen 1977, 19–20, sec. 7:15; 21; 1926, 35:25).

Second, Chalfon Ha-Cohen considered bloodshed in World War I to be a result of people's negligence and indifference toward each other:

> The voice of the people murdered in the world war, the voice of the blood wounded in the world war, . . . the voice of life of the oppressed and

tormented by hunger and thirst, waiting for death, yet we were naught . . . the voice of the exiled from city to city and from country to country . . . ringing in the ears of all those who seek the truth and love it, and whose heart is flesh and has not frozen. His heart is like a stone! (Chalfon Ha-Cohen 1992)

Examining the causes that led to this war, Chalfon Ha-Cohen sought ways to prevent such atrocities from happening again. For example, he applied rabbinic literature to the contemporary context, "a person who brings peace between husband and wife . . . between countries, no calamity shall befall them" (Sifra 20:17). In general, he called for *tikkun olam* (reparation of the world).

Finally, Chalfon Ha-Cohen viewed Jewish and global redemption through the lens of historical events. With the formation of the League of Nation, Jewish lobbying became possible on behalf of a Jewish state. He posited that this state would serve not only as a fulfillment of biblical prophecy but also as a model for all nations which follow international law (Chalfon Ha-Cohen 1992, 1:103). Notably, his propositions were not based on halakhah but on an international legal framework. As such, he did not propose that his words be understood as *pesiqah halakhah* (legal rulings) but as stemming from compromise and common sense. Experts and thinkers could thus participate in the international peace-building process apart from Jewish law (Chalfon Ha-Cohen 1926, 12). Indeed, Chalfon Ha-Cohen maintained that no nation would have absolute sovereignty, including the Jewish nation; rather, all nations would be subject to a universal government representing all countries. This international law body would regulate all matters pertaining to war, military, and the use of weapons (Zohar 2002). In fulfillment of biblical prophecy, he proposed that the international legal consensus establish its headquarters in Jerusalem, thereby serving as a lasting influence on Jewish culture (Chalfon Ha-Cohen 1977, 24).

Rabbi Dr. Isaac Breuer, a contemporary of Chalfon Ha-Cohen, was the leader of the Agudath Yisrael movement, the Haredi Jewish political party in Israel, which opposed twentieth-century Zionism. As such, he held a positive outlook on international law and the League of Nations. He was born in Frankfurt, Germany, where he was trained in Jewish law, secular law, and jurisprudence under the tutelage of his father. He practiced law there until 1936, when he emigrated to Jerusalem (Mittelman 1990; Horovits 2006, preface). Breuer published numerous works and articles in German and

Hebrew. He expressed his attitudes toward international law mainly in *Ṣione Derekh* (Horovits 1923).

The social and political context of halakhah played an important role in Breuer's conception of it. He maintained that although Torah law is eternal, its application must always establish justice a priori. In his mind, it was not possible to apply Jewish law independently of the changes that occurred in the world (Breuer 1953, preface). In *Moriyah* (1953) , Breuer opens by stating, "The nation of Israel is part of humanity, and it is impossible to understand its nature without taking a stance on behalf of humanity in general" (ibid.). Here, one gains entry into Breuer's worldview regarding the Jewish people and the international legal consensus. Like the Sephardic jurists from the School of Eẓ Ḥaim, Breuer established universal justice on the seven Noahide laws (ibid., 49).

Breuer held that sovereignty of states was inherently evil because they struggle among themselves. Human sovereignty, whether of individuals, states, and peoples or the whole world, contradicted his vision of law and justice. He argued that divine intervention was necessary, "[I]t was no longer necessary to bring a new flood on the land. The hateful waters of the states, the ones running out of their sovereignty are enough. And all this seditious water turns into blood" (ibid., 29). In a similar vein, Thomas Hobbes (1588–1679) had written:

> For the Lawes of Nature (as Justice, Equity, Modesty, Mercy, and (in summe) doing to others, as we would be done to,) of themselves, without the terrour of some Power, to cause them to be observed, are contrary to our naturall Passions, that carry us to Partiality, Pride, Revenge, and the like. And Covenants, without the Sword, are but Words, and of no strength to secure a man at all. (Hobbes 1984, XVII [85] 223)

Hobbes identified might as the root cause of human suffering within a sovereign state. Without the power of the sovereign, accords are meaningless (Faur 2010, 101). In the same way, Breuer argued that the political always triumphs over the legal.

Breuer's conception of international law accorded with his view of the Jewish tradition. He envisioned a decentralized international law to which diverse nations would submit themselves voluntarily under joint control. This universal legal authority would then strive to establish common justice backed up by decentralized enforcement (Breuer 1953, 125–26). For that matter, he argued that the League of Nations had three goals: the pursuit of world peace, the promotion of equality and sufficiency for all humans, and ensuring that law takes precedence over interests (Israel-Vleeshhouwer 2011, 70). He criticized the failure of the League of Nations to prevent wars: "For a long time, it was correct for the people of the great countries, not to permit such a serious sacrifice before the League of Nations, with its vision of law and justice . . . but the states had the upper hand, because only they possessed an army, while the League of Nations was the weakling before an armed world" (Breuer 1953, 233). In his view, it was not possible to achieve the League's goals without unity among international legal institutions, halakhah, and justice (ibid.). Ultimately, Breuer thought that only law was of supreme value, being above the institution of the state (Breuer 2024, 88).

As we finalize this chapter, we discuss the international legal theory of Hersch (Zvi) Lauterpacht. He was born to a middle-class Jewish family in Galicia, a center of rabbinic discussion on law (today part of eastern Poland and Ukraine). As a fluent speaker of Yiddish and Hebrew, he was immersed in the world of the Talmud and halakhah. His membership in a Zionist youth group led to his expulsion from the Austrian army in 1917. Lauterpacht studied law under Hans Kelsen and obtained a doctorate in law in 1921 and another in political science in 1922. A year later he moved to London, where he joined the London School of Economics and Political Science as an assistant lecturer in public international law.

Lauterpacht expressed his attitudes toward international law through the lens of Talmudic jurisprudence. Here we analyze his ideas through his dissertation, articles, and books. At the center of Lauterpacth's conception of international law was the natural tradition. In his article "The Grotian Tradition in International Law," he states:

> Undoubtedly the law of nature has often been resorted to in support of causes dubious and retrogressive. But this ambivalence of the ideology of natural law is only slightly relevant in the field of international law. There, by and large, it has acted as a lever of progress. The law of nature has been rightly exposed to the charge of vagueness and arbitrariness. But the uncertainty of the "higher law" is preferable to the arbitrariness and insolence of naked force. These considerations explain the significance of this aspect of the Grotian tradition in the history of the law of nations. He secularized the law of nature. He gave it added authority and dignity

> by making it an integral part of the exposition of a system of law which became essential to civilized life. By doing this he laid, more truly than any writer before him, the foundations of international law. (Lauterpacht 1946, 23:1–53, 24)

Despite the darkest moments in European history, Lauterpacht never ceased to argue that humans can find goodness through right reason. This idea served as the basis for the cosmopolitan tradition of Western liberalism. Furthermore, he maintained that natural law was the foundation and essence of international law, as applied in Article 38(1)c, Statute of the International Court of Justice: the general principles of law recognized by civilized nations (Lauterpacht 1946, 23). Thus, the implied consent between the nations to establish good relations stemmed from the natural law of international relations. In sum, Lauterpacht posited that natural law was the legal source that supplemented ordinary sources of positive law.

Lauterpacht applied natural legal theory in international law to promote principles of universalism against national particularisms. In the wake of World War II, he developed a theory of human rights:

> [W]hat is required at this juncture of history is not the recognition and not even the formulation of inalienable human rights but their effective protection, by an instrumentality higher than the state itself, against the arbitrariness of wilful men and against the complacent or selfish indolence of entrenched interests. (Lauterpacht 1949, 33, 410, 412)

In his book *International Law and Human Rights*, he highlights Western traditions and principles from Greek philosophers through Grotius and Vattel. To his dismay, the states unanimously rejected the legally binding force of the 1948 Universal Declaration of Human Rights. Consequently, he sought to translate morality and ethics into legal norms. As such, he asserted that jurists had to become diplomats within international judiciaries, as opposed to political bodies (Lauterpacht 1950, 397–408).

Lauterpacht sought to solve conflicts through law, not politics. His training in the Talmud and halakhah played a major role in his legal reasoning. The legal scholar Reut Yael Paz suggests that Lauterpacht resembled rabbinic exegetes in his approach to law (Paz 2012, 438). She begins her discourse by citing a *mishnah* which may have influenced Lauterpacht in combating extreme Hegelianism, based in Hobbesian politics (*b.Meẓia* 59b).[5] This discussion details a dispute between the majority of justices of the Jewish High Court and R. Eliezer, the wisest of his generation. After many phenomenological experiences attesting to R. Eliezer's argument, the majority did not recognize them as valid evidence to be considered within legal reasoning. This Talmudic passage strengthens the jurisprudential tradition that once the Torah was revealed to the people of Israel, it became the responsibility of the people in every generation to ascribe meaning to it through interpretation. Thus, not even God can infringe on this right granted to the people (Faur 2010, 58). Therefore, interpretation of law is the instrument by with the community builds itself, not the subjective ideas of a sovereign person.

In Lauterpacht's legal analysis, the institution of the state is equated with God in the *mishnah* cited. R. Eliezer represents justices who want to grant ultimate political power to the state, while the other group of rabbis represents the judiciary who want to maintain legislative authority. Paz argues that the failures of the powerful sovereign to prevent wars and the security of the Jews in Europe motivated Lauterpacht toward this change. In proposing a Bill of Rights for universal human rights, he asserted:

> A Bill of Rights worthy of the name is not a consummation which can be achieved without some States giving up practices and constitutional principles in a way necessary to ensure an irreducible minimum standard of respect for fundamental human rights and of the requisite international guarantees. In current terminology, that consummation cannot be

[5] "There is a Mishna (Kelim, V., 10) which treats of an oven which R. Eliezer makes clean and the sages unclean, and it is the oven of a snake. What does this mean? Said R. Jehudah in the name of Samuel: It intimates that they encircled it with their evidences as a snake winds itself around an object. And a *baraitha* states that R. Eliezer related all answers of the world, and they were not accepted. Then he said: Let this carob-tree prove that the halakhah prevails as I state, and the carob was (miraculously) thrown off to a distance of one hundred ells, and according to others four hundred ells. But they said: The carob proves nothing. He again said: 'Let, then, the spring of water prove that so the halakhah prevails.' The water then began to run backwards. But again, the sages said that this proved nothing. He again said: 'Then, let the walls of the college prove that I am right.' The walls were about to fall. R. Joshua, however, rebuked them, saying: 'If the scholars of this college are discussing upon a halakhah, wherefore should ye interfere!' They did not fall, for the honor of R. Joshua, but they did not become again straight, for the honor of R. Eliezer [and they are still in the same condition]. He said again: Let it be announced by the heavens that the halakhah prevails according to my statement, and a heavenly voice was heard, saying: Why do you quarrel with R. Eliezer, who is always right in his decisions! R. Joshua then arose and proclaimed [Deut. 30:12]: 'The Law is not in the heavens.' How is this to be understood? said R. Jeremiah: It means, the Torah was given already to us on the mountain of Sinai, and we do not care for a heavenly voice, as it reads [Exod. 23:2]: 'To incline after the majority.' R. Nathan met Elijah (the Prophet) and questioned him: 'What did the Holy One, blessed be He, at that time?' (when R. Joshua proclaimed the above answer to the heavenly voice), and he rejoined: 'He laughed and said, My children have overruled me, my children have overruled me.'"

> accomplished without some sacrifices of sovereignty not only in respect of the substance of the Bill but also of its enforcement. The essence of a Bill of the Rights of Man is that it implies a limitation upon the existing and the future powers of the State. There is no country so advanced or entitled to such absolute conviction of the excellence of its law and its institutions as to not be able to make a contribution to the common stock of a Bill of Rights by consenting to some change in its legal and constitutional system. (Lauterpacht 1950, 305–6).

Simply put, Lauterpacht maintained that the welfare of human beings depended on diminishing power and modifying the politics of sovereign states, whereby a universal court of justices would rule supreme. Ultimately, he argued that justice and morality should not be in the "hands of heaven" but in the realm of contemporary legal scholars (Paz 2012, 442). This idea was best expressed by US Supreme Court Justice Benjamin Cardozo (1870–1938):

> I have made myself today the self-appointed spokesman and defender of the philosopher in the field of law. I am not concerned to vindicate philosophy, either in jurisprudence or outside of it as an inquiry of cultural value or speculative interest. My concern is with the relationship of philosophy to life. . . . You think perhaps of philosophy as dwelling in the clouds. I hope you may see that she is able to descend to earth (Cardozo 1924, 22–23).

It is clear that both Cardozo and Lauterpacht drank from the same waters, namely, the Talmud.

A Summary of Jewish Intellectual and Legal History

This chapter has explored the legal history of the interaction between halakhah and international law from the early modern period to the establishment of the State of Israel. This intellectual history covers the domain of natural law, the law of nations, just war, slavery, sovereignty, treaties, maritime law, trade law, human rights, arbitration, and jurisdiction of courts. In the early modern period, with the contribution of the printing press, Jewish scholarship thrived with the publishing and dissemination of legal codes and manuals throughout the Jewish diaspora. In public international law, Jewish jurists equated the rabbinic concept of the seven Noahide precepts with natural law, thereby linking humanity under a universal code. At the same time, Sephardic legal scholars in the School of Eẓ Ḥaim arbitrated and adjudicated cases within the realm of private international law among the Nação.

At the dawn of the modern era, Jews were emancipated in Europe and the Americas, where the function of the *Shulḥan Arukh* as a code of international law dwindled. With the emancipation of European Jews and the establishment of nation-states, many gained access and entry to university education. Many Jews studied law and became prominent jurists. At the same time, Jewish jurists in the Ottoman Empire envisioned a sovereign Jewish state in the Holy Land. The chapter has thus explored different legal opinions regarding Jewish sovereignty, just war, humanitarian law, and the role of the international legal consensus. In the aftermath of two world wars, Hersch Lauterpacht applied rabbinic reasoning to argue in favor of universal justice, leading to the development of human rights. Human rights discourse thereafter would play a central role in the halakhic discussions pertaining to the treatment of Arabs within the State of Israel.

Bibliography

Primary Sources

Aboab, Immanuel. *Nomologia o Discursos Legales.* Venice, Italy: 1629.

Alkalai, Judah. *Mebaser Tob.* London, UK: S. Solomon Publishers, 1857.

Babylonian Talmud. *Baba Meẓia.* Edited by Jerome Schottenstein. Rahway, NJ: Artscroll Mesorah Publications, 1997.

Babylonian Talmud. *Gittin.* Edited by Jerome Schottenstein. Rahway, NJ: Artscroll Mesorah Publications, 1997.

Babylonian Talmud. *Ketuboth.* Edited by Jerome Schottenstein. Rahway, NJ: Artscroll Mesorah Publications, 1997.

Babylonian Talmud. *Nedarim.* Edited by Jerome Schottenstein. Rahway, NJ: Artscroll Mesorah Publications, 1997.

Babylonian Talmud. *Yebamoth.* Edited by Jerome Schottenstein. Rahway, NJ: Artscroll Mesorah Publications, 1997.

Breuer, Isaac. *Moriyah.* Jerusalem, Israel: ha-Merkaz le-maʿan sifrut ḥaredit, 1953.

Breuer, Isaac. *Mein Weg.* Second Edition. Basel, Germany: Verlag Morascha AG, 2024.

Bynkershoek, Cornelius Van. *A Treatise on the Law of War. Translated from the Original Latin. The First Book of his Quaestiones Juris Publici.* Clark, NJ: The Lawbook Exchange, 2008.

Cardozo, Benjamin. *The Growth of the Law.* New Haven, CT: Yale University Press, 1924.

Cardoso, Isaac. *Excelencia de los Hebreos.* Amsterdam, Netherlands: David de Castro Trata, 1679.

Chalfon Ha-Cohen, Moshe. *Matteh Moshe.* 1926.

Chalfon Ha-Cohen, Moshe. *Geulath Moshe,* 1977.

Chalfon Ha-Cohen, Moshe. *Wa-Yaqhel Moshe,* 1977.

Chalfon Ha-Cohen, Moshe. *Darke Moshe.* Netiboth, Israel: 1992.

Gemeente Archief Amsterdam [GAA], NA.nr. 334, 875, 17 Menahem Ab 5483.

Gemeente Archief Amsterdam 334:10, fol. 60.

Hirschensohn, Ḥayim. *Ha-Misderonah*. Vol. 1, Frankfurt Mein, Germany: 1889–1890.
Hirschensohn, Ḥayim. *Malki ba-Qodesh*. Jerusalem, St. Louis, Missouri: 1919.
Hirschensohn, Ḥayim. *Eleh Dibere ha-Berith*, 3 vols. Jerusalem, Israel: Defus Ha'ivri, 1926–1928.
Hirschensohn, Ḥayim. *Musage Shaw we-ha-'emeth*. Hoboken, NJ: 1932.
Hobbes, Thomas. *Leviathan*. London, UK: Penguin Classics, 1984.
Israel, Menasseh b. Thesouro dos Dinim. Tractate No. 3. Rosenthaliana Collection. 1645–1647, http://cf.uba.uva.nl/en/collections/rosenthaliana/menasseh/1859j47/index.html.
Leeuwen, Simon van. *Rooms Hollands Regt*., Book 2. London, UK: A. Straham, 1820.
London Metropolitan Archives. Archives of the Spanish and Portuguese Congregation, Minutes of the Mahamad of Shaar Hashamayim, MS 103, 1678–1724.
Maimonides, Moses, Yeḥi'el M. Zilber, and Me'ir A. Horoṿits. *Mishneh Torah: Hilkhoth Abadim*. Jerusalem, Israel: Mekhon Moreshet haNesher Hagadol, 2010.
Maimonides, Moses, Yeḥi'el M. Zilber, and Me'ir A. Horoṿits. *Mishneh Torah, Hilkhoth Mekhirah*. Jerusalem, Israel: Mekhon Moreshet haNesher Hagadol, 2010.
Maimonides, Moses, Yeḥi'el M. Zilber, and Me'ir A. Horoṿits. *Mishneh Torah, Hilkhoth Shebuoth*. Jerusalem, Israel: Mekhon Moreshet haNesher Hagadol, 2010.
Maimonides, Moses, Yeḥi'el M. Zilber, and Me'ir A. Horoṿits. *Mishneh Torah: Hilkhoth Sheluḥin we-Shuttafin*. Jerusalem, Israel: Mekhon Moreshet haNesher hagadol, 2010.
Meldola, David de Raphael. *Responsa Peri Eẓ Ḥaim*. Vols. 1, 3, 11. Amsterdam, Netherlands: Talmud Torah Eẓ Ḥaim, 1767.
Sefaria. "Shulḥan Arukh, Eben ha-Ezer 93." https://www.sefaria.org/Shulchan_Arukh%2C_Even_HaEzer.93?lang=bi.
Sefaria. "Shulḥan Arukh, Ḥoshen Mishpaṭ 225." https://www.sefaria.org/Shulchan_Arukh%2C_Choshen_Mishpat.225?lang=bi.
Sefaria. "Tur, Ḥoshen Mishpat 104:5." https://www.sefaria.org/Tur%2C_Choshen_Mishpat.104.5?lang=bi.
Spinoza, Benedictus. *A Political Treatise*. Translated by R. H. M. Elwes. EBooks @ University of Adelaide, 2014, https://ebooks.adelaide.edu.au/s/spinoza/benedict/political/index.html.
Spinoza, Benedictus. *Politik İnceleme* [Tractatus Politicus]. Ankara, Turkey: Dost Kitabevi, 2015.
Suárez, Francisco. *De virtute et statu religionis*. Reprint ed. London, UK: Forgotten Books, 2018.
Victoria, Francisco de. Las relecciones *de indis y de iure belli.* Washington, DC: Union Panamericana, 1963.

Secondary Sources

Abrahams, Israel. *Jewish Life in the Middle Ages*. London, UK: Routledge, 2010.
Besson, Samantha. "Sovereignty, International Law and Democracy." *The European Journal of International Law* 22, no. 2 (2011): 373–87.
Brown, Benjamin. "'The People Do Not Understand': R. Ḥayim Hirschensohn and Political Elitism in Modern Judaism (The Vilna Gaon, Rabbi N.Ts.Y. Berlin, I. B. Levinsohn, and Herzl)." *Harvard Theological Review* 115, no. 3 (July 2022): 441–65. [Online by Cambridge University Press, August 23, 2022].
Davis, Scott. "Humanist Ethics and Political Justice: Soto Sepúlveda, and the 'Affair of the Indies.'" *Annual of the Society of Christian Ethics* 19 (1999): 193–212.
Davis, Moshe. "Sabato Morais: A Selected and Annotated Bibliography of his Writings." *Publications of the American Jewish Historical Society* 37 (1947): 55–93.
Elazar-DeMota, Yehonatan. Nação Legal Consciousness and Its Contribution to the Seventeenth-Century Dutch Republic Debate on Slavery and the Slave Trade. PhD diss., University of Amsterdam, 2021.
Faur. José. *The Horizontal Society: Understanding the Covenant and Alphabetic Judaism* . Boston, MA: Academic Studies Press, 2010.

Fishman, Talya. "The 'Our Talmud' Tradition and the Predilection for Works of Applied Law in Early Sephardi Rabbinic Culture." In *Regional Identities and Cultures of Medieval Jews*, edited by Javier Castaño, Talya Fishman, and Ephraim Kanarfogel, 124–45. Liverpool, UK: Liverpool University Press, 2018.

Frankel, Steven. "Spinoza's Response to Maimonides: A Practical Strategy for Resolving the Tension between Reason and Revelation." *International Philosophical Quarterly* 45, no. 3 (2005): 309–25.

Güneysu, Gökhan. "Spinoza and International Law: Bleak Take on Self-Help or a Strong Belief in Humanity?" *Uludağ University Faculty of Arts and Sciences Journal of Philosophy* 28 (Spring 2017): 173–80.

Horovits, Rivkah. *Isaac Breuer: Ṣione Derekh*. Jerusalem, Israel: Mossad HaRab Kook, 2006.

Israel-Vleeshhouwer, Amos. The Attitudes of Jewish Law towards International Law: Analyzing the Jewish Legal Materials and Processes. PhD diss., Tel-Abib, Israel: Tel-Abib University, 2011.

Jewishencyclopedia.com. "Amsterdam," https://jewishencyclopedia.com/articles/1442-amsterdam.

Jiménez Fonseca, Manuel. "Jus gentium and the Transformation of Latin American Nature: One More Reading of Vitoria?" In *International Law and Empire: Historical Explorations*, edited by Martti Koskenniemi, Walter Rech, and Manuel Jiménez Fonseca, 123–48. Oxford: Oxford University Press, 2017.

Kaplan, Yosef. "'This Thing Alone Will Preserve Their Nation Forever.' Circumcision and Conversion in the Early Modern Western Sephardic Communities." In *The Conversos and Moriscos in Late Medieval Spain and Beyond*, edited by Kevin Ingram and Juan Ignacio Pulido Serrano, 218–43. Leiden, The Netherlands: Brill, 2016.

Katchen, Aaron L. *Christian Hebraists and Dutch Rabbis*. Cambrdige, MA: Harvard University Press, 1984.

Kennedy, David. *A World of Struggle: How Power, Law, and Expertise Shape Global Political Economy*. Princeton, NJ: Princeton University Press, 2016.

Kiron, Arthur. " 'Dust and Ashes': The Funeral and Forgetting of Sabato Morais." *American Jewish History* 84, no. 3 (September 1996): 155–88.

Koskenniemi, Martti. *The Politics of International Law*. Oxford: Hart, 2011.

Lauterpacht, Hersch. *International Law and Human Rights*. New York: Praeger, 1950.

Lauterpacht, Hersch. *An International Bill of the Rights of Man*. New York: Columbia University Press, 1949.

Lauterpacht, Hersch. "The Grotian Tradition in International Law." *British Year Book of International Law* 23 (1946): 1–53.

Menzel, Adolf. "Spinoza und Das Völkerrecht." *Zeitschrift für Völkerrecht* 2 (1907): 17–30.

Mittelman, Alan L. *Between Kant and Kabbalah: An Introduction to Isaac Breuer's Philosophy of Judaism*. Albany, NY: State University of New York Press: 1990.

Morgenstern, Matthias. *From Frankfurt to Jerusalem: Isaac Breuer and the History of the Secession Dispute in Modern Jewish Orthodoxy*. Leiden, The Netherlands: Brill, 2002.

Morais, Sabato. "A Letter by Maimonides to the Jews of South Arabia." *The Jewish Quarterly Review* 25, no. 4 (1935): 351–52.

Morais, Sabato. "The Dispersed of Judea: Is There Any Truth in the Reported Return of the Jews to Palestine? An Interesting Sermon by the Rev. S. Morais, at the Seventh Street Synagogue on Saturday." [Philadelphia] *Evening Telegraph*, January 29, 1877, 102.

Mortera, Saul Levi. *Tratado da Verdade da Lei de Moisés*, edited and translated by Herman Prins Salomon. Coimbra, Portugal: UC Biblioteca Geral, 1988.

Oliel Grausz, Evelyne. "Dispute Resolution and Kahal Kadosh Talmud Torah." In *Religious Changes and Cultural Transformations in the Early Modern Western Sephardic Communities*, edited by Yosef Kaplan, 228–57. Leiden, The Netherlands: Brill, 2019.

Paz, Reut Yael. "Hersch Lauterpacht's Rabbinical Approach to International Law." *Goettingen Journal of International Law* 4, no. 2 (2012): 417–45.

Pereyra, Abraham. *Espejo de la vanidad del mundo*. Amsterdam: Alexandro Janse, 1671.

Rothberg, Yeshayahu. "The Democracy of the Tradition of the Jewish State: Rabbi Hayyim Hirschenson's Political Doctrine and Its Torah Origins." PhD diss., Hebrew University, 2008.

Shumway, Edgar S. "Freedom and Slavery in Roman Law." *The American Law Register* 41 (1901): 636–53.

Weinstein, Roni. "Jewish Modern Law and Legalism in a Global Age: The Case of Rabbi JosephKaro." *Modern Intellectual History* 17, no. 2 (2018): 1–18.

Zohar, David. *Jewish Commitment in a Modern World: Rabbi Hayyim Hirschenson and His Attitude to Modernity* (Hebrew). Jerusalem: Hebrew University, 2005.

Zohar, Zvi. *Medinath Israel Ha-'Atidith.* Jerusalem, Israel: Mossad HaRab Kook, 2002.

6

Jewish Law and International Law: The Present

Introduction

In the twentieth century, the worldwide Jewish community faced a nemesis that claimed at least six million Jewish lives in the Holocaust. Many Jewish centers of learning, which had thrived for centuries, were devastated. Ultimately, World War II accounted for the deaths of around seventy to eighty million people. The sheer scale of human suffering and loss of life was unprecedented.

After the League of Nations failed to prevent war, the United Nations was established in 1945 to ensure that these kinds of tragedies would not reöccur. Consequently, human rights law and international criminal law became the focus of international lawyers (Neff 2014, 402). Equally important, the destruction of European Jewry, which left a lasting scar on the Jewish people and the world, served as a catalyst for the establishment of the State of Israel in 1948.[1] The trauma and suffering experienced by the Jewish community during the Holocaust led to a renewed sense of urgency for a Jewish homeland where Jews could live safely and freely. The establishment of Israel was seen as a symbol of Jewish resilience and a testament to the indomitable spirit of the Jewish people.

The impact of World War II on international law was significant. The Nuremberg Trials (1945–1949) were a landmark moment in the development

[1] "The catastrophe which recently befell the Jewish people—the massacre of millions of Jews in Europe—was another clear demonstration of the urgency of solving the problem of its homelessness by re-establishing in *Ereṣ Israel* the Jewish state, which would open the gates of the homeland wide to every Jew and confer upon the Jewish people the status of a fully privileged member of the comity of nations. Survivors of the Nazi holocaust in Europe, as well as Jews from other parts of the world, continued to migrate to Eretz Israel, undaunted by difficulties, restrictions, and dangers, and never ceased to assert their right to a life of dignity, freedom, and honest toil in their national homeland. In the Second World War, the Jewish community of this country contributed its full share to the struggle of the freedom- and peace-loving nations against the forces of Nazi wickedness and, by the blood of its soldiers and its war effort, gained the right to be reckoned among the peoples who founded the United Nations." Declaration of Independence of the State of Israel, May 5, 1948.

Jewish Law and International Law. Michael J. Broyde and Yehonatan Elazar-De Mota, Oxford University Press.
 DOI: 10.1093/9780197805275.003.0006

of international criminal law, as they held individuals accountable for their role in committing atrocities during the war. The Nuremberg Principles, which emerged from these trials, established the concept of individual criminal responsibility for crimes against humanity and war crimes.

The postwar period also saw the development of human rights law, with the adoption of the Universal Declaration of Human Rights (UN General Assembly 1948) and the Geneva Conventions (1949). These instruments aimed to protect individuals from abuse and ensure they were treated with dignity and respect.

In the following years, Jewish legal scholarship flourished in the Middle East. A plethora of questions emerged without legal precedents within Jewish law. The establishment of the State of Israel by the United Nations was a watershed moment in the relationship between Jewish law and international law. The framing of Israel's establishment under international law forced numerous Jewish law authorities to ponder what international law could contribute to halakhah and whether international law ought to be binding and incorporated into halakhah as a matter of public international law and private international law.

This chapter examines the uses of international law in the Jewish tradition after World War II. The corpus—almost all found in Israel and its rabbinical community and nearly exclusively in Hebrew—provides a fascinating lens through which to look at both the Jewish law and the international law community. Because the corpus is so vast, we limit ourselves to the relationship between Jewish law and international law on four crucial topics: intellectual property rights, international agreements and conventions, war and humanitarian law, and human rights. We also survey four views about the relationship between Jewish law and international law: nonexistent or forced relationships, hierarchical relationships, interaction, and comparative law.

Several Israeli jurists of Jewish law contributed to the discourse on how halakhah views international agreements and conventions. Here, we analyze the relationship between the Hebrew concept of *berith* (pact) and the legal term treaty. In our survey of war halakhah and international law, we surveyed the material that covers humanitarian, penal, and criminal law. The chapter concludes with a discussion of halakhah and human rights. The focus there is on women's rights, children's rights, minority rights, and immigration law. Overall, this chapter highlights the intellectual history and contemporary issues—from the establishment of the State of Israel until the present—through an analysis of rabbinic responsa, letters, interviews, and newspaper entries.

Four Jewish Views of International Law

Poseqim (halakhic decisors) assume different positions when faced with the structural relations between Jewish law and international law. In his doctoral thesis, Amos Israel-Vleeschhouwer identified four perceptions: nonexistent or forced relationships, hierarchical relationships, interaction, or comparative law (Israel-Vleeschhouwer 2011, 270). Surveying these four perceptions provides access into the world of the jurists of Jewish law who deal with international legal discourse.

One group of jurists maintains that Jewish law and international law cannot function together, with the exception of commercial law. They argue that halakhah does not recognize other legal systems and that Jewish law is the only legitimate international law. Rabbi Eliyahu Zini (b. 1946), Rabbi Yitzchak Ginsburg (b. 1944), Rabbi Israel Ariel (b. 1939), and Ḥakham José Faur (1934–2020) belong to this camp. In general, they recognize that international law might influence Jewish law to a small extent and sometimes be forced on *poseqim*. But these rabbinic jurists posit that Jewish law prohibits Jews from "walking in the ways of the nations" and from "seeking justice through gentile courts" (Lev. 18:3; *Shulḥan Arukh, Ḥoshen Mishpaṭ* 26:1).

This group of *poseqim* hold that international law and justice are based on Christianity, which Jewish law renders as *abodah zarah* (alien worship) (*Mishneh Torah, Hil. Abod. Zar.* 9:4). This premise echoes the thesis of Rabbi Eliyahu Benamozegh, a nineteenth-century Italian Sephardic jurist and kabbalist. In his work, Benamozegh asserts that Jewish and Christian morality are divergent in that the former combines religion and politics while the latter separates them. Benamozegh states, "[L]e judaïsme est un système double, à la fois un code civil et une morale, une politique et une religion" (Judaism is a double system, simultaneously being a civil and moral code, a political and religious one) (Benamozegh 1867). On the other hand, "Le christianisme a annulé en lui le code pour ne garder que la morale" (Christianity has annulled this code, while keeping the moral one) (ibid.). Thus, the contradiction between Jewish tradition and Christianity has led Christians to attack Jews for their political aspirations.

When the State of Israel decided to remove the settlers from Gush Katif (2005), Rabbi Zini criticized the Zionist and the Israeli state leadership for surrendering to Christian morality. He viewed the state's position as the result of external pressure and an internal desire to assimilate among the nations (Zini 2005). The Torah does not teach Western abstractions; its ethics are part and parcel of its national law. Rabbi Ginsburg views international law as competing against the Torah and the Jewish nation (Ginsburg 1999). Rabbi Israel Ariel emphasizes that Israel and the nations differ from each other in degrees, but not in the sense of race, since racism leads to the notion of superiority and domination. His model deals with hierarchical steps within a ladder, on which all the steps are subject to the unity of the ladder, and one is not allowed to harm the other (Ariel 1999, 258). Hakham Faur maintained that human rights proclaimed by governments and institutions rest on the subjection of individuals to a person or a group of persons who represent the very same governments and institutions awarding the so-called rights (Faur 2010, 195). He had a negative outlook on the promises made by the United Nations since the individual has no power to summon for default and breach of trust (ibid.).

While this position can be substantiated, it can also be refuted. International law expert Martti Koskenniemi posits that for the most part, international law has been essentially a Euro-Christian project (Koskenniemi 2019, 21). Antony Anghie has argued the same: It is a history of the incorporation of the peoples of Africa, Asia, the Americas, and the Pacific into an international law that is explicitly European and yet universal (Anghie 2004, 6). However, legal historian Gilad Ben-Nun asserts that due to the structural similarities between Talmudic law and international law, many East-Central European Jewish international jurists played principal roles in the elaboration of some of the most important treaties of post-World War II modern international law (Ben-Nun 2020, 1–33).

A second point of contention is the prohibition of Jews appearing before Gentile courts. This is viewed as blasphemy since it portrays Jewish law as too limited and Jewish courts as too weak to rule on any given matter (*Mishneh Torah, Hil. Sanhedrin* 26:7). However, this rule is not applicable when Jewish parties are forced to comply by Gentile law or when one party cannot appear before the Jewish court. Israel-Vleeschhouwer argues that within an international context, it is often not possible to handle matters through Jewish courts (Israel-Vleeschhouwer 2011, 280). Therefore, when the situation *forces* the parties to litigate within the realm of international law, Jewish law is set aside. In essence, Zini, Ginsburg, Ariel, and Faur view a cooperation of Jewish law with a legal system based on Christianity as surrendering to a foreign religion. They take this stance based on the supremacy of the Torah and halakhah.

Another group of *poseqim* posits that if international law and Jewish law are to work together, Jewish law will always take precedence. This group of jurists—Rabbi Eliezer Melamed (b. 1961), Rabbi Eliyahu Horowitz (1951–2003), and Rabbi Shelomo Aviner (b. 1943)—hold a Kelsian jurisprudential view and hierarchical structure. They generally maintain that a Jewish global government is the only stable international entity. However, they also hold that international law is a tool in the divine plan, albeit subordinated to halakhah. Melamed explains that there is a minimal obligation to adhere to the norms of international law on the principle *dina demalukhta dina*: "In other words, the conventional government is allowed to enact laws and amend regulations, and even the courts. . . . The rabbis, when they come to pronounce halakhah, should consider these laws as binding" (Melamed 2005, 137). Thus, this group of rabbinic jurists finds a limited relationship between Jewish law and international law.

A third group of Jewish jurists holds that international law is a recognized legal system that interacts with Jewish law. Ḥakham Ḥayyim David Halevi (1924–1998), Rabbi Abraham Yisrael Sharir, Rabbi Yitzhak Roness (1941–2015), and Ḥakham Eliezer Papo hold that *poseqim* must deal and interact with international law. During an interview on the interaction between Jewish law and international law in the State of Israel, the chief rabbi of Bosnia and Herzegovina, Eliezer Papo, said:

> The State of Israel is not governed by the Halakhah. This Jewish national state is inspired from time to time by Jewish religious tradition and culture, the same way that France is inspired by Catholicism or French folklore. If it is not better than other national states, it is certainly not worse than them. By definition, it is much better than any western state with their sad record of colonization, exploitation, genocide, etc. In the entire Judeo-Arab conflict, less [sic] people have died in a hundred years than in the Yugoslavian civil war (1991–2001). . . . It is not a halakhic state on any level, proclamational [sic], practical, theoretical, or utopic. It is not to be checked by the Halakhah but by international standards. . . . I mean, this is not a halakhic state. It should not be checked by the Halakhah, it's stupid. The same way that France is not checked by canonical law of the Catholic

> Church, or the same way Great Britain is not governed by the Protestant interpretation of the Bible . . . the national state of the Jews uses Judaism for iconography, but it is governed by politics and not by Judaism. So, it's not embodiment of Jewish ideals. It's not embodiment of whatever. Nobody wants it to be, by the way. Nonreligious Jews don't, and religious Jews. (Papo, interview with the author, February 19, 2019)

In Ḥakham Papo's view, religion and politics should be separate. He explains that Israeli politics relies on Jewish iconography for some things but is not governed by halakhah. For that matter, Ḥakham Papo holds that the State of Israel should be held accountable by international legal norms. This behoves Jewish legal authorities in Israel to interact with international law.

Ḥakham Ḥayyim David Halevi was the chief rabbi of Tel-Aviv-Jaffa. He perceived the United Nations and its charter to be prophetic and a divine tool in promoting world peace and order. In his mind, Jewish law and international law must interact with each other to inaugurate universal redemption and justice (Zohar 2007, 426:26; Israel-Vleescchower 2009, 171). Recalling the halakhic principle *dina demalkhuta dina* (the law of the land is the law), Rabbi Sharir posits, "The agreements between nations are not binding on us because of hostility, or because of the prohibition to violate treaties and alliances signed by Israel, . . . but because of *dina demalkhuta dina* which also applies between nations" (Sharir 2005, 435). Sharir promotes *darke shalom* (the ways of peace) as the reason why the State of Israel must comply with international law. Noncompliance would be tantamount to creating hostility among the nations. Rabbi Roness views international law interacting with halakhah in the realm of war:

> If all the nations come to an agreement to prohibit war, in such a way that it is ruled as a customary law among nations, war will no longer be legal nor will occupation. And the nation who goes to war would be condemned by the law as murderous and engaging in bloodshed. However, as long as the practice of war is accepted among the nations, war is not prohibited legally. (Roness 2007, 3)

Roness thus agrees that international legal norms within the domain of international humanitarian law can influence Jewish law.

Overall, while these rabbinic jurists maintain the supremacy of halakhah for the Jewish people, they posit that halakhah does not develop in a vacuum but incorporates international law as a vehicle to promote universal divine justice.

A fourth outlook on international law and halakhah is one held by *poseqim* who argue that Jewish law can be enriched by international law through a comparative process or as an interpretational tool: Rabbi Dr. Yitzchak Herzog (1888–1956), Rabbi Naftali Bar-Ilan (1880–1949), and Ḥakham Isaac S. Sassoon (b. 1946). This process is internal to Jewish law, whereby a halakhic decisor can compare or interpret international legal norms and internalize them as rulings. During an interview on the State of Israel's relationship with international law, renowned scholar Ḥakham Dr. Isaac S. Sassoon stated:

> The Rabbinate is corrupt and should be dismantled; it is dis-useful. I don't blame the individuals, but the institution. It has outlived its time. State and Religion should be separate. No country can exist without it today. In Israel, religion and politics are entangled. Israel should not be called a Jewish State. . . . We cannot use the Bible to justify the political claims of Israel today. Had it not been for the Six Day War, Israel would have been a wonderful place, but it has become very different. (Sassoon, interview, February 20, 2019)

Ḥakham Sassoon is adamant about the separation of religion and state. He supports the idea that Israeli *poseqim* must utilize international legal norms as an interpretative tool in their decision-making, yet not at the national level. This view supposes that local communal jurists should compare both legal systems and interpret global justice in the language of halakhah.

In developing a proposal for the Constitution, Israel's first chief Ashkenazi rabbi, Yitzchak Herzog, declared, "The principles of international law, recognized by all peoples, will be part of Israeli law" (Radziner 2009, 506). He opposed granting any foreign law a comparative role within Jewish jurisprudence. Indeed, he argued that since the State of Israel was created by the United Nations and under its auspices, halakhic decisors must put aside Jewish jurisprudence from time to time in favor of the international legal consensus (Herzog 1989, 740). In committing the State of Israel to compliance with international legal norms, Herzog acknowledged human rights and religious minority rights (Herzog 1981, 13).

Rabbi Naftali Bar-Ilan held that a Jewish legal constitution for a contemporary state should be written within the parameters of democratic states that adhere to international legal norms (Bar-Ilan 2009, preface, 33). In developing a treatise on Jewish constitutional law, he implemented international law as a vital source of comparative law. Bar-Ilan maintained that compliance with international law is halakhically mandatory, especially within the realm of humanitarian law (Bar-Ilan 2009). Essentially, this group of jurists holds that halakhah and Israeli constitutional law should be inspired by global governance and justice.

The four positions presented here portray a complex discourse among jurists of Jewish law. The discussion on the attitudes of Jewish law toward international law is far from simplistic and monolithic. Contemporary issues and potential conflicts between Jewish law and international law could perhaps be solved with the reestablishment of a Jewish High Court, whose judges should be scholars of international law.

International Law within a Jewish Framework

With the establishment of the State of Israel, many legal opinions converged and diverged simultaneously. In examining the role of international law within a Jewish framework, Jewish jurists view the relationship as either nonexistent (or forced), hierarchical, interactive, or comparative/interpretative. Ultimately, a Jewish state cannot exist without its most important institution, namely, the Sanhedrin. Indeed, Jews pray three times a day, "May You return to us our judges as before."[2]

The aftermath of two world wars in the twentieth century witnessed a plethora of legal projects to promote world peace. The UN Charter, signed and ratified in 1945, serves as an instrument of international law, codifying the major principles of international relations to prohibit the use of force. The Charter has been amended three times—1963, 1965, and 1973. The International Court of Justice, comprising fifteen judges, was also established in 1945 as one of six principal organs of the United Nations. Its main role is to give advisory opinions on international legal matters and settle differences between states through international law. In 1948, the Universal Declaration of Human Rights (UDHR) was drafted by representatives

[2] See Ricardo (1993). The Rambam (Moses Maimonides) also codifies that the Davidic (Messianic) kingdom will not be restored without this governing body (*Mishneh Torah, Laws of Kings and Their Wars*, 11–12).

worldwide.[3] It declares that human rights are universal, irrespective of geography or social status, and include civil, political, economic, social, and cultural rights. Since then, the UDHR has inspired and prepared the way for more than seventy human rights treaties, including the United for Peace Resolution (1953), Jus Cogens at the Vienna Convention (1969), the Chemical Weapons Convention (1993), and the Arms Trade Treaty (2014), to name a few.

Rabbinic decisors take different positions concerning the institution of the United Nations, the UDHR, and the treaties ratified in the twentieth century. Rabbi Shlomo Aviner avers that in times of peace, international agreements are valid and should be followed, but never against halakhah. He argues that war should be avoided as much as possible. However, in times of war, trust is broken, and international law loses its power (Aviner 2000, 155). Rabbi Eliezer Melamed asserts that violating international agreements can put worldwide Jewry in danger. Therefore, it is forbidden to violate them (Melamed 2005, 108). He applies this within the realm of humanitarian law, especially when dealing with terrorists. Melamed argues that the only solution at the present time is to surrender to international legal norms (ibid., 164). As stated previously, Rabbi Yitzchak Herzog held that the State of Israel was established on the basis of international legal consensus. Agreeing with Melamed, Herzog stated, "This choice stems from the law of reciprocity for ensuring the possibility of having normal relations with the surrounding peoples; also, not to give a reason to the nations to take a stance against the Jews living in their countries" (Herzog 1989, III:7).

Rabbi Eliyahu Horowitz viewed the entire human race as one organism. Thus, he posited that international law is a tool that trains humans in global cooperation and coordination (Horowitz 2007, 238). Despite this position, he had a negative outlook on peace based on human morality:

> Any peace founded on human morality which rises above all, is doomed to failure. . . . Therefore, only when the nations abandon the thought that they are the ones who will bring solutions to the conflicts between the nations and the long-awaited world peace; Only when they free themselves from the thought that what they understand and determine in their universities, is the truth that defines reality; Only when they come to the realization that

[3] UN General Assembly, The Universal Declaration of Human Rights (UDHR) (New York: United Nations General Assembly, 1948), https://www.un.org/en/about-us/universal-declaration-of-human-rights.

> true peace depends on the emergence of divine morality of "being good to all," which is apparent and is revealed in the world through the people of Israel, only then can we talk about real and sustainable peace. . . . Therefore, if the nations of the world really want to do good to the world and reach peace between nations, the perfect and right way to do this is, to elevate themselves to the source of morality as it appears in Israel (ibid., 240–41).

Critical of an international world order, Rabbi Eliyahu Horowitz wrote:

> Non-Jews also have human morals and the ability to live honest lives governed by laws. They have the wisdom of human laws and civility and even the wisdom of morality, things that sometimes we should learn from them. . . . But the desire to do good and build a better world among gentiles is always too narrow. . . . Thinkers and philosophers . . . came to the conclusion that defining a moral action is to do something that is good for all, but the "simple question" is what is good for all—this is a very difficult question since humankind cannot come up with a system that is for the equal benefit of all humanity. (Horowitz 2007, 227)

For Horowitz, true peace can be initiated only through the agency of the Jewish people by implementing Torah law and the Noahide laws throughout the world. All other sources of morality will result in failure time and again.

Rabbis Aryeh Stern[4] (b. 1944), Avraham Moshe Avidan[5] (d. 2021), and Simon Federbush[6] (1892–1969) posit that the State of Israel has the right to decide whether it accepts a legal norm of international law or not, and that halakhah ratifies the state's decisions. R. Federbush and R. Stern maintain that halakhah upholds all international norms and even preempts them. In their vision, the collaboration of Israeli national law and international law is a type of reformulation of halakhah. They agree that halakhah has no say whether to accept an international legal norm or not; that decision is in the hands of the prime minister of the State of Israel.[7]

[4] Rabbi Aryeh Stern is the Ashkenazi chief rabbi of Jerusalem, a member of the Chief Rabbinate Council of Israel, and the chief editor of the Halacha Brura and Berur Halacha Institute.

[5] Rabbi Avidan was a chaplain of the Israeli military and the dean of the Sha'albim Rabbinic Seminary from 1987 until 1992.

[6] Rabbi Federbush was born in Narol, Galicia. He was rabbi, author, and Zionist leader of the Mizraḥi movement of America from 1942 to 1948.

[7] They establish their position on the principle *dina demalkhuta dina* (*b.Shebuoth* 35b).

Ḥakham Ḥayyim David Halevi advocated for compliance with international treaties as an integral part of Israel's foreign policy. He also argued that Israel should be a leading advocate of international law and order as a fulfillment of its prophetic role (Halevi 1967). However, concerning the return or handing over of the occupied territories, he did not mention international norms or institutions (Israel-Vleeschhouwer 2011, 211).

The consensus among *poseqim* is that international treaties and agreements should be kept unless they threaten the existence of the State of Israel and its inhabitants. The main points of contention are found within the laws of war and humanitarian law. Some *poseqim* accept all international legal norms, whereas others remove halakhah from the discourse completely, granting sole authority to the prime minister of Israel. The plethora of positions on Israeli foreign policy as it relates to the Judeo-Arab conflict contributes to the constant internal debate and discourse between the State of Israel and the international community.

Human Rights

The establishment of the State of Israel brought new challenges and questions regarding the relationship between international law and Jewish law on human rights. Israeli *poseqim* either embraced the conventions or not. Law professor Samuel Moyn asserts that human rights have become the measuring stick for indicating the strength of our cosmopolitanism—how we deal with discrimination on the basis of gender, race, and sexual orientation (Moyn 2018, 6). Political philosopher John Rawls (1921–2002) theorized that peace among democratic societies rests on whether they protect human rights within their *internal* structure (Rawls 1999, 8). The UDHR was created in the aftermath of World War II as a means to peace. However, when it comes to the Jewish tradition, religious leaders have hesitated to embrace the moral foundations of human rights discourse.

Hakham Avraham David Shalem (1928–2014) placed human rights discourse at the center of his practice of the Jewish tradition. He studied at the Sha'are Ṣion Yeshiba. He was conferred as *dayan* (judge) by Ḥakham Ben-Ṣion Meir Ḥai Uzziel and relocated to Lima, Peru, in 1950 to serve the Jewish community. Ḥakham Shalem expressed his humanism throughout his lifetime:

> It is not sufficient to live by a dry and mechanical observance of Jewish law. In addition to living by our precepts, we Jews must impress upon all of humanity the importance of balancing human intellect with acts of charity and kindness, with teachings that reflect truth and equality, and with promoting a way of life that protects the human rights of all human beings created in God's image, without discriminating based on race, colour, or creed. Repairing the world in the spirit of God, for the good of all of humanity, can only happen through loving our fellow man, protecting their human rights, and performing acts of charity and kindness, for this is the ultimate will of God. (Shalem, interview with the author, 1998)

Ḥakham Shalem envisioned the reparation of the world by protecting the human rights of all, Jews and non-Jews alike. Ultimately, his humanism stemmed from *imago Dei* anthropology.

R. Shelomo Goren was also a proponent of the human rights of non-Jews living within the borders of Israel. In harmonizing halakhah with human rights law, R. Goren wrote:

> The minority problem in the Jewish state requires a comprehensive religious solution. Their [the minorities'] legal status, legal or social rights should be determined taking into account international laws on the rights of minorities. The nature of each country and the morality of any nation are determined and measured by their attitude to the minorities in their midst. The Jewish people, suffering for all the days of exile for being always a minority, will have to set an example to the world. (Herzog 1989, 1:152–33)

Jewish exile was the motivating factor in rebuilding a commonwealth in the Holy Land, yet that hope of a Jewish homeland should not diminish the rights of non-Jews living there. R. Goren's approach to human rights was grounded on the collective experience of the Jewish people, who often lived under oppression within host populations. This experience obligates the Jewish people to empathize with anyone in a similar position.

Women's Rights

One of the most controversial areas of human rights law and Jewish law is women's rights and equality. Certain sectors of religious Jewish communities in Israel hold a traditional stance on the position of women. Generally speaking, this means that women are not permitted to obtain high-level Torah education as men do. Moreover, many Jewish wives are *chained* to their estranged husbands who refuse to issue them a *geṭ* (bill of divorce). Furthermore, Jewish women within these circles are discouraged from getting abortions, no matter the circumstance. Overall, Jewish women within the Haredi (ultra-Orthodox) Jewish community lack agency.

Gender equality was at the forefront of the ratification of the UDHR. The first two articles state, "All human beings are born free and equal in dignity and rights," and "Everyone is entitled to all the rights and freedoms set forth in this Declaration, without distinction of any kind, such as race, colour, sex, language, religion, . . . birth or other status."[8] Despite this global initiative, Samuel Moyn criticizes the indifference of welfare states to uphold the human rights agenda:

> The welfare state shouldered the burden of provision for males above all, and ethnic and racial insiders among them. Women and children certainly mattered, but the welfare state's schemes treated their plight as derivative, and its very generosity entrenched their subordination to the destiny of the male working nation, especially when welfare states took up natalist policies—a fact that the Universal Declaration's prohibition of discrimination did shockingly little to affect for a long time. (Moyn 2018, 14)

Not until the 1970s did women gain higher prominence within the profession of international law, including law faculties, courts, and tribunals. By 2012, there were two women (of fifteen judges) on the World Court, one (of twenty-one) on the Law of the Sea Tribunal, ten (of eighteen) on the International Criminal Court, and two (of thirty-four) on the International Law Commission (Neff 2014, 464). Feminist movements surely contributed to these changes.

In 1951, Israel legislated the right for women to live in dignity by providing equality in work, education, health, and social welfare. Israel's Ministry

[8] United Nations, *Universal Declaration of Human Rights*, 1948, arts. 1, 2.

of Education requires the state's schools to offer equal opportunities for members of both sexes and introduce programs designed to encourage a culture of gender equality. However, ultra-Orthodox and some Orthodox Jewish circles uphold the opinion of the Talmudic sage Rabbi Eliezer, "Whoever teaches his daughter Torah, teaches her obscenity" (*b.Sotah* 21b). In the same vein, the Andalusian sage Maimonides codifies the law in his *Mishneh Torah*: "The Sages legislated that a man should not teach his daughter Torah, since the majority of women cannot focus their minds in learning, and [are] incapable of making deductions due to their poor mental states. The Sages said, he who teaches his daughter Torah, it is as if he taught her uselessness" (Maimonides, *Hil. Talmud Torah* 1:13).

Ḥakham Dr. Isaac Sassoon (2011) states that "Halakhah's classification of people by gender for religious purpose rubs against the grain of our collective psyche" (Sassoon 2011, viii). One wonders how it is possible to have so many advances in global education yet see so little of it within certain Jewish religious communities. The Ḥaredi Jewish ethos promotes the notion that "the new is prohibited by Torah (*ḥadash asur min ha-torah*)." As such, any social changes that threaten traditional standpoints are forbidden.

When the question was raised whether women in Israel were allowed to vote, the Mizraḥi ultra-Orthodox Jewish party opposed the referendum. Ḥakham Ben-Ṣion Meir Ḥai Uzziel countered:

> If anyone should tell us that women should be excluded from the voting public because "their minds are flighty (*da'atan qaloth*)"[9] and they know not how to choose who is worthy of leading the people, we reply: Well, then, let us exclude from the electorate also those men who are "of flighty minds" (and such are never lacking). However, reality confronts us clearly with the fact that, both in the past and in our times, women are equal to men in knowledge and wisdom, dealing in commerce and trade and conducting all personal matters in the best possible way. Has it ever been known that a guardian is appointed to conduct the affairs of an adult woman, against her will? (Uzziel 1929, 44)

Ḥakham Uzziel granted women equal status on the basis of past and contemporary capacity for agency equal to that of men.

[9] *b.Shabbat* 33b; *b.Qiddushin* 80b.

In the twentieth century, a debate arose about whether Jewish women could participate in positions of leadership within Israeli society. Once again, the Ḥaredi community opposed the election of female judges and leaders on the basis of tradition. Ḥakham Uzziel rebutted their claims:

> It is clear that even according to the *Sifre*,[10] a woman may be accepted as judge (i.e., leader), and she may make decisions just as one can accept a relative as judge. Therefore, in appointment by election, which is the public's acceptance of those elected as their representatives and leaders, the law is that they can also elect women, even according to the positions of the *Sifre* and the Rambam. And in the writings of the *Rishonim*[11] in general no dissenting opinion has been found. (Uzziel 1929, 44)

Consulting the halakhic sources, Ḥakham Uzziel found no legal source to prohibit the election of women into office nor to the judiciary. Clearly, his humanistic perspective permeated his halakhic decisions. Eventually, in 1969, the State of Israel led most nation-states by electing its first female prime minister—Golda Meir (1898–1978).

According to divorce halakhah, marriage unions are severed upon the issuing and receiving of a *geṭ*. The Torah establishes that when a wife loses favor in the eyes of her husband, he should give her a bill of divorcement (Deut. 24:1–2). Men's right to initiate divorce already positions women in a vulnerable situation, especially where there are no legal mechanisms to protect the wife in the face of abuse. Gail Labovitz, a professor of rabbinic literature at the American Jewish University, underscores this fact: "There is no need to sugarcoat the fundamental fact that Jewish heterosexual marriage is based on an embedded inequity between the male and female partners" (Labovitz 2017, 91). Author and activist Keshet Starr views the refusal of a *geṭ* as a form of spiritual abuse, where religion is turned into a weapon of power and control in an abusive relationship (Starr 2017, 37). To the dismay of many Orthodox Jewish women whose husbands refuse to issue them a *geṭ*, they are not able to move on with their lives and remarry. According to halakhah, these liminal women are *agunoth* (singular *agunah*, chained).

[10] Sifre refers to either of two works of *midrash halakha*, or classical Jewish legal biblical exegesis, based on the biblical books of Numbers and Deuteronomy.

[11] The *Rishonim* were the leading rabbis and halakhic decisors who lived approximately during the eleventh to fifteenth centuries, in the era between the *Geonim* (589–1038 CE) and the writing of the *Shulḥan Arukh* (1563 CE).

Agunoth in Israel fall under the jurisdiction of the chief Rabbinate, regardless of whether they are religiously observant or not. Even though the Rabbinate has the authority to impose sanctions on the wayward husband, such as freezing his bank account, revoking his driver's license, or incarcerating him, these mechanisms are rarely applied. Thus, women in a situation of financial and physical abuse are left in dangerous positions (Starr 2017, 43). In a study conducted by Ruth Halperin-Kaddari on Israeli Jewish women going through a divorce, she concluded that 28 percent of the cases involved *geṭ* abuse. One-third of those cases ended with settlements to the detriment of the women. Within the ultra-Orthodox community, almost half of the women involved in divorce proceedings succumbed to extortion to receive the *geṭ* (ibid., 44). It suffices to say that the *agunah* crisis reveals the inherent inequality of Jewish women within the institution of religious marriage.

While Talmudic law offers solutions to avoid the abuse of *agunoth*, many Orthodox rabbis and *poseqim* are reluctant to implement them.[12] In 1929, the *beth din* of Constantinople issued a ruling to implement *tenna'im* (stipulations) during the *qiddushin* (wedding ceremony), whose fulfillment would annul the marriage without the need for a *geṭ* (Bejarano 1924). The Conservative Jewish movement in the United States implemented the Lieberman Clause in the *ketubah* (prenuptial agreement), which stipulates that divorce will be adjudicated by a contemporary *beth din*. Orthodox rabbis rejected this legal mechanism due to a disagreement between R. Saul Lieberman (1898–1983) and R. Joseph Soloveitchik (1903–1993). Ronit Irshai, professor of gender studies at Bar-Ilan University, criticizes R. Soloveitchik's approach to halakhah: "However, the notion that a religious person is required to bend his will to the yoke of halakhah, even if this is not in harmony with his moral sensibilities, has gained favor among the Modern Orthodox sector under the decisive influence of the writings of R. Soloveitchik" (Irshai 2014, 418). She goes on to say:

> We can then perhaps understand why the halakhic notion that one cannot treat an injured non-Jew on Shabbat has (usually) been rejected on the basis of such religious principles and values as *darke shalom* ["ways of peace"]. But we have yet to hear rabbis rejecting the reduction of female

[12] See Michael Broyde, "The 1992 New York Get Law," *Tradition: A Journal of Orthodox Jewish Thought* 29, no. 4 (1995): 5–13.

> humanity in the name of religious principles and values such as *kebod ha-beriyoht* [human dignity] or plain justice (Irshai 2014, 420).

Irshai highlights a serious issue within halakhic decision-making by comparing how rabbinic jurists find solutions to deal with non-Jews (against what is written), and their lack of compassion toward women. In her opinion, Jewish women play a lesser role in Jewish jurisprudence than non-Jews do.

The discourse on human rights proposes that everyone possesses bodily autonomy. Therefore, women have the right to decide to have an abortion if they desire it. The UN Human Rights Committee, like the Committee on the Elimination of Discrimination Against Women, has taken note that prohibiting abortions leads to the disproportionate implementation of illegal, unsafe abortions by poor and marginalized women who are unable to travel outside a jurisdiction where abortion is banned. The UN Committee on the Rights of the Child has reported that punitive abortion laws constitute a violation of children's right to freedom from discrimination. Noticing the lack of a focus on feminist issues within the Orthodox Jewish community, Ronit Irshai writes:

> Although on the surface, many of its demands—such as the struggle on behalf of agunot and women whose husbands refuse to grant them a *geṭ*, the (today almost self-evident) demand that women be allowed to study Torah, or the incipient discourse on women's fertility rights—appear to focus on the realm of human rights, it is difficult to find a systematic, Orthodox-feminist philosophical treatment of these issues in these terms. (Irshai 2014, 413)

Irshai points out the obvious gap between human rights law and Jewish law.

Amos Israel-Vleeschhouwer notices that most of the discourse on women and halakhah is limited to their femininity and "role in giving birth and raising children, and not on their humanity, their personal development and personality" (Israel-Vleeschhouwer 2011, 218). He also points out that *poseqim* shy away from discussing equality in political and class power (ibid.). Israel-Vleeschhouwer asserts that rabbinic jurists refrain from the implementation of certain international treaties concerning women's equality within the religious sector (ibid., 323). Consequently, the state ratifies a particular religious position against international law (ibid.).

Despite the hesitance of rabbinic jurists within the ultra-Orthodox world to adhere to human rights discourse as it relates to gender equality, significant changes have been made. Within the realm of education, one can see Jewish women in advanced Torah learning programs in Israel and in the United States. Moreover, women participate at the highest level of government, the judiciary, and the military. Where there is still much work to be done is in the sphere of marriage, divorce, and bodily autonomy. Only then will Jewish women be truly free and equal to men.

Jewish Law and Refugees

In 1954, Israel ratified the UN Convention Relating to the Status of Refugees (1951), which protects the rights of refugees without "discrimination as to race, religion or country of origin."[13] While war and political strife are among the main reasons why people migrate to other locations, historian David Kennedy explains how economic expansion in one place can have detrimental effects in other places (Kennedy 2016, 203). He argues that the wealthy attract resources to their locations while creating challenges for the less fortunate at their locations. This, in turn, contributes to a cycle of migrants with skills leaving for places of wealth and opportunities (ibid.). Religious freedom and liberty of conscience also prompt migration, as John Rawls demonstrated in arguing that inequality and subjection of women lead them to migrate to locations where they are granted equal participation in politics and are guaranteed education (Rawls 1999, 8–9). Nonetheless, the ratification of the Convention Relating to the Status of Refugees did not come without a debate.

At present, there are tens of thousands of African refugees in Israel. In 2018, Israeli Prime Minister Benjamin Netanyahu implemented a policy that sought to deport many of the African migrants who had entered the country illegally (Dahir 2018, 5). This policy provoked a global outcry, with many critics accusing the Israeli government of violating its international obligations by deporting refugees to countries where they may face danger or imprisonment (ibid.). Within the Jewish religious sector, questions were raised about how to interpret the law of "strangers" and what freedoms

[13] United Nations High Commissioner for Refugees (OHCHR), Convention Relating to the Status of Refugees, Preamble, 1951, https://www.ohchr.org/en/instruments-mechanisms/instruments/convention-relating-status-refugees.

minorities may exercise within the borders of the Holy Land. The concept of strangers or aliens in biblical law is sharply different from Talmudic law. The former considers the children of Israel *gerim* (strangers) in the land of Egypt (Exod. 23:9; Lev. 19:34; Deut. 10:19). Whether they lived and worked in Egypt voluntarily or involuntarily, they never gave up their ancestral faith and customs. The Rashi, a French exegete, comments that "*gerim* are persons who settle to live in a country in which they were not born" (Rashi ad Exod. 22:20).

On the other hand, the Talmudic jurists reworked the term *gerim* by distinguishing between a stranger who became a *ger ṣedeq* (Jewish proselyte) and a *ger toshab* (a stranger who did not) (*b.Abod.Zara* 64b). Thus, Talmudic law applies the biblical injunctions to love the strangers and treat them as your equals only to Jewish proselytes, while discriminating them from non-Jewish residents of the Holy Land (Cohn 1984, 165). The Talmudic jurists settled that "adherents of the monotheistic religions, like Christianity and Islam, are to be classified as 'strangers' (*gerim*), and strangers 'thou shalt love as thyself'" (Lev. 19:34; Deut. 10:19). Medieval Jewish authorities decided that "all the rules which govern your conduct towards Jews must govern your conduct towards monotheist non-Jews"[14] (Cohn 1984, 160).

The issue at stake is how to treat those minorities who are not of the monotheistic faiths. R. Yehudah Gershuni (1908–2000) presents the conflict:

> Until now, no [rabbinic authority] has said whether a *ger toshab* requires the reception [of the yoke of the seven Noahide laws], from the time when they were idolators, who now desires to become a Noahide . . . if the Noahides accustom themselves as commanded by the Holy One, blessed be He, to the first human [Adam] and his descendants, keeping the seven Noahide laws, it is simply understood that they are complete *gerim toshabim*. And it is clear that they have not violated all of the seven Noahide laws, thereby requiring them to accept anew the yoke of the seven Noahide laws. (Gershoni "Ger Toshab," 3)

This halakhic debate implies that nonmonotheistic minorities in Israel must agree to keep the seven Noahide laws as a basic requirement to settle there.

[14] See Num. 15:16; Naḥmanides *Sefer ha-Miṣwoth* 16; *Responsa Ribash* 119; Beth Yosef ad Tur, *Ḥoshen Mishpaṭ* 266; Ba'er Hagola ad *Ḥoshen Mishpaṭ* 425; et al.

The difficulty for rabbinic jurists is whether they have to receive the yoke of the seven laws or not since the Rambam stipulates that non-Jewish residents may not be received at a time when the Jubilee year is not kept (*Rambam Hil. Issure Bi'ah* 14:7–8).

Ḥakham Ḥayyim David Halevi reconciles this difficulty:

> However, in our times, since there are no longer idolators, but those who are led by their hands by their ancestors . . . there is no basis to consider the gentiles of our times as idolators, whether they live in the Land [of Israel] or in the diaspora, they are considered to be as fellow citizens of the nation-states. As such, there is need to treat them equally only on the basis of *darke shalom* [the ways of peace], but out of the obligation of human morality. (Levi "Ger Toshab," 4)

Ḥakham Halevi puts aside the halakhic controversy by recalling the notions of *darke shalom* and human rights. He circumvents the problem of the *ger toshab* by explaining that non-Jews are not real idolators but have been led astray by their ancestors. Undeniably, they are human beings created in the image of God, and it thus behooves the Jewish people to treat them as equal citizens of the world.

Children's Rights

The human rights of children are violated every day around the world. Young people and children are exposed to poverty, malnourishment, and abuse because they are dependent on adults. Children who are disadvantaged because of divorce are highly vulnerable and tend to be challenged in their ability to "acquire the political virtues required of future citizens in a viable democratic society" (Rawls 1999, 160). In 1989, almost all UN member states ratified the Convention on the Rights of the Child (UNCRC) to protect children's rights to speak out and express opinions and rights to equality, health, and education.[15]

[15] United Nations, *Convention on the Rights of the Child*, adopted November 20, 1989, Treaty Series, vol. 1577, p. 3, https://www.ohchr.org/en/instruments-mechanisms/instruments/convention-rights-child.

Halakhah affords children rights to shelter, sustenance, education, safety, and limited freedom of speech and expression.[16] While it is incumbent upon children to honor their parents, they are granted agency in vetoing any command that violates Torah law (*Shulḥan Arukh, Yoreh De'ah* 240:15).[17] According to Jewish law, boys and girls enter adulthood at puberty.[18] From that time, they are held responsible for their actions within society and before God. From this standpoint, Jewish law grants children agency at an earlier age than human rights law (UNCRC 1989, art. 1).[19]

Jewish law and human rights law converge when it comes to protecting the best interest of children after the separation of their parents. The Mishnah establishes that a child under the age of six is still attached to his mother (*m. Ketuboth* 12:1). Therefore, in a case of divorce, boys stay with their mothers until the age of six, after which they will live with their fathers.[20] Daughters, however, may continue to reside with their mothers (*m.Ketuboth* 12:1). In this regard, human rights law states, "Children should not be separated from their parents unless it is for their own good. For example, if a parent is mistreating or neglecting a child. Children whose parents have separated have the right to stay in contact with both parents, unless this might harm the child" (UNCRC 1989, art. 9).

Racial and ethnic discrimination against children within the Israeli education system is an issue that continues to thwart social harmony. According to the UNCRC, it is a right that "education should develop each child's personality and talents to the full. It should encourage children to respect their parents, their cultures, and other cultures" (UNCRC 1989, art. 29). Also, "Children have the right to learn and use the language and customs of their families, whether or not these are shared by the majority of the people in the country where they live, as long as this does not harm others" (UNCRC 1989, art. 30). Unfortunately, children of religious and ethnic minorities in Israel suffer from discrimination. Schools are highly segregated—Arab and Jewish children attend their respective schools. This poses a challenge for learning about each other's cultures. Moreover, fewer resources are allocated to

[16] Human rights law ensures that "children have the right to good quality health care, clean water, nutritious food and a clean environment so that they will stay healthy": UNCRC 1989, art. 24.

[17] Similarly, human rights law states, "children have the right to say what they think should happen when adults are making decisions that affect them and to have their opinions taken into account": UNCRC 1989, Art. 12.

[18] Boys are considered *bar miṣwah* at the age of thirteen and girls *bat miṣwah* at the age of twelve.

[19] Humans rights law stipulates that a child reaches adulthood at the age of eighteen years.

[20] For other applications, see *Mishneh Torah, Hil. Erubin* 6:1; *Shulḥan Arukh, Oraḥ Ḥayyim* 414:1–2; *b.Sukkah* 28a; *Shulḥan Arukh, Oraḥ Ḥayyim* 640:1–2; *b.Yebamoth* 102b.

Arab-Israeli schools, thereby hindering their students from meeting the same educational benchmarks as their Jewish counterparts (Arlosoroff 2016).

Children from Jewish ethnic minorities also suffer discrimination within the Israeli school system. In 2010, Sephardic Jewish girls were discriminated against in the Israeli town Emmanuel. Deputy Education Minister Meir Porush, of United Torah Judaism, asserted that any Sephardic girl who wanted to be in the "ḥassidic" track could get in, under the condition that she agreed to speak Hebrew with an Ashkenazi accent and give up Sephardic customs at home. He justified this discrimination on the grounds that Sephardic girls are on a "lower spiritual level" than Ashkenazic girls. According to Porush, 30 percent of the girls of Sephardic origins in the ḥassidic track agreed to the school's ethnic demands, while seventy-four girls who were separated refused to comply (Sztokman 2010). Attorney Yael Biton wrote, "This repulsive and mentally abusive treatment towards *Mizraḥi* students has already inflicted profound damage. . . . The students have expressed deep feelings of pain, discrimination, shame, confusion, poor self-esteem, and inferiority to their Ashkenazic fellows" (ibid.). Two rabbis ordered the school administrators not to abide by the Supreme Court order to integrate. R. Shalom Elyashiv, a leading authority of the Ashkenazi community, charged his followers to disobey the ruling and even go to jail, calling the court order "dreadful" (ibid.). In support of this position, the Slonimer rebbe commanded his followers in Emmanuel to disregard the court ruling, stating, "I am willing to be the first to sit in prison over this issue. . . . Jews sat in Russian prisons over their children's education" (ibid).[21] Evidently, the influence of rabbinic jurists is stronger than the Supreme Court within ultra-Orthodox communities in Israel.

Jewish children of Ethiopian backgrounds face similar discrimination in Israeli schools. In 2019, a group of Ethiopian Israeli parents presented a legal claim on the grounds of discrimination since their children were not allowed to register for the upcoming school year in ultra-Orthodox schools in Jerusalem (Surkes 2019). Four Talmud Torah schools rejected the students. In previous years, the children had to travel very far because the local schools would not accept them. After a careful investigation, officials noticed a pattern of not accepting Ethiopian Israel children into their schools. One parent said, "They don't look at us as human beings" (ibid.). After a petition had

[21] See the works by Dr. Lotem Perry-Hazan on discrimination within the Israeli educational system.

been filed in court, one school did not respond, another said that its response was not yet ready, and the other two denied having received the petition. Sefy Bililin, mother of a three-year-old daughter, was shocked to find that her daughter was placed in a classroom with exclusively Ethiopian Israeli children (Sokol 2019). She posted on Facebook that these children "never did anything wrong in their lives. . . . Because of the colour of their skin they cannot mix with other children" (ibid.). After Bililin's post went viral, her municipality replied that children were directed to schools by a computerized system that sorted students "according to geographic area and parental requests for state and state-religious schools" (ibid.). One can conclude that unless parents become aware of such discrimination, school administrators will continue to get away with child abuse.

It is not uncommon for persons within a Jewish community to know of a rabbi or authority who has been accused of sexual abuse of minors. Article 34 of the UNCRC states, "Governments should protect children from sexual abuse." However, when it comes to Jewish communities, this human right has been pushed aside. A survey of newspapers in and outside of Israel reveals how widespread this problem is within the Jewish community.[22]

Jewish victims of sexual abuse as children have reported spiritual stagnation and doubt about the religious system. They question everything that they learned in school and synagogue. In a survey of sexual abuse victims, two respondents commented:

> Seeing the rabbis constantly ignore abuse in the community. Plus, the complete lack of checks and balances plus transparency amongst the hierarchy of the entire system. And so, once I peeled away at the hierarchy, my entire belief system collapsed. Even when people do leave and have been abused, it's not the abuse that causes dislike of the community. It's usually that the abuse causes them to question the community, and question what we have been told, to the point that we eventually cannot reconcile the answers. (Trencher 2020, 206)

[22] See https://forward.com/news/472617/in-israel-activists-and-families-push-for-stiffer-sentences-for-child-sex/; https://www.haaretz.com/2013-11-13/ty-article/.premium/half-of-israeli-children-suffer-abuse/0000017f-dbf0-df9c-a17f-fff8163e0000; https://www.i24news.tv/en/news/israel/1634741790-israel-report-says-24-increase-in-child-sexual-abuse-cases-in-2020; https://www.haaretz.com/israel-news/2022-07-07/ty-article/.premium/israel-grants-residency-status-to-rabbi-convicted-of-child-sex-abuse/00000181-d80b-d9a3-a3e1-fdbb8dc00000; https://www.timesofisrael.com/israel-extradites-brooklyn-rabbi-accused-of-molesting-children/; https://www.bbc.com/news/world-middle-east-62984847.

This is indeed a tragedy. Religious leaders have what Stephen Covey calls, "principle-centered power":

> They are trusted. They are respected. They are honored. And they are followed because others want to follow them, want to believe in them and their cause, want to do what the leader wants. This is not blind faith, mindless obedience, or robotic servitude; this is knowledgeable, wholehearted, uninhibited commitment. This is *principle-centered power*. (Covey 2003, 102)

Children who have been abused sexually by a rabbi suffer twice: the physical act and the spiritual damage.

Sexual offenders against minors within the Jewish community cannot get away with their crimes without assistance. Victims, parents of victims, and coreligionists are pressured with halakhah to keep silent. The taboo of *mesirah* (informing non-Jewish authorities) serves as a tool for perpetrators to get away with their crimes. The Rambam codifies in his *Mishneh Torah*, "those who hand over Jews to non-Jewish authorities have no portion in the world-to-come" (Maimonides, *Mishneh Torah, Hil. Teshubah* 3:6). Thus, community leaders use halakhah to protect sexual predators from judgment in non-Jewish civil courts. Erica Brown, vice provost for values and leadership at Yeshiva University, notes that criminals can escape judgment for months, years, or even decades, while many others could have been protected from harm had someone taken the proper measures (Brown 2017, 87). She argues that the claim to *mesirah* must be scrutinized (ibid.). Others claim that defaming a religious authority or Jewish institution constitutes *lashon hara*[23] (slandering) and creating *ḥillul Ha-Shem*[24] (profanation of the Divine Name) (Blau 2017, 56). As in the scandal in the Catholic Church regarding sexual abuse of children, "there has been reluctance of victims and their families to sue the abusers or the institutions that covered up the abuse" (ibid., 55).

In the absence of *poseqim*, there are halakhic sources for defending children's rights. The argument that one violates the Torah by speaking ill of a religious leader has no place before a person who is a threat to the many. Halakhah

[23] Torah law prohibits slandering and defamation (Lev. 19:16).

[24] Profanation of the Divine Name is a serious offense which warrants punishment by the "hands of Heaven" (Maimonides, *Mishneh Torah, Hil. Yesode Ha-Torah* 5).

permits reporting abusers to secular authorities in such cases (Maimonides, *Mishneh Torah Hil. Hobel wu-Mazziq* 8:11). One precept states that "whenever a person can save another person's life, but he fails to do so, he transgresses a negative commandment, as Leviticus 19:16 states: 'Do not stand idly by while your brother's blood is at stake'" (ibid., *Hil. Roṣeaḥ wu-Shemirath Nefesh* 1:14). Finally, it has been said that reporting abuse before Gentile authorities constitutes a profanation of the Divine Name. On the contrary, when a religious leader of high repute commits such crimes, they are guilty of *ḥillul Ha-Shem* (ibid., *Hil. Yesode Ha-Torah* 5:11). Overall, with careful analysis and consideration, one can raise many halakhic arguments to empower and defend victims of sexual abuse without undermining the integrity of Jewish law.

Conclusion

This chapter has explored the legal history of the interaction between halakhah and international law, from the establishment of the State of Israel until today. We have explored the relationship between halakhah and international agreements and conventions, war halakhah and international law, and halakhah and human rights. The analysis of rabbinic responsa, case studies, letters, newspaper entries, and interviews has permitted us to delve into the vast corpus with a specific focus in mind, namely, to understand where, why, and when halakhah converges with or diverges from international law.

Concerning the decisions of UN conventions, some rabbinic jurists posited that the international community's morality is based on Christian values, thereby conflicting with the Jewish tradition. Others within the State of Israel maintained that since it was founded on international consensus, it must follow the dictates of international law. The realm of conflict became very clear within the domains of *jus ad bellum* and *jus in bello*, where some rabbinic authorities held a position of fear of the international community and the profanation of the Divine Name, while others relied on the notion of defense within Torah law. Interestingly, none of the authorities agreed that the occupied territories of Judea, Samaria, or Gaza should be returned to the Arabs.

When it comes to women's issues, such as advanced religious education and the *agunah* crisis, while there has been some progress in the overall

Jewish world, some Orthodox and ultra-Orthodox jurists have been reluctant to change. Similarly, Jewish and non-Jewish children have been subjected to all kinds of abuse, against the articles of the UNCRC. Perpetrators have managed to masquerade behind the misconstruing of halakhic principles and taboos.

Another challenge to human rights law within the State of Israel has been the protection of refugees and minorities. With Arabs as the supposed enemies of Jews on the one hand, and migrants on the other hand, some Israeli rabbinic decisors have stood up in their defense, while others have practiced silence.

Within the rabbinic literature of the twentieth century, one can find brushstrokes of optimistic visions for the world at large. These rabbis, among others, saw international law as a means to achieve a more just and peaceful world by establishing clear standards for human rights, protecting individuals from abuse and ensuring their dignity, encouraging cooperation between nations through standard rules and norms for behavior, promoting dialogue and diplomacy, helping to prevent conflicts from arising or escalating, and promoting social justice to address issues of poverty, inequality, and environmental degradation.

These visions for a more just world through international law reflect the values of the Jewish prophetic tradition, which emphasizes the importance of social justice, compassion, and human dignity. Those visionaries viewed international law as a tool and vehicle for making positive change on a global scale. Indeed, it was the Prophet Isaiah who said:

> Many nations will go and say, "Come, let's go up to the Lord's mountain, to the house of Jacob's God so that he may teach us his ways and we may walk in God's paths." Instruction will come from Zion; the Lord's word from Jerusalem. God will judge between the nations, and settle disputes of mighty nations. Then they will beat their swords into iron plows and their spears into pruning tools. Nation will not take up sword against nation; they will no longer learn how to make war. (Common English Bible, Isa. 2:3–4)

And also: "The earth will surely be filled with the knowledge of the Lord, just as the water covers the sea" (Isaiah 11:9). This is the everlasting hope of the Jewish people and the desire of all nations.

Bibliography

Primary Sources

Al-Fayyumi, Se'adya Gaon. *Al Ha-Torah we-Al Nakh*, Vol 2. London, UK: Hebrewbooks, 1960.

Anghie, Antony. *Imperialism, Sovereignty, and the Making of International Law*. Cambridge: Cambridge University Press, 2004.

Ariel, Israel. *Al Yisrael Geuto*. Jerusalem, Israel: Gal 'Enay Publisher, 1999.

Aviner, Shelomo. *Meḥayil el Ḥayil*. Beth El, Israel: Hava, 2000.

Bar-Ilan, Naftali. *Mishtar wu-Mishpat be-Medinath Yisra'el*. Jerusalem, Israel: Eretz Hemda, 2009.

Bejarano, Moshe Haim. *Qiddushin 'Al Tena'i*. Istanbul, Turkey: Hebrewbooks, 1924.

Benamozegh, Élie. *Morale Juive et Morale Chrétienne*. Paris: Michel Lévy frères, 1867.

Cohn, Haim Hermann. *Human Rights in Jewish Law*. New York: KTAV, 1984.

Covey, Stephen R. *Principle-Centered Leadership*. New York: Free Press, 2003.

Faur, José. *The Horizontal Society: Understanding the Covenant and Alphabetic Judaism*. 2 vols. Boston, MA: Academic Studies Press, 2010.

Etzion. "Rabbi David Haim Levi: Ger Toshab." http://www.etzion.org.il/vbm.

Etzion. "Rabbi Yehudah Gershuni: Ger Toshab." http://www.etzion.org.il/vbm.

Ginsburg, Yitzchak. *Malkut*. Jerusalem, Israel: 1999.

Halevi, Ḥayyim David. "Ge'ulath 'Olam we-Ge'ulath 'Olamim." *She'arim* 20, no. 6 (1967): 20–21.

Herzog, Yitzchak. *Teḥuqah Le-Yisrael 'Al Fi ha-Torah*. Vols. 1–3. Jerusalem, Israel: Mossad HaRav Kook, 1989.

Herzog, Yitzchak. "Zekhuyoth ha-Mi'utim le-Fi he-Halakhah." *Teḥumin* 169 (1981): 175–79.

Horowitz, Eliyaho. *Milḥemeth ha-Tarbut*. Jerusalem, Israel: Ṣion Derekh, 2007.

Kennedy, David. *A World of Struggle: How Power, Law, and Expertise Shape Global Political Economy*. Princeton, NJ: Princeton University Press, 2016.

Maimonides, Moses, Yeḥi'el M. Zilber, and Me'ir A. Horoyits. *Mishneh Torah: Hilkhoth Melakhim wu-Milḥamoth*. Jerusalem, Israel: Mekhon Moreshet haNesher Hagadol, 2010a.

Maimonides, Moses, Yeḥi'el M. Zilber, and Me'ir A. Horoyits. *Mishneh Torah: Hilkhoth Sanhedrin we-ha-Oneshin*. Jerusalem, Israel: Mekhon Moreshet haNesher Hagadol, 2010b.

Maimonides, Moshe. *Mishneh Torah, Laws on Kings and Wars*, chaps. 11–12. https://mechon-mamre.org/i/e505.htm.

Melamed, Eliezer. *Penine Halakhah: Me-Inyane Ha-Am We-Ha-Aretz*. Jerusalem, Israel: Koren Publishers, 2005.

Moyn, Samuel. *Not Enough Human Rights in an Unequal World*. Cambridge, MA: Harvard University Press, 2018.

Neff, Stephen C. *Justice among the Nations: A History of International Law*. Cambridge, MA: Harvard University Press, 2014.

Rawls, John. *The Law of Peoples: With the "Idea of Public Reason Revisited."* Cambridge, MA: Harvard University Press, 1999.

Ricardo, B. Israel. *Tefillath Qol Pe Prayer Book: Ke-Minhag Q"Q Ha-Sefaradim*. Amsterdam, Netherlands: P.I.G, 1993.

Ravitsky, Aviezer. "Prohibited Wars in Jewish Religious Law." *Meorot* 6, no. 1 (2006): 1–17.

Roness, Yitzhak. "Family Planning and Halakha: The Postponement of Mitzvat Peru U-Revu." *Milin Havivin* 3 (2007): 73–84.

Sassoon, Isaac S. *The Status of Women in Jewish Tradition*. New York: Cambridge University Press, 2011.

Sefaria. "Rabbi David Kimḥi." https://www.sefaria.org/Joshua.9.5?lang=en&with=Radak&lang2=en.

Sefaria. "Rabbi Levi ben Gershon." https://www.sefaria.org/Joshua.9.5?lang=en&with=Ralbag&lang2=en.

Sefaria. "Rabbi Shelomo Isaac." https://www.sefaria.org/Numbers.31.3?lang=en&with=Rashi&lang2=en.

Sefaria. "Seforno." https://www.sefaria.org/Genesis.34.30?lang=en&with=Sforno&lang2=en.

Shalem, Abraham. *Eshed Naḥalim*. Jerusalem, Israel: 1998.

Sharir, Abraham Yisrael. "Atiqah Ṣebi'ath 'Al Pi he-Halakhah." *Teḥumin* 25 (2005): 426.

United Nations. *Convention on the Rights of the Child*. Adopted November 20, 1989. Treaty Series, vol. 1577, p. 3. https://www.ohchr.org/en/instruments-mechanisms/instruments/convention-rights-child.

United Nations. *Universal Declaration of Human Rights*. Adopted December 10, 1948. General Assembly Resolution 217A.

Uzziel, Ben-Ṣion Meir Ḥai. *Responsa Mishpate Uzziel*. Tel-Aviv, Israel: 1929.

Uzziel, Ben-Ṣion Meir Ḥai. *Mikhmane Uzziel: Ma'amarim Wu-Ne'umim*, Vol. 4. Tel-Aviv, Israel: 1939.

Uzziel, Ben-Ṣion Meir Ḥai. *Mikhmane Uzziel: Ma'amarim Wu-Ne'umim*, Vol. 5. Tel-Aviv, Israel: 1939.

Uzziel, Ben-Ṣion Meir Ḥai. *Public Address: Seventh Day of Passover*, April 1948.

Uzziel, Ben-Ṣion Meir Ḥai. *Hegyone Uzzi'el*, Vol. 2. Jerusalem, Israel: Mossad HaRav Kook, 1953.

Uzziel, Ben-Ṣion Meir Ḥai. *Public Letter Following the 1947 U.N. Partition Plan*. 1947.

Yisraeli, Shaul. *Ḥavot Binyamin*. Jerusalem, Israel: Makhon Ha-Torah we-Ha-Areṣ, 1992.

Zini, Eliyahu. "Gerush Me-Gush Qatif Ke-Pesha Neged Ha-Enushuth." *Yeshibath Or Wi-shua*, 2005. http://www.orvishua.org.il/heb/files/art/1123700191.pdf.

Zohar, Ṣebi, and Abi Sagi. *Universalith, Ereṣ Israelith we-Ṣionith-Datith: Hashqafatho Shel ha-Rab ha-Lewi*. Jerusalem, Israel: Yahaduth Shel Haim Press, 2007.

Secondary Sources

Arlosoroff, Meirav. "An Arab Child Scores Ninety Percent Lower than a Jewish Child." *The Marker Online*, January 5, 2016. https://www.themarker.com/news/2016-01-05/ty-article-opinion/0000017f-e5bd-da9b-a1ff-edffe2360000

Ben-Nun, Gilad. "How Jewish Is International Law?" *Journal of the History of International Law* 23, no. 2 (2020): 1–33.

Blau, Yosef. "Sexual Abuse in the Orthodox Jewish Community." *Tradition: A Journal of Orthodox Jewish Thought* 50, no. 2 (2017): 50–59.

Brekke, Torkel. *The Ethics of War in Asian Civilizations: A Comparative Perspective*. London, UK: Routledge, 2006.

Broyde, Michael. "The 1992 New York Get Law." *Tradition: A Journal of Orthodox Jewish Thought* 29, no. 4 (1995): 5–13.

Broyde, Michael. "A Jewish Law View of World Law." *Emory Law Journal* 54 (2005): 79–93.

Broyde, Michael. "Military Ethics in Jewish Law." *Jewish Law Association Studies* 16 (2007): 1–36.

Brown, Erica. "Standing Idly By." *Tradition: A Journal of Orthodox Jewish Thought* 50, no. 2 (2017): 78–92.

Dahir, Abdinor Hassan. *African Migrants in Israel: Neither Safe nor Sound*. Ankara, Turkey: TRT World Research Centre, 2018.

Eisen, Robert. "War, Revenge, and Jewish Ethics: Rabbi Shaul Yisraeli's Essay on Kibiyeh Revisted." *AJS Review* 36, no. 1 (2021): 141–63.

Irshai, Ronit. "Judaism, Gender, and Human Rights: The Case of Orthodox Feminism." In *Religion and the Discourse of Human Rights*, edited by Hanoch Dagan, Shachar Lifshitz, and Yedidia Stern, 412–38. Jerusalem, Israel: The Israel Democracy Institute, 2014.

Israel-Vleeschhouwer, Amos. The Attitudes of Jewish Law Towards International Law: Analyzing the Jewish Legal Materials and Processes. Doctoral dissertation, Tel-Aviv University, 2011.

Israel-Vleeschhouwer, Amos. "As the World Changes: International Law in the Halakhah." In *Philosophy of the Halakhah*, edited by Avinoam Roznek, 150–80. Jerusalem, Israel: Gefen, 2009.

Koskenniemi, Martti. "Histories of International Law: Dealing with Eurocentrism." *Rechtsgeschichte* 19, no. 152 (2019): 152–77.

Labovitz, Gail. "With Righteousness and with Justice: To Create Equitable Jewish Divorce, Create Equitable Jewish Marriage." *Nashim: A Journal of Jewish Women's Studies & Gender Issues* 31 (2017): 91–122.

Radziner, Amichai. "Yeḥasu shel ha-Gri'a Herzog la-Mishpat ha-Shawa'ti." In *Mesho'ah Le-Yitzchak*, edited by Yitzhak Herzog, 506–32. Jerusalem, Israel: Rambi Publications, 2009.

Rosenak, Avinoam. "The Conquest of the Land of Israel and Associated Moral Questions in the Teachings of Rabbi Kook and His Disciples: Thoughts in Light of the Book Herev Pipiyoth Be-Yadam." In *The Gifts of the Land and the Fate of the Canaanites in Jewish Thought*, edited by Katell Berthelot et al., 399–428. Oxford: Oxford University Press, 2014.

Sokol, Sam. "After Ethiopian-Israeli Kindergarten Scandal, Ministry Vows to End Segregation." *Times of Israel*, December 15, 2019. https://www.timesofisrael.com/after-ethiopian-israeli-kindergarten-scandal-ministry-vows-end-to-segregation/.

Starr, Keshet. "Scars of the Soul: Get Refusal and Spiritual Abuse in Orthodox Jewish Communities." *Nashim: A Journal of Jewish Women's Studies & Gender Issues* 31 (2017): 37–60.

Surkes, Sue. "Ethiopian-Israeli Parents Petition Against Haredi School's Rejection of Children." *The Times of Israel*, July 18, 2019. https://www.timesofisrael.com/ethiopian-israeli-parents-petition-against-haredi-schools-rejection-of-children/.

Sztokman, Elana. "Religious Girls' School Fails To Integrate Ashkenazic and Sephardic Students." *Forward*, April 13, 2010. https://forward.com/life/127209/religious-girls-school-fails-to-integrate-ashkenaz/.

Trencher, Mark. "Leaving the Fold: Dissent from Communal Authority in the Orthodox World?" In *Authority and Dissent in Jewish Life*, edited by Leonard J. Greenspoon, 195–210. Lafayette, IN: Purdue University Press, 2020.

7

Jewish Law and Antisemitic Legal Systems: The Past, Present, and Future

Introduction

The history of international law begins with the Spanish exploration of the West Indies (1492) and gains prominence with the Treaty of Westphalia in 1648. After the Thirty Years War, a series of religious wars in Europe, sovereign states agreed to the Westphalia treaty to end great wars and promote peace. The Treaty of Westphalia marked a significant turning point in the development of international law, as it formalized the concept of state sovereignty and established the principles that would shape European international relations for centuries to come. Prior to the Treaty of Westphalia, the Catholic Church had played a dominant role in shaping international law and politics. The concept of sovereignty was not yet clearly defined, and the idea of states as independent political units was not universally accepted. Westphalia recognized the independence and sovereignty of several German states, the Holy Roman Empire, Sweden, France, and Spain, among others.

Minority groups and stateless peoples, such as Jews, did not have a voice in the political and legal framework established at Westphalia. Many Euro-Christian jurists viewed the Jews as a problem to the social order within their respective states. For instance, Thomas Hobbes argued that religious unity within borders promotes bonds of peace necessary to create a republic. The republic has a body and a soul; the body must be protected for the soul to flourish. He believed that their cultural differences would make Jews a constant challenge to the peace of the commonwealth (Bredekamp 2007). After the reentry of Jews in England (1655), James Harrington proposed that Jews should have their own territory in Ireland. He expressed dismay that they would never integrate into a Christian state and held that Jews were like an extra limb that sucked the life force from the rest of the body (Harrington 2012). Jean Bodin maintained that borders protected the citizens from

Jewish Law and International Law. Michael J. Broyde and Yehonatan Elazar-De Mota, Oxford University Press.
 DOI: 10.1093/9780197805275.003.0007

enemies and promoted inner peace and unity, but, he said, without land, Jews could not defend their own religion or liberty. He argued that Jews were, therefore, hated because they practiced strange customs in Christian territories (Bodin 1975, 471). The Westphalia treaty thus laid the foundations for a European Christian model of international law but excluded Jews from political and international legal discourse.

Some legal scholars find certain limitations to the concept in the historiography of international law. For instance, Bhupinder Chimni asserts that the standard approach to legal history is state-centric, pivoting around a narrow set of male European figures (Chimni 2017). Antony Anghie argues that international law has had a civilizing mission animated by what he crudely terms the question of "cultural difference" (Anghie 2004, 3), as only European sovereign states formed part of this axiomatic framework. Laura Benton agrees that the contemporary discourse on the history of international law is focused on rights, empire-building, and sovereignty (Benton 2018, 473–78). Assaf Likhovski posits that the study of the history of legal consciousness calls for more attention from scholars of Jewish law (Likhovski 2018).

This chapter focuses on the long and detailed interactions the Jewish tradition has had with antisemitism in structured legal systems, including international law, and how the Jewish tradition responded to legal systems that either treated Jews and Judaism as invalid or were grossly unfair to the Jewish community. It commences with Christian Europe and moves through the law history to examine specific cases where antisemitism was a factor. This is an important legal chapter for the historiography of law and for the substantive way the Jewish tradition responded to legal systems that might have merited incorporation but were excluded because of concerns about antisemitism or fundamental unfairness. Deciding whether a legal system is decent enough to merit incorporation is central to this chapter. The chapter is both specific to the Jewish tradition and yet has extremely important lessons to teach about deciding when the legal culture around a community is unethical, thus making incorporation impossible.

Conditions of Equality and Fairness

One of the basic conditions upon which the obligation to observe secular law (as a function of *dina demalkhuta dina*) is predicated is the fairness or equality of the secular law in question. As R. Dr. Shmuel Shilo writes, "There is no dispute among the Sages with regard to the principle that the law of the government must apply equally on all members of the community."[1] There is no doubt that if international law (or portions of it) is ever incorporated into halacha through *dina demalkhuta*, international law—like national law—will need to be subject to the test of equality and fairness. Jews specifically and the Jewish state generally need not show fidelity to a legal system that codifies injustice.

However, the halachic test for determining equality and fairness has been subject to a great deal of analysis and discussion. Even though most medieval rabbinic authorities seem to indicate that full equality is a prerequisite for a valid secular law under *dina demalkhuta*,[2] Maharik lays claim to a startling analysis: a secular law can be considered proper according to halacha even if that law treats Jews differently as a group from members of other religions or other citizens, at least as a matter of taxation.[3] Indeed, Rama states that this is the proper understanding of the halacha. The *Shulḥan Arukh* says: "When does taxation become like robbery: . . . when the taxation comes from the king with no limitations and precision, but rather the king takes what he wishes; however, a taxation enacted for a finite amount [is valid]."[4] Rama adds, "Even if [the government] directs that the Jews pay more than the non-Jews, nonetheless, this is called a finite amount."[5]

Other halachic authorities—including R. Karo himself—simply disagree with the Rama and posit that for any law to be valid as a form of *dina demalkhuta dina*, it must apply equally to all in a given area and may not discriminate based on religion.[6] However, many halachic authorities are open to distinctions in secular law that seem rational, such as distinctions between citizens and noncitizens,[7] the wealthy and the impoverished,[8] particular professions,[9] geographical regions,[10] and other distinctions that seem consistent with the best interest of the society or community.

1 R. Shmuel Shilo, *Dina demalkhuta Dina*, p. 109.

2 The obligation of fairness in secular law was first noted by the Ri Migash commenting on *Bava Batra* 54b, and is seconded by Rambam, *Hil. Gezela we-Abeda* 5:14 and *Or Zarua, Baba Qamma* 447. Rabbeinu Tam is also quoted as endorsing this principal (see Rosh, *Nedarim* 3:11). It is quite possible that Rosh himself does not fully accept this principle, as he raises a series of questions about Rabbeinu Tam's prooftext.

3 *Mahariq, teshubah* 195 (194 in other editions).

4 *Shulḥan Arukh, Ḥoshen Mishpaṭ* 369:6.

5 Ibid.

6 See *Shulchan Aruch, Ḥoshen Mishpaṭ* 369:6–9 and *Radvaz* 3:968. For more on this and a full listing of these authorities, see R. Shmuel Shilo, *Dina demalkhuta Dina*, p. 112.

7 *Chachmat Shlomo, Ḥoshen Mishpaṭ* 369:8

8 Rabbi Yosef Eliyahu Henkin, "On the Matter of *Dina demalkhuta Dina*," *Hapardes* 31:54, pp. 3–5 (5717).

9 See the view of R. Yaakov Yisrael cited in *Beth Yosef, Ḥoshen Mishpaṭ* 369.

10 *Shut Orach Latzadik, Ḥoshen Mishpaṭ* 1.

We would suggest the possibility that Rama and Maharik might actually recognize these distinctions and permit distinctions based on religion in the area of *dina demalkhuta* only when they are consistent with fair government generally and not motivated by antisemitism. Consider, for example, a general secular law that prohibits surgical procedures outside a hospital and requires that a physician supervise such procedures. No doubt such regulations are valid as a matter of *dina demalkhuta* according to Rama, yet they also recognize that an exception to such a regulation allowing circumcision of Jewish children by an authorized mohel would be a valid exception to the general application of *dina demalkhuta dina.*[11] Indeed, there are many other situations where faiths are provided specific exemptions from general laws due to unique religious needs, and Rama should be understood as permitting such faith-specific exceptions to secular law.[12] Thus, even where the beneficiary of an exception is not an adherent of Jewish law, and legal discrimination against Jews seems to occur by denying them exemptions, Jewish law would still recognize the validity of such secular laws, such as one that exempted Santeria sacrifice rituals from animal cruelty laws.

R. Yosef Eliyahu Henkin, one of the first *poseqim* to ponder the application of *dina demalkhuta* in a just democracy, noted that the proper formulation of the halacha is as follows:

> That which the *poseqim* stated, which is that a law that does not treat all equally has created no obligation to obey it under *dina demalkhuta dina*, their intent is when such a law distinguishes between people and groups because of evil motives, such as when a government decrees against the conduct of the Jewish people, Heaven forbid, or simply generally taxing individuals with no just cause, but with malice of the heart.[13]

[11] Indeed, many states in the United States have exactly such an exception. Consider for example, the following statute in Illinois: "A person commits the offense of ritual mutilation, when he mutilates . . . another person as part of a ceremony, rite, initiation, observance, performance or practice, and the victim did not consent or under such circumstances that the defendant knew or should have known that the victim was unable to render effective consent.The offense ritual mutilation does not include the practice of circumcision or a ceremony, rite, initiation, observance, or performance related thereto." *Ill.Rev.Stat.* ch. 38, para. 12–32 (1992).

[12] Consider for example, the use of peyote in American Indian religious practice or animal slaughter in Santeria ritual, both of which have sought exemption from secular law (See *Employment Div., Ore. Dept. of Human Res. v. Smith*, 494 U.S. 872 (1990) and *Church of the Lukumi Babalu Aye, Inc. v. City of Hialeah*, 508 U.S. 520 (1993)). For other examples and an analysis of this issue in American law, see Eugene Volokh, "A Common-Law Model for Religious Exemptions," *UCLA Law Review* 46 (1999): 1465.

[13] Rabbi Yosef Eliyahu Henkin, "On the Matter of *Dina de-Malchuta Dina*," *Hapardes* 31:54, pp. 3–5 (5717) (validating rent control laws).

This standard ought to be equally applicable in incorporating international law into everyday life through *dina demalkhuta dina*. A brief conclusion is needed: First, Jewish law recognizes a test of rational fairness in the doctrine of the law of the land. Second, Jewish law is of the view that distinctions based on religion are rational in some circumstances, although to the modern American ear, it is hard to construct such a case.

The Example of Anti-Jewish Sentiments in Medieval Spain

During the Reconquista (722–1492), as a consequence of many attempts to convert as many Jews as possible to Catholicism, a number of Jewish communities throughout Spain were devasted. The Moors had invaded Spain in 711, and under the Umayyad Caliphate, they dominated most of the Iberian Peninsula for centuries. Although Jews had been there since before the first century CE, under Christian rule, they were subject to forced conversions, massacres, and persecution. When the Muslims entered Iberia, Jews were protected as *dhimmis*, since they were considered *ahl kitab* (People of the Book).[14] The death of Al-Hakam II Ibn Abd-ar-Rahman in 976 marked the beginning of the end of the Córdoba Caliphate (Gottheil and Kayserling, Granada). For the following centuries, Spanish Jews saw many massacres and persecutions in the name of the cross.[15]

In 1391, Ferrán Martínez blamed King Henry III for allowing the Jews to injure the state through usuries and commerce. He preached hatred of the Jews throughout the streets of Seville. Martínez considered it a "Christian duty" to convert all the synagogues to churches and to settle the Jewish quarters (Baer 1961, 99). At that time, riots broke out throughout the various Spanish kingdoms. Christian mobs ruthlessly murdered four thousand Jews on June 6, 1391. In addition to many Jewish martyrs, however, there were many converts to Catholicism (Baron 1942, 15). Eleven thousand Jews in Valencia submitted to baptism to save their lives (Nirenberg 2002, 9).

Solomon Ha-Levi converted to Catholicism in 1391, adopting the name Pablo de Santa María, and rose to high positions within the Catholic Church.[16] He was one of the most wealthy and influential Jews of Burgos, a

[14] People of the Book (Arabic: أهل الكتاب 'Ahl al- Kitāb) is an Islamic term referring to Jews, Christians, and Sabians, and sometimes applied to members of other religions, such as Zoroastrians.

[15] For more context see Samuel Kohn Jr., "The Black Death and the Burning of Jews," *The Past and Present Society* 196 (2007): 3–36.

[16] He is also known as Paul of Burgos.

Talmudic scholar and a rabbinic judge of the Jewish community (Abrahams 1895, 149). He was appointed Bishop of Cartagena in 1402 and Archbishop of Burgos in 1415.

In 1412, under the authority of John II of Castile, de Santa María issued a law with twenty-four clauses. This law ordered Jews to move to enclosed *juderías* (Jewish quarters) within eight days or lose their property. They were prohibited from practicing medicine, surgery, and pharmacy and selling bread, wine, flour, and meat. They could not engage in trade, fill public offices, or act as money-brokers or agents. They were prohibited from employing Catholic servants, lamplighters, farmhands, or gravediggers. To distance them from Catholics, they were not permitted to eat, drink, bathe, or visit with them or give them presents (Baron 1942, 11). Jews were not endowed with any self-jurisdiction as they had been in previous generations. Jews were not allowed to levy taxes for communal purposes, bear arms, or trim their hair or beards. They could not assume the title of "Don" and were forced to wear simple, long mantles made of coarse material. If they attempted to flee the country, they would lose their properties and even be sold into slavery. All of this was to humiliate them in the hope that they would embrace Christianity.

To the dismay of the Church, these laws did not compel all the Jews to convert to Catholicism. In 1415, Pope Benedict XIII issued a bull with twelve articles. This bull prohibited Jews from studying the Talmud, reading anti-Catholic works, or pronouncing the names of Jesus, Mary, or any of the saints. Jews were not allowed to produce communion cups or other church articles or to build new synagogues. Only one synagogue was permitted per community. With Jews stripped of self-jurisdiction, the communal judges could no longer convict *malshinim* (accusers) (ibid., 34). Most of the articles mirror de Santa María's twenty-four clauses. However, this bull went further, prohibiting Jews from baking or selling *maṣoth* (matzoh), unleavened bread for the Passover. Furthermore, Jews always had to wear a badge, and children over twelve had to listen to a sermon.

The implementation of these laws aggravated Jewish life in Christian Spain. Without contact between Jews and non-Jews, the former would have complications in keeping the Sabbath due to the prohibition of certain works on that day. In stripping Jews of the political-religious autonomy they had enjoyed under Muslim rule, the new regime placed all their political and social laws under the jurisdiction of the civil court. Hence, the monarchy handled monetary disputes, marriages, divorces, and criminal punishment.

Unable to sell bread, wine, and meat, Jews could not produce *kasher* (kosher) meat or *kasher* wine for ritual purposes.[17] In the same vein, the prohibition against baking or selling *maṣoth* undermined the distinctive character of the Jewish Passover, when Jews are commanded to eat unleavened bread for seven days in the spring (Lev. 23:4–8). These laws were clearly fueled by anti-Jewish sentiments from the Church and the monarchy, and it was clear to Jews that such was the case.

Spanish Jews responded to anti-Jewish legal systems in several ways: emigrating to safe spaces, publishing anti-Christian literature, or writing rabbinic responsa concerning those who were coerced into converting to Christianity. Jews who were fortunate enough to emigrate went to North Africa or to the nonpapal states of Italy. This class of Jews knew from halakhah that in the face of a *shemad* (general persecution), it was better to flee than to suffer martyrdom. Maimonides codifies in his *Mishneh Torah*, "all the house of Israel is commanded to sanctify this great Name [YHWH] . . . and are commanded to not profane it (*Mishneh Torah*, *Yesode Ha-Torah*5:1). He explains further that should a non-Jew coerce a Jew to violate one of the precepts of the Torah (except for illicit worship, bloodshed, or sexual immorality), one should transgress the commandment because one's life is more important than the precept (ibid., 5:2). However, should there be a *shemad* and one is not able to escape, one should submit to martyrdom (ibid., 5:3). Many Spanish Jews were not able to escape and chose conversion and baptism as a means of momentary survival (Faur 1992, 117). This is what gave rise to the crypto-Jewish phenomenon, that is, persons living as Christians in public but as Jews in private (*conversos*).

Thousands of Jews and hundreds of rabbinic leaders were immersed in the baptism waters of the Church. In response to this reality, some rabbis produced anti-Christian polemical literature. Ḥasdai Crescas (1340–1410) produced a treatise in Catalan against ten main Catholic doctrines. The book, whose original title is lost to history, is known today as *The Refutation of Christian Principles*, available only in the medieval Hebrew translation of R. Yosef Eben Shem Tob and in modern English and Spanish translations from the Hebrew. Referring to the Christian Bible, Aristotelian logic, and Jewish sources, Crescas critiques various Catholic doctrines: original sin, liberation from this sin, the Trinity, the Incarnation, the virginity of Mary,

[17] *Kasher* (Hebrew) or *kosher* (Yiddish) refers to the status of meat and wine which are fit according to halakhah.

transubstantiation, baptism, the coming of the Messiah, new laws, and demons. Crescas had hoped to convince Jews not to succumb to Christianity and for Jewish apostates to return to the Jewish tradition (Sadik 2020, Crescas).

Another writer of anti-Christian polemics was the scholar and physician Profiat Duran (born Isaac ben Moses Ha-Levi, d. ca. 1414). After his conversion to Christianity, he lived publicly as a Christian but secretly as a Jew. Later, he reverted to the Jewish tradition. He prepared a work in Hebrew called *Ma'aseh Efod*, which is regarded as the most important of his writings and represents the clearest expression of his vision and beliefs. He encodes a double message throughout this work, expressing his lifestyle as a Christian yet also as a moderate and traditional Jew. In his use of irony, coded language, and other rhetorical techniques, Duran writes for two audiences—his fellow *conversos* and unconverted Jews (Maud 2015, 161). Duran also wrote *Kelimmat ha-Goyim* (The Shame of the Gentiles), in which he discredits the Gospels and early Christian writings. Duran surveyed the writings of the Church Fathers and highlighted inaccuracies and interpolations in the translations of Jewish writings by those who challenged the Jewish tradition. This work fueled more anti-Jewish sentiments among the Christian majority (Maud 2015, 162).

Another form of response to the crisis of forced conversion at the time came from rabbinic judges. The Ribash (R. Isaac ben Shéshat Barfet, 1326–1408) wrote a responsum on the Jewishness of the *anusim* (the *conversos*) after having fled to Algeria: "These are *anusim*, who remained in the lands of persecution all this time and did not surrender to the death, as many did . . . and their presumption of their status has expired, and it is necessary for a *Ḥakham* to investigate whether they behave correctly among themselves" (Reponsum Ribash, 4; 11). The Ribash takes a stricter position than his contemporaries, requiring the investigation of each individual to see who is fit to serve as a witness and to prepare wines. It is interesting that he did not decide on a general law but rather required a sociological investigation of the family and the environment of the person in question.

Ḥakham Shime'ón ben Sémaḥ Durán (Tashbeṣ, 1361–1444) decides that the *anusim* of Spain have *ḥazaqah* (legal presumption) that they do not marry non-Jews; they marry among themselves, and only a minority mix. Therefore, only those who do not have Jewish mothers and wish to return to their Jewish tradition should make *tebilah* (ritual immersion) and receive the Torah yoke, as is necessary for the *gerim* (proselytes) (Responsum

Yakhin Wu-Bo'az 2:31). The Tashbeṣ decided in this way based on the *ḥazaqah* that the Spanish *conversos* did not mix with non-Jews. In Majorca, for instance, "old" Christians did not want to marry "new" Christians, lest they mix with Jewish blood. In Spain, the *anusim* used to marry their cousins to ensure the identity of their descendants as Jews. This *ḥazaqah*, therefore, is based on the practice of a majority of cases that the Tashbeṣ observed in his day. He constructed it on the *sugya* (legal discussion) in tractate Ḥullin, where R. Hanina decides that the majority of Jews who do the *sheḥitáh* (ritual slaughter) have *ḥazaqah*, because they know what they are doing (*b.Ḥul.* 12a).

The Tashbeṣ also establishes the *ḥazaqáh* of the *anusim* as Jews on the basis of another *sugya* of the same tractate. The rabbis ask if you can eat meat sold by a non-Jew on the street in a town where there are ten butcher shops—nine Jewish and one non-Jewish. R. Levi decides that it is possible since it is presumed that the meat comes from the nine and not from the non-Jewish butcher shop. The principle here is that a portion drawn from a majority reflects that same majority (*Kol defarish meruba farish*) (*b.Ḥul.* 95a).

Overall, the Catholic monarchy was successful in complicating Jewish life throughout Spain using anti-Jewish legal systems. While thousands of Jews were killed or converted to Christianity, others chose to leave or fight back with literature. Anti-Christian apologetic literature served not only as a way to delegitimize Christianity but also as a tool for convincing those who converted to revert to the Law of Moses. Simultaneously, rabbinic responsa served as legal decisions that explained the phenomenon of the Jewish tradition as a covenant and not a religion. As such, even though many Jews were baptized into Christianity, they remained Jews according to halakhah. Thus, in the rabbinic mind, while the Spanish monarchy may have won the physical battle against the Jews, they did not defeat the Jewish tradition.

The Ottoman Example

At the end of the fifteenth century, Iberian Jewry ended when Jews were expelled from the peninsula or were forced to convert to Christianity. Most Sephardi exiles relocated to the lands of the Ottoman Empire. After the Ottoman Empire acquired the region of the land of Israel, imperial leaders started taxing Jews as *dhimmi*, or non-Muslim subjects. As a revenue crisis increased in the latter part of the sixteenth century, taxes for the Jews increased. This resulted in "more centralized community structures" (Levy 1994, 65). As it had been customary in medieval Islamic Spain to collect taxes from Jews, the function of *Ḥakham Bashi* was instituted (ibid., 45) to assist in the relationship between the Jews and the government. Since large sums were given by *dhimmis* to the poll tax as well as to bribe Ottoman officials in the land of Israel, the result was a deficit that overwhelmed the Jewish communities. Occasionally, the *qadi* (Islamic judge) in Jerusalem would request more money, thereby adding to the Jewish communal deficit.

According to some schools of Islamic law, religious scholars were exempt from paying the *djizya* (Al-Nawawi 2005, 337–38). Torah scholars were generally exempted from paying. Within Ottoman communities, special arrangements were made for scholars who held recognized positions (Ashtor, Kharaj, and Jizya); however, scholars who did not hold communal positions had to pay the tax. Around 1560, Ḥakham David Ibn Zimra (Radbaz) decided that all Jerusalem Torah scholars had to pay the *djizya* (ibid.).

A new law was promulgated in 1691 to reestablish the old system of individual payment. Previously, only the males of every household had to pay the annual tax. The new law required every member of Jewish households to pay (Bornstein-Makovetsky 1988, 131, 181–82, 188). Ottoman rabbinic scholar and physician Raphael Mordecai Malki estimated that the Jewish community in Jerusalem was paying about 5,000 kuruş a year in taxes, although official documents in the eighteenth century suggest that only about 2,000 kuruş of *djizya* were collected (Lehmann 2014, 24). Malki also estimated the financial needs of the Jerusalem community, demonstrating that most of the budget was needed to keep up with the poll tax and other payments to the Ottoman provincial authorities (ibid.).

Jewish communities in the Holy Land responded to this unfair legal system through bribery, a centralized communal bank, collecting funds from the worldwide Jewish community, and deception. For instance, when it came time for Ottoman government authorities to perform new censuses, many Jews would leave the city and hide when the officials came to write new lists of *djizya* taxpayers (ibid.). Generally, the number of persons in the *jizya* lists did not represent a true number of community members. Accordingly, the community paid the Ottomans less in taxes.

Much of the funds collected for the Jerusalem Jewish community came from the wealthy Sephardi communities of Western Europe and the West Indies. Rabbinic emissaries were sent throughout the Jewish world to collect pledges and contributions, which were then sent to Istanbul or distributed in Jerusalem (Lehmann 2014, 2). Sephardi scholars from the land of Israel traveled to the tropics of South America and the Caribbean to support the Jewish community's continued existence in Jerusalem. The Nação in the Netherlands, England, and Italy also established funds for this purpose. Nação communal records of charities and distribution of funds reveal that the Portuguese Jewish community in Recife regularly contributed to the Holy Land via Amsterdam (Emmanuel 1970, 484). It was customary to make pledges on *Shabbath Naḥamu* (the Sabbath after the ninth day of the month of Ab) for donations on behalf of the poor of the Holy Land (Wiznitzer 1953, 243).

Although the payment of the *djizya* promised protection and security for Jews living in Ottoman lands, changes in legal policies often created stress. The arbitrary increase of poll taxes by local Islamic judges exemplifies a clear case of an unfair legal system. Many times, Jews were happy to pay because doing so afforded them security. However, when higher demands were unjustified, they had to find ways to circumvent payment or rely on other communities to help them pay. Theoretically, the forms of bribery and deceit performed by Ottoman Jews would not have existed within a fair legal system. With no halakhah on how to handle unfair legal systems, Ottoman Jews had to maneuver through extralegal practices to secure their welfare.

Nazi Germany

The emergence of the Nazi regime in the twentieth century bore the seeds of devastation for many Jewish communities in Europe and Africa. The Nuremberg Laws, promulgated by Nazi Germany in 1935 with subsequent elaborations, represent one of the vilest antisemitic legal systems in modern Jewish history. The goal of these laws was to distinguish and segregate Jews from non-Jews (Stoltzfus 2011, 379). In 1938, Hitler granted privileges to Jews who had married non-Jews, thereby reducing complaints from the minority of "full Jews" (ibid.). Indeed, Jews who had married Germans were not required to wear the star. Further legislation based on the Nuremberg Laws defined Jews as persons having three or four Jewish grandparents or persons having two Jewish grandparents who were members of the Israelite Congregation or were married to a Jew (Tammes 2007, 548). The German News Bureau (*Deutsches Nachrichtenburo*) distinguished Jews from Germans, calling the former Jewish *Volk* and the latter German *Volk*

(Pegelow 2002, 208). Overall, the Nuremberg Laws of 1935 stripped Jews of full Reich citizenship, codified who was Jewish, and prohibited marriages between Jews and non-Jews (ibid., 383).

The "Aryan Paragraph" in section three, paragraph one states, "Officials who are of non-Aryan descent are to be placed in retirement; in the case of honorary officials, they shall be discharged from official positions" (Heymann 1938, 40). This law essentially barred Jews from holding public office. Consequently, Jews were not allowed to exercise their professions as lawyers, physicians, military officials, or dentists, among others. Wherever Jews held salaried positions, whether professional or semiprofessional, Nazi legislation was implemented to limit them. However, it was much more difficult to do so for those who held freelancing positions in commerce, business, and trade (ibid., 43). Under the Currency Law, Germans Jews who emigrated were allowed to take one-fifth of their property with them, leaving four-fifths to the National Socialist government.

As the Nazis' political influence gained more territory by military conquest of European and North African states, the Nuremberg Laws were implemented there as well. The Yugoslav government passed two laws in 1940: the Decree on Measures Concerning Jews and the Performance of Activities with Items of Human Nutrition; and the Decree on the Enrollment of Persons of Jewish Descent at the University, Secondary School, Teacher Training College, and Other Vocational Schools. The former decree was intended to ban wholesale food enterprises owned or co-owned by Jews. The latter decree was designed to reduce the percentage of Jews in the total population from the first school grade through university. Similar laws were enacted in France and North Africa. The *numerus clausus* was imposed on Jews in Algeria, limiting the number of Jewish doctors, lawyers, architects, and notaries to 2 percent of the whole. The percentage of Jewish students was capped at 14 percent. By July 1941, further legislation allowed the confiscation of Jewish property. The Status des Juifs in Morocco and Tunisia restricted Jews' legal status along racial lines. Anti-Jewish legislation forced Moroccan Jews out of the *ville nouvelle*, or central parts of cities, and into the *mellah*, or Jewish quarter. Libyan Jews were affected by the Fascist Race Protection Laws in 1940. They could not send their children to public or private Italian schools and were barred from government employment and skilled professions. Their passports were stamped with the phrase "Jewish race." Essentially, the Nuremberg Laws were implemented similarly throughout Europe and North Africa.

French Jews responded to the Nuremberg Laws through protests. Before the anti-Jewish measures were promulgated throughout France (in October 1940), Grand Rabbi Isaiah Schwartz protested the decree before the secretary general. Recalling the Crémieux Decree of 1870, which granted French citizenship to Algerian Jews, Schwartz reminded the minister that no French citizen would be discriminated against because of race or religion (Kaplan 1945, 89). Schwartz declared:

> By imposing on the Jews this dishonorable statute, the new legislation only increases their sorrows. . . . The law promulgated against the Jews, containing an arbitrary definition of the Jewish race, thus most seriously violates their freedom of conscience. Nonetheless, the Jews declare that they are neither a racial minority nor a political minority but only a religious community. The Jews protest against the infamous accusations of internationalism and anarchism which have been levelled against them and proudly affirm their love of their fatherland; those Jews who have fallen by the side of their comrades-in-arms have, moreover, given striking proof of that fact. (ibid.)

Clearly, Schwartz attempted to deconstruct the Nazis' claims that Jews were an inferior race, guilty of political anarchy. Indeed, he presented Jews as model citizens of France, differing from their countrymen only in religious beliefs and practice.

Similarly, Jacques Helbronner, president of the Central Consistory of French Jews, protested on numerous occasions before Marshal Pétain. He declared:

> The Central Consistory again solemnly protests against this measure which tends to deprive French citizens and foreigners of the Jewish faith, their religious communities as well as their charitable institutions, of the protection of the law, and constitutes one step more toward the re-establishment of a real Ghetto. In the religious and cultural field, the Consistory refuses to take into consideration a text which is so contrary to the fundamental tenets of French public order: freedom of conscience, freedom of religion, freedom of association, and equality of all French citizens before the law. Nevertheless, the Consistory considers that it is its duty, in the social and philanthropic field, urgently to call the attention of the authorities to the grave dangers which such a dissolution of the already coordinated private

> institutions of Jewish welfare, would entail, without having first considered the serious consequences for the thousands of unfortunate human beings for whom they are providing. (Kaplan 1945, 91)

It was clear to the Jewish leaders that the new decrees promulgated by the Nazis ran contrary to French liberalism, but Helbronner appealed to the French revolutionary spirit of *liberté, fraternité, egalité* to no avail.

Other protests came from decorated ex-military officials and their descendants:

> We solemnly declare that we renounce any exceptional benefits we may derive from our status as ex-servicemen. The French Jews who died for France, whom we represent, and those who have fought for her do not wish to beg in humiliating fashion for exceptions to a law which, as you yourself have declared, does not except any Jews anywhere—and by the same token, his family—from all of the consequences resulting from his juridical status as a Jew. Among the French Jews, those who have given their lives, the wounded who have given their blood, the living who wear its decorations did not think that they had given their lives or received their honors for a country which would reject them. Through our voice, the fathers and descendants of our dead, our surviving wounded and crippled declare that, far from denying France despite all that they have suffered, they mean to add their silent sacrifice of today to their sacrifices of former years. So, in a juster and freer future, they hope to deserve doubly the name of Frenchmen which they will never relinquish in their hearts even if it is taken away from them by force. (ibid., 92)

This plea offered proof that French Jews participated in the political interests of the country and that, on the merit of those ex-servicemen, French Jewry should be granted equal standing with their non-Jewish countrymen. However, the government replied by stating, "There is no antisemitism in the Government's attitude, simply the application of reasons of state" (Kaplan 1945, 117).[18] The French government did not deny any of the merits

[18] Reply of the General Commissariat for Jewish Affairs to the letter of Rabbi Kaplan, dated August 5, 1941: "Vichy, August 5, 1941 Rabbi J. Kaplan 2 bis, Rue Carnot Cusset. Dear Rabbi: I have the honor to acknowledge receipt of your letter of July 31 in which you quoted to me a certain number of texts which are of course quite well known. They would never have been refuted in any French legislation if there had not been, during the past few years, an invasion of our territory by a host of Jews having no ties with our civilization. I do not intend to refute in detail a certain number of your

of French Jewry but raised the issue of foreign Jews who have no ties with the country. Either way, French Jews were affected. In replying that there was no antisemitism or ill-feelings toward French Jews, the French government took a similar stance as Pontius Pilate before the Nazarene.

A legal analysis of the Nuremberg Laws merits our attention. A number of Jewish legal experts have done just that. In his book *The Dual State*, Ernst Fraenkel (2001) discussed the Nuremberg Laws indirectly while describing a Reich Supreme Court decision of 1936. The case involved a film contract with a Jewish director, which ended in February 1933 (Morris 2016, 385). The director sued after the film company terminated the contract because of his Jewish descent. The contract permitted cancellation exclusively in the event of the director's illness or death. Upon further investigation, it was concluded that the Reich Supreme Court ruled that being of Jewish descent was tantamount to being dead. In losing his rights, the Jewish director was considered legally dead (*unbeden klich*). Fraenkel viewed this decision as gross and dangerous, making more than six hundred thousand persons essentially dead to German society (ibid.; Fraenkel 2001, 148).

Legal historian and criminal defense attorney Douglas Morris argues that Jewish defense lawyers probably did not respond with personal commentaries on the Nuremberg Laws because the Nazis put prosecutions to political use (Morris 2016, 386). He posits further that Jewish defense lawyers took the Nuremberg Laws as a given and tried to construe the law against the prosecution in cases of sexual misconduct between Aryans and Jews. Indeed, they would not try to make the case political but would find ways to prove that the parties involved were not of the said "races." Various cases of this nature led to the Supreme Court decision of December 9, 1935 (Friedländer 1997, 158–59).[19]

It is within the Jewish community that one finds legal analyses concerning the Nuremberg Laws. The legal question was whether Nazi Germany validated the *Rechtsstaat* doctrine, that is, the "legal security when [one] can

arguments, in particular the statistics you give of the Jews who have entered the armed forces and died for France. That is a matter which deserves too much respect to become the object of a controversy. Let me simply point out that in the government's attitude there is no antisemitism, simply the application of reasons of state. Please be assured, Rabbi, of my genuine regard. Signed: Jarnieu For the General Commissaire By his Chef de Cabinet."

[19] Germany's chief prosecutor urged the court to expand the provision beyond the language of *beischlaf* [coitus], that is, all natural and unnatural sexual intercourse besides coitus, and all sexual activity with a member of the opposite sex which may substitute coitus in satisfying the sexual urges of at least one of the individuals involved.

predict the consequences of [one's] behavior based on reasonable laws that are clear, neutral, and equal—equally applicable to everyone" (Morris 2016, 387). By stripping Jews of this equal security, the Nuremberg Laws were rendered as antisemitic within Jewish communities. Jewish lawyers in the communities questioned whether the clarity of their status as Jews secured their protection and well-being. Ironically, while the Nuremberg Laws led to the inequality of Jews on the one hand, they also resulted in a firm legal basis for Jews. Thereafter, the uncertainty that many Jews felt about their status vanished, leading to Jewish migration to Palestine, England, the United States, and elsewhere (ibid., 388).

Another form of protest of the Nuremberg Laws was the use of satire before Nazi courts. Such was the case of German Jewish lawyer Max Hellman. After converting to Lutheranism, he married a non-Jewish woman and considered himself German first, Jewish second. In fact, he despised Eastern European Jews, arguing that they undermined the character of German Jews. Unhappy with his situation under the Nuremberg Laws, he wrote various letters to Hitler (Oberstaatsan 1938, 4–5). His letters received no response.

After the death of Hellmann's wife, prosecutors charged him with violating section 3 of the Law on German Blood and Honor. According to this law, Jews could not employ Aryan women younger than forty-five in their households. Witnesses stated that after the death of Hellmann's wife, a thirty-four-year-old cook, Gertrud Dittrich, prepared his meals.[20] She would cook the meals in her home and deliver them to his place. Prosecutors argued that he must have acted with intent, since as a lawyer he knew the law. In his defense, he focused on the language of the law—*beschäftigen*, which can be translated into English as to "employ," "occupy," or "busy oneself." Hellman argued that Dittrich busied herself with her own affairs at her home, and that he did not "busy her" with his own affairs (Hellmann 1937, 4). Section 3 of the Law on German Blood and Honor lacked additional language to criminalize Hellmann. For that matter, the law required interpretation of the legislator's intent—that is, Hitler's intent. After many failed attempts to deliver a subpoena to Hitler, Hellman was convicted for employing an Aryan woman younger than forty-five years old in his household, however minor the daily housework was (Morris 2016, 391). After serving his two-month sentence,

[20] See Robert M.W. Kempner, *Ankläger einer Epoche: Lebenserinnerungen*. Frankfurt/Main: Ulstein, 1983.

he was sent to Dachau concentration camp and died three weeks later, on October 13, 1939.

This tragic story demonstrates both humor and mockery of the Nazi regime. After Hellmann's letters received no reply from Hitler, Hellmann tried to bring Hitler to the courtroom to make a public spectacle of the ridiculous nature of Nazi laws. The subpoena became public knowledge through the radio, thereby ridiculing the *Führer*. If he had appeared in the courtroom, it would have been a spectacle to see how insufficient Section 3 of the German Blood and Honor Law was. If he did not appear, everyone would see that Nazi laws were not just but were promoted by a tyrant. Overall, Hellman highlighted the futile role of German judges before the leadership principle, which gave Hitler ultimate power to interpret Nazi legal doctrine. Hellmann's mockery of German bureaucracy demonstrated not only that there was no separation of powers but that judges had lost their ability to interpret law. This case stands as a testimony to the antisemitic nature of the Nuremberg Laws.

Laws about Circumcision

In recent decades, a debate has arisen within the European Union (EU) concerning child ritual circumcision. In some cases, states have proposed legislation to ban male ritual circumcision.[21] According to Jewish ritual and practice, males must be circumcised on the eighth day after birth (Gen. 17:11–14). The issue is whether an infant's human rights, defined by the European Convention on Human Rights, are violated because he is unable to consent to the procedure.[22] Generally speaking, European states have been tolerant of male ritual circumcision (Fox and Thompson 2009). Legislators have been content to maintain the status quo and courts have kept at a cautious distance.

In 2011, the Finnish Union of Medical Doctors (Suomen Laakariliitto) expressed its opposition to nonmedical circumcision because the procedure involves risk, inflicts pain and injury, and violates the child's right to decide about his body (Askola 2011, 104). This position received much media coverage after a Finnish Jewish couple was fined 1,500 euros in damages to be

[21] This does not include circumcision due to medical necessity.
[22] Article 8 of the European Convention of Human Rights establishes the right to respect for private life and family life.

paid to their child because they brought in a British rabbi who was not a medical doctor. After the circumcision, the son was hospitalized for heavy bleeding (Elgot 2010). One of the expert witnesses in the case was Dr. Harry Lindahl, who is renowned for his position against nonmedical circumcision in the Finnish press (ibid.). Fortunately for the Finnish Jewish community, this case did not lead to prohibitive legislation on male ritual circumcision.

In May 2012, a court in Cologne, Germany, ruled that circumcision constituted child abuse under German law. The Bundestag undertook immediate action to legislate the legality of the practice (Yurdakul 2016). Contrary to the court in Cologne, the judicial consensus has practiced distance from such cases, ruling that parental discretion covers the right to male ritual circumcision (Svoboda 2013). As a result of this case, paragraph 1631 of the German Civil Code now permits parents of newborn sons to have someone carry out ritual circumcisions "if they are performed according to rules of medical art" (Ahren 2012). This ruling reflects a compromise between religious law and human rights discourse.

In 2018, Iceland's Progressive Party proposed a bill to ban male ritual circumcision for the same reasons promoted by the Cologne court. This bill united Iceland's tiny Islamic and Jewish communities, evoking outrage from both. Cardinal Reinhard Marx, president of the Catholic Church in the EU, declared the bill was a "dangerous attack on religious freedom. . . . The criminalization of circumcision is a very grave measure that raises deep concern" (Sherwood 2018). At least Marx saw it as antisemitic. Icelandic politician Silja Dögg Gunnarsdóttir argued, "We are talking about children's rights, not about freedom of belief. Everyone has the right to believe in what they want, but the rights of children come above the right to belief" (Sherwood 2018). This bill proposed to penalize violators with up to six years in prison. After a three-month national debate and worldwide lobbying, Iceland's parliament dropped the proposed ban.

In 2020, several Danish medical organizations withdrew from a working group that proposed to regulate national guidelines for male infant circumcision. Six political parties were in favor of banning male ritual circumcision: SF, Enhedslisten, Liberal Alliance, Dansk Folkeparti, Nye Borgerlige, and Alternativet. After the Danish prime minister, Mette Frederiksen, declared her commitment to protecting Jews after World War II, and in the face of public disfavor against the ban, the larger Muslim community became upset because it, too, was affected by the proposed ban (Bendixen 2020). Although Frederiksen did not mention her support for the Muslim community in this debate, one can say that she understood the proposed ban as antisemitic. Overall, the Danish Ethical Council voted against the ban on the grounds that it was oppressive and disrespectful of minority groups.

Rabbi Andrew Baker, director of International Jewish Affairs at the American Jewish Committee, has responded to the issue of European bans on male ritual circumcision. He highlights a paradox within the European political arena:

> What these opponents of the practice don't discuss is circumcision as a religious practice, likely because European countries have strong provisions protecting freedom of religion and belief, which one might imagine would prevent any outright ban. But Western Europeans are also strongly secular and tend to view organized religion with skepticism and even disdain. (Baker 2020)

R. Baker points to anti-Muslim policies from right-wing parties that promote these bans. He argues that European politicians are not really concerned for the rights of children or for bodily autonomy but are attacking Muslims. Consequently, European Jews are affected as "collateral damage" (ibid.). R. Baker concludes that "as European governments have woken to the need to fight antisemitism, they should adopt a common European approach to guarantee this religious practice" (ibid.).

The case studies of Iceland, Germany, Denmark, and Finland demonstrate how the worldwide Jewish community protested the potential ban on male ritual circumcision of infants through powerful lobbying. Such prohibitions would undermine the religious freedom of not only Jews but also other minorities in EU states. Since ritual circumcision is a religious act, connecting the current generation with previous ones, a political ban would undermine the Jewish tradition at its core. These attempts have not been unfair, but they have been antisemitic in nature.

Legislation about Ritual Slaughter

The European Parliament has attempted to pass legislation banning ritual slaughter of animals for food consumption. Analyzing those laws, one can conclude that while it is not possible to prove intention, they have an antisemitic impact.

The European Union's Council Regulation 1099/20092 and the Council of Europe's Convention for the Protection of Animals for Slaughter (ECPA) stipulate that animals should be stunned before they are slaughtered (ECPA 1979, art. 4). A similar rule emerged from Nazi Germany when, in 1933, Hitler ordered that all animals be paralyzed by an electric shock before slaughtering (Lavi 2021). The claim was that this would prevent unnecessary suffering of the animal. However, according to halakhah, animals must be slaughtered with sharp knives (*Mishneh Torah*, *Sheḥitah* 1:14). Therefore, anything that would harm the integrity of animals' bodies before the ritual slaughter would render them unfit for consumption by Jews. Consequently, the European Convention of Human Rights and international human rights laws on freedom of religion are implicated (Lerner and Rabello 2007).[23] How do EU legislators reconcile the evident contradiction between protecting animal rights and protecting human rights? How do contemporary Jewish authorities view this EU stipulation on ritual slaughter? Is it unfair or antisemitic?

Every EU country applies the law differently, but in general, there are four positions: stunning prior to slaughtering, concurrent sedation, stunning a posteriori, and permission of ritual slaughtering. Countries that require stunning before slaughter are Sweden, Iceland, Denmark, Slovenia, and Norway. Switzerland and Lichtenstein do not require stunning poultry beforehand. Two of the three regions of Belgium have enacted laws requiring prior stunning. Finland is the only country to require concurrent sedation. Countries that require stunning after slaughter are Austria, Greece, Latvia, and Estonia. Cyprus, France, Germany, Luxembourg, Spain, and Poland all permit ritual slaughter.

One of the first countries in Europe to lead the debate on ritual slaughtering bans was the Netherlands. In the summer of 2011, the Party for the Animals presented a proposal to prohibit the slaughtering of animals without stunning them beforehand (Zoethout 2013, 651–52). While most members of the Dutch Parliament voted in favor of the proposal, after heated debates and campaigns by many Jewish and Muslim groups, the proposal was set aside (ibid., 652). The proposed bill would have overturned the 1920 royal decree exempting Jews from stunning animals before ritual slaughter (ibid., 660). With over two million animals slaughtered every year, it is no surprise that animals suffer before and during slaughter. Besides the stress, pain, and

[23] European Convention on Human Rights (ECHR), 1950. *Treaty Series*, 213 U.N.T.S. 221.

suffering caused to animals slaughtered without stunning, reports in the Netherlands concluded that the production of ritually slaughtered meat exceeded the demands of Dutch religious groups. Thus, the Netherlands was serving as a base for an export market of ritually slaughtered meat (ibid., 659).

Both the Dutch and the worldwide Jewish communities responded to the Dutch Parliament's attempt to undermine ritual slaughter. Moshe Kantor, president of the European Jewish Congress, stated, "Some of those who try and ban our customs are in essence trying to make Europe more uncomfortable for Jews, because the essence and centrality of our life are our ancient traditions, and if our customs are not welcome nor are our communities" (Siegal 2017). Motti Rosenzweig, the only Jewish ritual slaughterer in the Netherlands, asserted, "The new rules dictate that if an animal is not insensitive to pain within 40 seconds of slaughter, based on measures called 'induced eyelid reflex' and 'cornea reflex,' it must be shot. . . . If you shoot it before you slaughter, it's not kosher at all. . . . They want to shoot it after it's slaughtered, and that's where the problem starts. They're shooting a piece of metal into the brain, and they call that stunning. . . . You tell me what's more humane" (ibid.).

Until 2017, Slagerij Marcus, the Jewish butcher shop in the Netherlands, relied on exporting meat for 40 percent of its income. The new ruling that ritually slaughtered meat production must meet the actual need of the religious communities in the Netherlands posed a new challenge to Slagerij Marcus. Ruben Vis, director of the Organization of Jewish Communities in the Netherlands (NIK), said, "The Jewish community's reaction will be, 'Not again, we're targeted again.'" He continued, "We have worked with the government to find a balance between our expression of freedom of religion and the general principle of the care for animals. I consider it as the best possible outcome" (Siegal 2017). However, rabbi and politician Lody van de Kamp, representing the Council for Ritual Slaughter, argued that "The government is concerning itself with issues such as how to perform the cut. That is the domain of rabbis and the Jewish community" (Liphshiz 2012). Van de Kamp also maintained that the NIK "had no authority to rule on rabbinical matters" (ibid.). Despite this opinion, the Jewish community in the Netherlands was willing to compromise between the laws and practices of ritual slaughter and EU legislation on the protection of animal rights.

In December 2020, the Court of Justice of the European Union ruled that "bans on slaughter of animals for meat without stunning do not violate

EU principles on freedom of worship" (Liphshiz 2020). In response to this ruling, Emmanuel Nachson, Israel's ambassador to Belgium, exclaimed that this was "a blow to Jewish life in Europe" (ibid.). Yohan Benizri, president of the Coordinating Committee of Jewish Organizations in Belgium (CCOJB), argued that the ruling "gives member states a free pass on banning ritual slaughter in Europe. . . . Europe no longer protects religious minorities" (ibid.). R. Menachem Margolin, head of the Brussels-based European Jewish Association, declared, "Judaism will not change halakhic requirements as per the demands of the EU Court of Justice" (ibid.). One can conclude from these responses that the Belgian Jewish community views the ban as antisemitic in nature. The protection of animal rights over religious freedom makes this legislation seem unfair. And although it is not possible to prove intention, the legislation has antisemitic effects.

Shortly after two Belgian provinces ruled in favor of stunning animals before slaughter, the Greek high court issued a similar ruling in October 2021. The court declared that there should always be ways to compromise between animal rights advocates and the religious dietary needs of Jews and Muslims. The court also asserted, "The government should regulate the issue of slaughtering animals in the context of worship in such a way as to ensure both the protection of animals from any inconvenience during slaughter and the religious freedom of religious Muslims and Jews living in Greece" (Liphshiz 2021). R. Margolin stated, "Jewish freedom of religion is under direct attack. It started in Belgium, moved to Poland and Cyprus and now it is Greece's turn" (ibid.). The ban on ritual slaughter disheartened the few thousand Jews living in Greece, making them feel unimportant to the Greek government (Shafran 2021). The chairman of the European Jewish Association highlighted the hypocrisy across Europe in depriving Jewish communities of kosher meat yet promising to protect them from antisemitism (ibid.). R. Avi Shafran, director of public affairs for Agudath Israel of America, maintains that Jews are portrayed as being less concerned about the welfare of animals than their fellow citizens (ibid.). One could then argue that although these bans did not have intentionally antisemitic motivations, they do contribute to antisemitism in the long run.

Israeli professor of law Shai Lavi compares the contemporary EU bans on ritual slaughtering to regulations in Nazi Germany. He asserts that "there was no doubt that the law was aimed not only at the Orthodox [Jews] but was intended to marginalize Jews of Germany whoever they were" (Lavi 2021). Lavi posits that these bans have contributed to coalitions between antisemites and associations acting on behalf of animal rights. As a result, more veterinarians view traditional practices as unhygienic and antiquated. During the Nazi regime, the dean of the Torah study academy for Orthodox rabbis, R. Yehiel Weinberg, did not view the ban on ritual slaughter as antisemitic. He maintained that the prohibition was not directed against Jews and that it would continue to exist for a long time after the end of the Nazi regime (ibid.). He asserted further that the desire to protect animals and casting doubt on the humaneness of ritual slaughter are not in themselves connected to antisemitism (ibid.). Weinberg concluded that even though there were antisemites who desired to prevent ritual slaughter, the moral basis for its prohibition could not be changed. Lavi concludes, "It is important to distinguish between assertions that are not, in themselves, antisemitic, but are liable to serve antisemitic interests and assertions that are founded in antisemitism" (ibid.).

Overall, Lavi holds that trying to prove that bans against ritual slaughter are antisemitic is complex and context-dependent.

Antisemitism versus Unfairness in Law

This chapter has focused on the challenge issued by Assaf Likhovski, which is that scholars of Jewish law should focus more on the history of legal consciousness (Likhovski 2018). We have focused on various interactions between halakhah and unfair or antisemitic structured legal systems. We have seen clear cases of antisemitic legal systems whose sole purpose was to humiliate or annihilate the Jewish people. We have also seen incidents of legal systems put into place within the realm of international law, which had antisemitic results, even though antisemitic intention could not be proven. There have also been cases of unfair legal systems that provoked the local Jewish community to circumvent them.

One can conclude from the historiography presented here that Jews were subject to abuse by their host countries because they lacked sovereignty and self-governance. It is also evident that a large part of halakhah developed under these dire circumstances. Rabbinic jurists in Europe and the Ottoman Empire had to establish legal mechanisms to implement legal notions prompted by the actions of civil authorities or international institutions. Wherever and whenever the Jewish tradition could flourish, Jews' general attitude was one of compliance. But when civil authorities have instituted unfair laws toward Jews, sometimes rabbinic scholars have been silent, while other members of the community have resorted to extralegal measures.

The case studies presented here should lead contemporary scholars of international law and Jewish law to ponder the limitations and dangers of law as a tool. As the Jewish world is experiencing greater globalization, it is simultaneously suffering from greater fragmentation. On one hand, some rabbinic scholars feel that international legal norms should inform halakhic norms, while others posit that international institutions undermine the particularity of the Jewish people. Indeed, the idea of the State of Israel as a Jewish state has contributed to that end. Regardless of the political and legal stance that one should take, the issue at stake is the preservation and continuance of the Jewish ethos. This will be the topic of Chapter 8.

Bibliography

Primary Sources

Babylonian Talmud. *Ḥullin*. Edited by Jerome Schottenstein. Rahway, NJ: Artscroll Mesorah Publications, 1997.

Barfet, Isaac ben Shéshat [Ribash]. *Responsum Ribash*. Spain, 1326–1408.

Convention for the Protection of Human Rights and Fundamental Freedoms. http://www.echr.coe.int/Documents/Convention_ENG.pdf, archived at http://perma.cc/H88Y-KGN9.

Duran, Shime'ón ben Sémaḥ [Tashbeṣ]. *Responsum Yakhin Wu-Bo'az*. Algiers, 1400.

European Convention for the Protection of Animals for Slaughter, May 10, 1979, E.T.S. No. 102. https://rm.coe.int/1680077d98, archived at https://perma.cc/8USA-GG5U.

Ha-Levi, R. Isaac ben Moses (Profiat) Duran. *Kelimat Ha-Goyim*, Vienna, Italy: 1350–1415.

Ha-Levi, R. Isaac ben Moses (Profiat) Duran, and R. Samuel D. Luzzatto. *Ma'aseh Efod*. Vienna, Italy: Holtvarteh, 1867.

Maimonides, Moses, Yeḥi'el M. Zilḅer, and Me'ir A. Horoṿits. *Mishneh Torah: Hilkhoth Sheḥitah*. Jerusalem, Israel: Mekhon Moreshet haNesher Hagadol, 2010.

Maimonides, Moses, Yeḥi'el M. Zilber, and Me'ir A. Horoṿits. *Mishneh Torah: Yesode Ha-Torah*. Jerusalem, Israel: Mekhon Moreshet haNesher Hagadol, 2010.

Secondary Sources

Abrahams, Israel. "Paul of Burgos in London." *Jewish Historical Society of England* 2 (1985): 149–52.

Ahren, Raphael. "Three Months after Circumcision Ban, German Government to Legalize Rite." *Times of Israel*, October 4, 2012.

Al-Nawawi. *Minḥaj At Talibin: A Manual of Muhammadan Law*. Translated by E. C. Howard. Coon Rapids, MN: Adam, 2005.

Anghie, Antony. *Imperialism, Sovereignty, and the Making of International Law*. Cambridge: Cambridge University Press, 2004.

Ashtor, Eliyahu. "Kharaj and Jizya." In *Encyclopaedia Judaica*, edited by Thomason Gale. New York: Keter, 1971. https://www.encyclopedia.com/religion/encyclopedias-almanacs-transcripts-and-maps/kharaj-and-jizya.

Askola, Heli. "Cut-Off Point? Regulating Male Circumcision in Finland." *International Journal of Law, Policy and the Family* 25, no. 1 (2011): 100–19.

Baer, Yitzchak. *A History of the Jews in Christian Spain*. Philadelphia, PA: Jewish Publication Society of America, 1961.

Baker, Andrew. "Banning Circumcision Is an Unnecessary Bar to Jewish Belonging in Europe." *Religion News Service,* November 19, 2020. https://religionnews.com/2020/11/19/banning-circumcision-is-a-unnecessary-bar-to-jewish-belonging-in-europe/.

Baron, Salo W. "The Jewish Factor in Medieval Civilization." *Proceedings of the American Academy for Jewish Research* 12 (1942): 1–48.

Bendixen, Michala Clante. EU Commission: "Denmark: Renewed Debate on Circumcision of Boys," September 10, 2020. https://migrant-integration.ec.europa.eu/news/denmark-renewed-debate-circumcision-boys_en#:~:text=In%202018%20a%20'citizen%20proposal,debated%20in%20the%20Danish%20Parliament.

Benton, Laura. "International Legal Theory. Made in Empire: Finding the History of International Law in Imperial Locations." *Leiden Journal of International Law* 31 (2018): 473–78.

Bodin, Jean. *Colloquium of the Seven about Secrets of the Sublime*. Princeton, NJ: Princeton University Press, 1975.

Bornstein-Makovetsky, L. "Toledot Yehudei Mitzrayim ba-Tekufah ha-Otmanit (1517–1914)." In *Ha-Yehudim Ba-Imperia Ha-Otmanith*, edited by Jacob M. Landau, 611–47. Jerusalem, Israel: Misgab Yerushalayim, 1988.

Bredekamp, Horst. "Hobbes' Visual Strategies." In *The Cambridge Companion to Thomas Hobbes*, edited by Patricia Springborg, 29–60. Cambridge: Cambridge University Press, 2007.

Chimni, Bhupinder. *International Law and World Order*. Cambridge: Cambridge University Press, 2017.

Crescas, Hasdai. *The Refutation of the Christian Principles*. New York: State University of New York Press, 1992.

Elgot, Jessica. "Couple Fined for Son's Circumcision by British Rabbi." *The Jewish Chronicle*, February 25, 2010. https://www.thejc.com/news/world/couple-fined-for-son-s-circumcision-by-british-rabbi-1.14164.

Emmanuel, Isaac Samuel. *History of the Jews of the Netherlands Antilles*. Cincinnati, OH: American Jewish Archives, 1970.

Faur, José. *In the Shadow of History: Jews and Conversos at the Dawn of Modernity*. Albany, NY: State University of New York Press, 1992.

Fox, Mary, and Michael Thompson. "A Covenant with the Status Quo? Male Circumcision and the New BMA Guidance to Doctors." *Journal of Medical Ethics* 31 (2005): 463–69.

Fraenkel, Ernst. *Der Dopplestaat*. Hamburg, Germany: Europäische Verlagsanstalt, 2001.

Friedländer, Saul. *Nazi Germany and the Jews*. New York: HarperCollins, 1997.

Gottheil, Richard, et al. "Granada." *Jewish Encyclopedia*. New York: KTAV, 1906.

Harrington, James. *The Commonwealth of Oceana*. Edited by J. G. A. Pocock. Cambridge: Cambridge University Press, 2012.

Hellmann, Max. *Zeugenladung* to Hitler, December 17, 1937.

Heymann, Curt L. "German Laws against the Jews." *Current History* 48, no. 3 (1938): 38–43.

Kaplan, Jacob. "French Jewry Under Occupation." *The American Jewish Yearbook* 47 (1945–1946): 71–118.

Kohn Jr., Samuel. "The Black Death and the Burning of Jews." *The Past and Present Society* 196 (2007): 3–36.

Lavi, Shai. "Who Is an Antisemite? Reflections on Jewish and Muslim Ritual Slaughter in Europe." *K-Larevue*, December 2, 2021. https://k-larevue.com/en/who-is-an-antisemite-reflections-on-jewish-and-muslim-ritual-slaughter-in-europe/.

Lehmann, Matthias. *Emissaries from the Holy Land: The Sephardic Diaspora and the Practice of Pan-Judaism in the Eighteenth Century*. Stanford, CA: Stanford University Press, 2014.

Lerner, Pablo, and Alfredo Mordechai Rabello. "The Prohibition of Ritual Slaughtering (Kosher Shechita and Halal) and Freedom of Religion of Minorities." *Journal of Law and Religion* 22

(2007): 17–26. http://www.istitutobioetica. org/Bioetica sociale/multiculturalismo/Lerner Rabello Macellazione.htm, archived at https://perma.cc/UPQ7-3ZGH.

Levy, Avigdor. *The Jews of the Ottoman Empire.* Princeton, NJ: Darwin Press, 1994.

Likhovski, Assaf. "Recent Trends in the Study of the Intellectual History of Law and Jewish Law Scholarship." *Diné Yisrael* 32 (2018): 227–60.

Liphshiz, Cnaan. "EU Court Upholds Belgian Bans on Ritual Slaughter, Dealing Major Blow to Jewish and Muslim Advocates." *Jewish Telegraphic Agency*, December 17, 2020. https://www.jta.org/2020/12/17/global/eu-court-okays-belgian-bans-on-ritual-slaughter-dealing-major-blow-to-jewish-muslim-advocates -:~:text=(JTA) – The European Union%27s,for additional bans across Europe.

Liphshiz, Cnaan. "Agreement Will Allow Ritual Slaughter in the Netherlands." *Jewish Telegraphic Agency*, June 6, 2012. https://www.jta.org/2012/06/06/global/agreement-will-allow-ritual-slaughter-in-the-netherlands.

Liphshiz, Cnaan. "Greece's Top Court Rules against Ritual Slaughter, Following Recent EU Decision Upholding Bans." *Jewish Telegraphic Agency*, October 27, 2021. https://www.jta.org/2021/10/27/global/greeces-top-court-rules-against-ritual-slaughter-following-recent-eu-decision-upholding-bans.

Maud, Kozodoy. "The True Wisdom of the Torah: Ma'aseh Efod." In *The Secret Faith of Maestre Honoratus: Profayt Duran and Jewish Identity in Late Medieval Iberia*, 161–81. Philadelphia, PA: University of Pennsylvania Press, 2015. https://doi.org/10.9783/9780812291810-012.

Morris, Douglas G. "The Lawyer Who Mocked Hitler, and Other Jewish Commentaries on the Nuremberg Laws." *Central European History* 49, nos. 3/4 (2016): 383–408.

Nirenberg, David. "Mass Conversion and Genealogical Mentalities: Jews and Christians in Fifteenth-Century Spain." *Past & Present* 174 (2002): 3–41.

Oberstaatsan, Leiter. *Anklagebehörde, Sondergericht*, Freiberg, to Reichsminister der Justiz, Berlin, letter, June 7, 1938.

Pegelow, Thomas. "'German Jews,' 'National Jews,' 'Jewish Volk' or 'Racial Jews'? The Constitution and Contestation of 'Jewishness' in Newspapers of Nazi Germany, 1933–1938." *Central European History* 35, no. 2 (2002): 195–221.

Sadik, Shalom. "Hasdai Crescas." *The Stanford Encyclopedia of Philosophy* (Summer 2020 ed.), edited by Edward N. Zalta. https://plato.stanford.edu/archives/sum2020/entries/crescas/.

Shafran, Avi. "Why Jewish Ritual Slaughter Bans Are Unnecessary—And Harmful to Jewish Life." *Religion News Service*, November 4, 2021. https://religionnews.com/2021/11/04/why-jewish-ritual-slaughter-bans-are-unnecessary-and-harmful-to-jewish-life/.

Sherwood, Harriet. "Iceland Law to Outlaw Male Circumcision Sparks Row over Religious Freedom." *The Guardian*, February 18, 2018.

Siegal, Nina. "New Slaughtering Rules Pit Dutch Religious Freedoms against Animal Rights." *The New York Times*, December 31, 2017. https://www.nytimes.com/2017/12/31/world/europe/netherlands-kosher-halal-animal-rights.html.

Stoltzfus, Nathan. "Societal Influences on the Promulgation and Enforcement of the Nuremberg Laws." *Soundings* 94, no. 3/4 (2011): 375–91.

Svoboda, J. Stephen. "Circumcision of Male Infants as a Human Rights Violation." *Journal of Medical Ethics* 39 (2013): 469–74.

Tammes, Peter. "Jewish Immigrants in the Netherlands during the Nazi Occupation." *The Journal of Interdisciplinary History* 37, no. 4 (2007): 543–62.

Wiznitzer, Arnold. "The Minute Book of Congregations Ẓur Israel of Recife and Magen Abraham of Murcia, Brazil." *Publications of the American Jewish Historical Society* 42, no. 3 (1953): 217–302.

Yurdakul, Goekce. "Jews, Muslims and the Ritual Male Circumcision Debate: Religious Diversity and Social Inclusion in Germany." *Social Inclusion* 4 (2016): 77–86.

Zoethout, Carla M. "Ritual Slaughter and the Freedom of Religion: Some Reflections on a Stunning Matter." *Human Rights Quarterly* 35, no. 3 (2013): 651–72.

8

Jewish Law and International Law: The Future

Contemporary Discourse: Jewish Law and International Law

A significant part of this book has focused on the convergence and divergence between Jewish law and international law. Throughout the discussion, we have also explored how law has been used to disenfranchise Jews. By the same token, legal mechanisms within international law have allowed Jews to flourish and succeed within the domain of commerce and private international law. International law and theory developed among European Christian institutions. Before the nineteenth century, European jurists theorized many conceptions of the law of nations and nature, which then evolved into positive law. Before 1948, without their own state, many Jews were subject to abuse from their host countries because they lacked sovereignty and self-determination. In the wake of World War II, the international legal community initiated the human rights discourse and implemented various treaties and conventions. Through the political institution of the State of Israel, Jews have been granted agency before the United Nations. While Israeli politicians and rabbinic jurists have not always agreed on international legal norms, nonetheless, agency has played an important role in contributing to the construction of a postwar Jewish ethos.

This analytical and predictive chapter explores what the future might bring, how international law might process future developments in Jewish law, and how the Jewish legal tradition might process future developments in international law. This concluding chapter reflects on what Jewish law can learn from its interactions with international law and vice versa.

At this moment, several major issues are shaping the course of human lives worldwide and will lead humanity into a very different future. Those issues are artificial intelligence, cybersecurity, Silicon Valley tech companies, global governance, and crimes against humanity. In this chapter, we use the contemporary discourse within these debates to analyze how Jewish law and international law may work together or learn from each other.

Jewish Law and International Law. Michael J. Broyde and Yehonatan Elazar-De Mota, Oxford University Press.
 DOI: 10.1093/9780197805275.003.0008

Urbanization and International Law

Globalization has brought about multiple economic opportunities and inspired national politicians to provide the conditions for stable economies. This has wrought a solid and reliable private legal order, security, and fiscal responsibility (Kennedy 2016, 24). However, while globalization has elevated the lives of some, it has also impoverished many around the world. As global markets grow increasingly competitive, workers, businesses, and consumers turn to their national politicians for help (ibid., 26). David Kennedy, professor of global law and policy at Harvard, highlights the problem with globalization, in that it increases the difference between "economic" and "political" structures and actors (ibid., 29). He, therefore, suggests that private actors, such as Amazon and Microsoft, should act in the public interest, and public actors (local government officials) should regulate borders. The lack thereof has led to the polarization of the global economy.

Antony Anghie agrees that globalization has had an impact on cultural, political, and social life. By globalization, he means the "economic phenomenon" of the 1990s, which internationalized production and financial services (Anghie 2004, 245). Anghie argues that contemporary governance provides political institutions to further globalization through human rights norms. Accordingly, he raises the inherent contradiction between human dignity, which human rights discourse is supposed to protect, and the inequalities promoted through globalization (ibid., 256).

Samuel Moyn asserts that although globalization has made neoliberalism and human rights more ubiquitous, there has never been a globalization of social justice (Moyn 2018, 196). Indeed, he raises the conflict between sufficiency and equality. Legal historian Stephen Neff has a negative outlook on globalization—freedom of trade and investment threaten local economic interests (Neff 2014, 467). He maintains that "economic liberalization contributes to greater inequality, to environmental degradation, and to oppressive labor conditions in poor countries" (ibid.). While globalization has provided new possibilities for business and enrichment, it has also disenfranchised many worldwide.

Another challenge to human equality brought about by economic globalization is the global housing crisis. According to the UN Department of Economic and Social Affairs, by the year 2030, urban areas are projected to house 60 percent of all people in the world, and one in every three people will live in cities with at least half a million inhabitants. The challenge will be to ensure that globalization and urbanization will benefit all humans, not a select few.[1] Besides the expansion of slums due to rapid urbanization, there is likely to be increased environmental pollution, migration, and cultural diversity, as well as concerns about access to water, sanitation, transportation, and inequality.

Amsterdam University law professor Janne Nijman presents six propositions on how international law will be affected by urbanization: direct, institutionalized relations between cities and global institutions will intensify; international law will be implemented and enforced by cities themselves; international law will be less formal; cities will become informal actors in international lawmaking; international law will address city matters directly; cities will become international legal persons. The issue at stake here is the role of the state. If the city acquires legal personhood, that will alter the state-centric system of today (Nijman 2011, 213–28). This would present a serious problem because it would undermine the international legal order and pose a threat to global governance.

Helmut Philipp Aust, professor of law at Freie Universität, raises some of the same issues as Nijman. Aust distinguishes between plenipotentiary powers possessed by states and conferred powers by which international organizations (IOs) operate. IOs can exercise only that authority transferred to them by states (Aust 2020, 82). Comparing cities to IOs, Aust identifies three pillars by which states and IOs recognize cities as international legal authorities: (1) international law increasingly relies on the local level directly through the globalization of urbanization; (2) in various international regimes, states have recognized that cities are important for enforcing agreed-upon international norms; (3) states have set up international agreements regulating transboundary cooperation among subnational authorities. For Aust, the city as an international legal authority is hybrid in nature, that is, it functions at the international level but is simultaneously conditioned by domestic law (ibid., 88).

It would seem that, as most humans will reside in urban areas in the future, sufficiency and equality will be under threat. At the same time, corporations established within cities will influence domestic and international policy to the detriment of the masses. The institution of the state will cease to have

[1] United Nations. 2016. Department of Economic and Social Affairs, Population Division. *The World's Cities in 2016*—Data Booklet ST/ESA/ SER.A/392.

importance in the face of such a predicament. For that matter, an institution that promotes global governance will be increasingly necessary.

Lessons from Silicon Valley

With the invention of the smartphone, the twenty-first century saw the emergence of a growing array of digital startups. Business-to-consumer platforms known by the acronym FAANGMULA (Facebook, Apple, Amazon, Netflix, Google, Microsoft, Uber, Lyft, and Airbnb) are changing the world. Just a decade ago, it was considered strange and dangerous to take a ride with a stranger or stay in an unknown person's home. Uber, Lyft, and Airbnb have changed how we travel, how governments regulate business, and how we define neighborhoods. Tech companies in Silicon Valley have contributed to the disruption of entire industries. Google has changed the way that we research. Overall, FAANGMULA companies are rewriting business ethics and challenging the rule of law.

Facebook has been in the spotlight a few times since its launch in 2004. To uphold the right to freedom of expression, the company established its Oversight Board. Comprising forty members from around the world, the board represents a diverse set of disciplines and backgrounds. The board's website reads: "The board uses its independent judgment to support people's right to free expression and ensure those rights are being adequately respected. The board's decisions to uphold or reverse Facebook, Instagram and Threads content decisions will be binding, meaning Meta will have to implement them, unless doing so could violate the law" (Facebook Oversight Board 2024).

The Oversight Board's attention to the rule of law and international human rights allows Facebook to avoid serious matters concerning ethical responsibilities to its users and the general public. After US President Donald Trump (between his discontinuous terms of office) was banned from Facebook, the Oversight Board approached Facebook seeking clarification about the extent to which the design decisions, algorithms, policies, and procedures amplified President Trump's posts, which may have contributed to the attack on the US Capitol on January 6, 2021. The Oversight Board addressed forty-six questions to Facebook, of which the latter declined to answer seven.[2]

[2] Oversight Board Case 2021-001-FB-FBR (decision to deplatform Donald J. Trump).

Later, in 2021, Frances Haugen, a whistleblower and former Facebook employee, revealed that Facebook had exempted high-profile users from its ordinary community standards (Horwitz 2021). Moreover, Haugen said that Facebook did not prioritize Instagram's harmful effects on teenage girls or demonstrate a willingness to protect the health and personal well-being of its users (Wells, Horwitz, and Seetharaman 2021). Haugen's testimony clearly demonstrated the limitation of the Oversight Board, as Facebook does not want zealous judges overseeing the activity of its users. The institution of the Oversight Board appears to be functionless before Facebook's executive power. At best, the board is an experiment at the intersection of technology and the rule of law, which Facebook has crafted for the advancement of its social media model.

The San Francisco–base company Airbnb functions as an online marketplace where people can enroll, search, and book accommodations worldwide. The company was founded in 2008 by Brian Chesky, Nathan Blecharzczyk, and Joe Gebbia. Among the legal concerns surrounding the digital platform are whether it is equivalent to a hotel, and whether hosts are considered rental agents or hotel employees. Some of the problems reported to date are inflation of local housing prices, gentrification of neighborhoods, straining of public resources, and overtourism. Since 2021, many countries have placed restrictions on Airbnb, including capping the number of days per year a host can rent, increasing the minimum amount of days for guests to stay in a home, requiring a tourist license from the host, prohibiting hosts from renting out on holidays, permitting hosts to rent only their primary residence, and, in some instances, banning a listing.

Airbnb has been challenged by international legal authorities on the grounds that it violates human rights. In November 2018, Airbnb announced that it would remove its two hundred Jewish-owned rental listings in the West Bank, on the basis that the region is the pivotal axis on which Israelis and Palestinians are conflicted. When American Jews lobbied against this policy, Airbnb overturned it in April 2019. American Jews filed a lawsuit on the grounds that they had been discriminated against for being Jews, since Palestinian Muslims and Christians could list their properties on the platform. Airbnb also stated that it did not support the BDS (Boycott, Divestment, and Sanctions) movement against Israel.

Saleh Higazi, Amnesty International's regional director for the Middle East and North Africa, issued a public statement on December 10, 2020:

> These settlements are a war crime under international law. Airbnb needs to do right by future investors and stop benefiting from illegal settlements built on stolen Palestinian land in the Occupied Palestinian Territories. . . . Shamefully, Airbnb has been promoting and benefiting from a situation that is a root cause of the systematic human rights violations faced by millions of Palestinians on a daily basis. (Staff 2020)

Airbnb responded that it would permit both Palestinians and Israelis in the contested area to promote their listings and that Airbnb would give its proceeds to charity. The nature of this private entity has surely affected international law and public policy in other parts of the world.

One of the world's fastest startups was Uber, founded in 2009. It has disrupted modern transportation, at one point making Uber the most valuable startup in the world. During its 2022 annual report, Uber announced a total of 7.6 billion trips, $31.9 billion in revenue, and a net loss of $9.1 billion. This ride-sharing platform has disrupted taxi companies around the world. Taxi companies raised legal claims on the grounds that they have to pay expensive license fees and that Uber bypasses local laws, essentially creating unfair competition. In 2014, taxi drivers in London, Berlin, Paris, and Madrid united to bring a case against Uber. The conflict began when Uber was introduced to the European market. Taxi drivers felt their livelihoods threatened and came together to slow down or block traffic in busy areas of their respective cities. In Madrid, the Ministry of Public Works warned ride-sharing companies and consumers of being fined thousands of euros. The verdict yielded in Uber losing its license to operate in London.

Netflix was found in 1997 by Reed Hastings and March Randolph as a DVD-by-mail service. Hastings conceived of the idea when he was charged a late fee for returning a movie. Adopting the subscription-based model, Netflix offered its consumers an online catalogue of films. This revolutionized the film industry on two fronts, first because consumers could watch movies from the comfort of their homes, and second because everyone worldwide had access to the same films. By 2016, Netflix had reached into 190 countries.

In Germany, Broadcom filed a lawsuit in 2018 against Netflix for infringing on their patent. Consequently, Netflix was ordered to stop its streaming services in Germany that use Broadcom's technology. The German Court found Netflix to be in violation of European patent EP 2 575 366, by which Broadcom registered its HEVC video technology. This patent is video coding crucial to delivering high-quality Ultra HD content. Despite the verdict, Netflix reported trading 1 percent higher the following Monday. This ruling attests to the importance of technology in the digital streaming world and the extent to which a US-based company affects public policy across the globe.

Various European countries have forced Netflix to invest in local films. By 2016, European film companies were forced to maintain 20 percent of their broadcasts European (produced by European-based companies). However, streaming companies such as Netflix had been excluded from this rule. France, Spain, and Germany applied restrictions to Netflix to protect local national culture. In Switzerland, Netflix must invest 45 percent of its income in Swiss audiovisual productions, a regulation that has been coined "Lex Netflix." Although Netflix initially penetrated the Chinese market initially, China's strict rules on internet usage have prevented Netflix from launching a library there. The same is true in Russia, North Korea, and Crimea. Consumers circumvent these restrictions by using VPNs, or virtual personal networks. Ultimately, Netflix's global influence challenged the rule of law in various countries. European countries saw the immediate threat that Netflix posed to their respective cultures, thereby placing restrictions on streaming companies.

Nowadays, whenever one wants to purchase books or just about anything else, Amazon is often the first website consulted. As of October 2023, Amazon was the twelfth most visited website in the world. The company was founded in 1994 by Princeton University graduate Jeff Bezos. Initially, it was dedicated to selling books within the United States and forty-five other countries. Within twenty years, Amazon saw $29 billion in net sales, and ten years later another $31.77 billion through Amazon Prime. During that time, Amazon expanded its e-commerce platform to various products, including baby products, apparel, jewelry, kitchen items, and more. During the COVID-19 pandemic, the company saw an increase of 28 million subscribers.

Amazon has been in the hotseat over various issues since going international. There have been allegations of the company aiding in the violation of human rights, fraud, and violating commercial laws. In 2022, the UK Buy Box Claim filed a class action lawsuit for £900 million against Amazon for breaching UK and EU competition law, directing consumers of its website and app to bids that are beneficial to Amazon, while hiding offers which could better suit those consumers (Hannah et al. 2022). The claim alleged that Amazon's practice resulted in customers paying more money for products that could have been bought more cheaply from other sellers.

The claim alleges that Amazon is guilty of breaching section 18 of the UK Competition Act 1998 and Article 102 of the Treaty on the Functioning of the European Union (TFEU). The UK Competition Act reads, "Subject to section 19, any conduct on the part of one or more undertakings which amounts to the abuse of a dominant position in a market is prohibited if it may affect trade within the United Kingdom."[3] This constitutes fraud because it betrays the trust of consumers, who wrongly assume that they are receiving the best deal. The suit alleges that Amazon uses algorithms that are systematically biased to favor its goods and/or those of third-party merchants who use the platform.

Amazon was also sued for breaching Article 102 of the TFEU, which "prohibits abusive behavior by companies holding a dominant position on any given market. Most abuse of dominance cases concern practices having an exclusionary effect on actual or potential competitors. The Commission adopted guidance on its enforcement priorities in the area of exclusionary conduct in 2008, promoting a so-called effects based approach to exclusionary abuses of dominance."[4] In November 2020, the European Commission began two antitrust investigations into Amazon for

[3] Competition Act 1998. The National Archives, https://www.legislation.gov.uk/ukpga/1998/41/section/18. The rest of the article states: Conduct may, in particular, constitute such an abuse if it consists in—

(a) directly or indirectly imposing unfair purchase or selling prices or other unfair trading conditions;
(b) limiting production, markets or technical development to the prejudice of consumers;
(c) applying dissimilar conditions to equivalent transactions with other trading parties, thereby placing them at a competitive disadvantage;
(d) making the conclusion of contracts subject to acceptance by the other parties of supplementary obligations which, by their nature or according to commercial usage, have no connection with the subject of the contracts.

(3) In this section—
"dominant position" means a dominant position within the United Kingdom; and
"the United Kingdom" means the United Kingdom or any part of it.

(4) The prohibition imposed by subsection (1) is referred to in this Act as "the Chapter II prohibition."

[4] TEFU art. 102.

self-preferencing. Then, in July 2022, the British Competition and Markets Authority (CMA) pursued an investigation following the one by the EU. The investigation concluded that Amazon had abused its dominant position by stipulating conditions on their purchases and logistics service in exchange for benefits to third-party retailers.

As if this were not enough, Steve Cockburn, Amnesty International's head of economic and social justice, raised concerns over abuses suffered by contract workers in Amazon warehouses in Saudi Arabia (Amnesty International 2023). Cockburn alleged that workers were duped by recruitment agents and labor-force companies. Contract workers were forced to live in unhabitable conditions, cheated of their earnings, and not permitted to engage in alternative employment or leave the country. This amounted to human trafficking. Human rights are violated by human trafficking when one lacks freedom of movement, freedom of association, or the right to life, liberty, and security. The result is slavery, servitude, forced labor, or bonded labor. Although workers complained numerous times, Amazon failed to make amends for the human rights violation. After a series of interviews, many workers were reported to be traumatized. Overall, Amnesty International suspected that hundreds had endured such treatment.

We have explored two instances where international law and national politics either worked in tandem successfully or, on the contrary, failed to uphold human rights law. In the former case, the UK government upheld EU commercial agreements ratified decades ago. In the latter case, neither the Saudi Arabian government nor its judicial system enforced UN legislation against human trafficking.[5]

Almost a century ago, Hersch Lauterpacht envisioned the diminishment of state powers and the modification of politics as the precursor to a universal court of justice ruling over all people. Instead of politicians meting out justice and morality, he held that contemporary legal scholars should interpret

[5] The Trafficking Protocol defines the term "trafficking in persons" as follows: (a) "'Trafficking in persons' shall mean the recruitment, transportation, transfer, harbouring or receipt of persons, by means of the threat or use of force or other forms of coercion, of abduction, of fraud, of deception, of the abuse of power or of a position of vulnerability or of the giving or receiving of payments or benefits to achieve the consent of a person having control over another person, for the purpose of exploitation. Exploitation shall include, at a minimum, the exploitation of the prostitution of others or other forms of sexual exploitation, forced labour or services, slavery or practices similar to slavery, servitude or the removal of organs; (b) The consent of a victim of trafficking in persons to the intended exploitation set forth in subparagraph (a) of this article shall be irrelevant where any of the means set forth in subparagraph (a) have been used; (art. 3)."

the rule of law (Paz 2012 , 442). Along the same lines, Martti Koskenniemi maintains that the "fight for an International Rule of Law is a fight against politics, understood as a matter of furthering subjective desires and leading into an international anarchy. . . . The health of the political realm is maintained by conscientious objection to the political" (Koskenniemi 1990, 5). By "subjective desires" he means economic pursuits mobilized by state actors, which in turn challenge the welfare of the citizens of the state. In short, an international rule of law can emerge only with the disappearance of national and corporate interests.

Lessons for and from Jewish Law

Jewish law can learn much from these cases because it functions similarly to international law and justice. Previously, we stated that national legislation in Jewish jurisprudence requires a Sanhedrin, that is, a senate or a supreme court. Without this essential element, justices from lower courts can only establish communal and generational decrees and ordinances. The cases concerning the activities of Facebook, Airbnb, Uber, and Amazon teach us that new technologies can challenge the interpretation of the rule of law. In some instances, cases have been brought before European courts. Since it has been a challenge, at best, to reassemble a Jewish senate since the fifth century CE, Jewish jurists could follow the European example and create regional tribunals to oversee cases of *agunoth* (chained wives), judge criminals within the Jewish community, and regulate international commerce between Jewish private actors.

Halakhah does not permit turning over a Jew to Gentile courts to be judged. There are exceptions to this rule, but they require legal consensus. When the separation of religion and state removes jurisdiction from Jewish courts, that creates a difficult challenge for enforcing verdicts in penal law within the domain of Jewish courts. Consequently, if Jewish criminals are not reported to Gentile authorities, those criminals go unpunished, to the detriment of not only the victims but the entire community. To resolve this issue, regional Jewish courts could create an app where their rulings and verdicts are published, just as the Oversight Board functions on behalf of Facebook. If Jewish regional courts could function like their EU counterparts, the Jewish rulings could then be implemented by respective local courts. At that stage, local courts could decide whether to turn over their criminals to the local civil authorities or not. They could also determine how to apply specific rulings according to the legal context.

In situations where Jewish criminals turn to civil authorities to overrule halakhic verdicts, regional courts could publish an internationalized *ḥerem* (excision or ban) through the use of their app. These individuals then would no longer fall under the jurisdiction of Jewish law, but the *ḥerem* would hold the equivalent status in the global Jewish community of a hefty fine within EU law. Jewish jurists could essentially serve as prosecutors and file lawsuit claims against culprits.

Ultimately, as regional Jewish courts emerge throughout the world, justices and jurists will see the need for international legal consensus. This could give birth to the long-awaited Jewish senate. Video-call technologies, such as Zoom, have facilitated global communication and meetings. During the COVID-19 pandemic in 2020 and 2021, we witnessed the use of video-call online platforms in courtrooms. Already, some Jewish courts have been using them to convene, where one or more of the justices could not be present. Indeed, this technology forced some halakhic authorities to reinterpret halakhah regarding the need for three or more judges present simultaneously in time and space. The reworking of legal terms and interpretation of law could permit many Jewish justices and jurists to convene around the world, with Jerusalem at the center. This consensus would select the most knowledgeable representatives to form the future Sanhedrin. Consequently, the need for chief rabbis and most political actors within the State of Israel would become obsolete.

In *Future Crimes*, US law enforcement official Marc Goodman provides an overview of how cybercriminals are ahead of law enforcement officials by at least two hundred days. This means that by the time the authorities figure out that a cybercrime has been committed, the criminals have already managed to abuse the software and internet systems used by individuals and companies. He thus presents a serious issue regarding jurisdiction, whereby a cybercriminal may be physically located in Russia but uses a proxy through Brazil to steal funds from a bank in the United States. When the culprit is caught, which court should try him? By which law should the culprit be accused? Goodman asserts:

> Though physical borders still matter, such divisions are much less clear in an online world. Bits and bytes flow freely from one country to the next without any border guards, immigration controls, or customs declarations

> to slow their transit. The traditional barriers to crime faced by former generations of thieves, thugs, and convicts have been demolished in the online world, allowing unsavory individuals to freely enter and exit any virtual location they please. (Goodman 2015, 11)

Indeed, we are all exposed to the dangers of having our information online. Ultimately, Goodman argues that antivirus software is futile in the face of a new generation of criminals.

In Chapter 5 we learned how Portuguese Jewish merchants created a global trade network under the auspices of the *Shulḥan Arukh.* This was a crucial element in their engagement with private international law. Within that domain, there were no law enforcement officials and no borders, only trust in the rule of law and local communal judges. They managed to create this system by drafting contracts stipulating that they would follow the civil laws found within the *Shulḥan Arukh.* In case of a breach of contract, any Jewish court had jurisdiction to hear the case and declare a verdict. This practice serves as a potential model for international law within the realm of cyber law and artificial intelligence.

With so many complex rules and regulations regarding jurisdiction of cyberspace, handing cases over to federal courts does not always yield the best results. According to the UN policy in the E4J University Module Series, territorial sovereignty is applicable to cyberspace. Thus, state sovereignty is violated when cybercrimes occur against a state's information and communications technology (ICT).[6] If there were a universal legal code and system on cyberlaw and cybercrimes, like a *Shulḥan Arukh,* it could eliminate the issues with jurisdiction altogether. The first step would be to establish cyberspace international treaties throughout the world. The next step would be to establish specialized courts around the globe that could hold hybrid hearings. Legal and IT experts would collaborate to ensure that the rule of law is upheld in cyberspace. Since there are no prisons for such crimes under international legal jurisdiction, federal prison systems where the culprits are arrested would be responsible for incarcerating cybercriminals. This style of global governance would function the way the Nação governed its business in the early modern period.

[6] UN Office on Drugs and Crime. 2013. "Cybercrime," Module 7. https://www.unodc.org/e4j/en/cybercrime/module-7/key-issues/sovereignty-and-jurisdiction.html.

Interactions between Jewish law and international law can be a rich field for exploration, offering insights and lessons for both systems. Each system can learn from the other's approaches to legal pluralism. Jewish law's long history of adapting to different cultural contexts and legal systems can offer valuable lessons for international law in addressing diverse legal traditions. Jewish law's emphasis on ethical principles and human dignity can contribute to discussions within international law on human rights.

Conversely, international human rights norms may challenge Jewish legal interpretations on certain issues, sparking dialogue and reflection within Jewish legal scholarship. Jewish legal traditions of arbitration and mediation can provide insights for international law in the realm of alternative dispute resolution. Examining how these methods are applied within Jewish communities can inform international efforts to promote peaceful conflict resolution.

The interactions between Jewish law and international law highlight the importance of cultural sensitivity and understanding in legal frameworks. Both systems can benefit from recognizing and respecting the cultural nuances and values that influence legal decision-making. Exploring historical interactions between Jewish law and various legal systems can offer valuable lessons for understanding contemporary challenges in the relationship between international law and religious legal traditions. Overall, through dialogue and comparative analysis, both Jewish law and international law can broaden their perspectives, enhance their approaches to legal issues, and foster mutual respect and collaboration in addressing global challenges.

In the wake of the Hamas attack on Israelis and foreign nationals on October 7, 2023, antisemitism has increased fourfold around the world. Jewish legal scholars suggest that international law can counteract antisemitism. International law can play a crucial role in countering antisemitism by providing a legal framework for addressing and combating acts of discrimination and prejudice against Jewish individuals and communities. International human rights law, including treaties such as the International Covenant on Civil and Political Rights and the International Convention on the Elimination of All Forms of Racial Discrimination, prohibits discrimination based on religion or ethnicity. These legal instruments provide avenues for individuals and groups to seek protection and redress against antisemitic acts. International law can also inform and support efforts to combat hate speech targeting Jews. Countries can adopt and enforce legal frameworks consistent with international standards that criminalize incitement to violence or hatred based on religion or ethnicity, including antisemitism.

Moreover, international law can promote education and awareness to foster tolerance and respect for diversity, including initiatives aimed at countering antisemitism. International bodies, such as the United Nations, can support educational programs that promote understanding and dialogue among different religious and cultural communities. International mechanisms, such as the Office for Democratic Institutions and Human Rights (ODIHR) of the Organization for Security and Cooperation in Europe (OSCE), can monitor and report on incidents of antisemitism, providing data and analysis to support efforts to combat this form of discrimination. International law can facilitate diplomatic engagement among countries to address and condemn antisemitic acts and policies. Through bilateral and multilateral channels, countries can collaborate to combat antisemitism and promote mutual understanding and respect. Essentially, by leveraging the tools and principles of international law, governments, civil society organizations, and individuals can work together to counteract antisemitism, uphold human rights, and build inclusive and tolerant societies.

In May 2024, Israel faced significant setbacks in the international legal arena. The International Criminal Court's prosecutor, Karim Khan, requested arrest warrants for leaders of both Israel and Hamas. This was followed by a ruling from the International Court of Justice (ICJ) that Israel must refrain from military actions in Rafah that could harm civilians. Upon closer examination, however, it appears that neither development would lead to an immediate end to the conflict.

The ICJ's ruling is more of a guideline on the appropriate conduct of the war rather than a judgment on its legality. Despite the many compelling reasons to bring a swift end to the war and alleviate the suffering of the people of Gaza, the ICJ's ruling has made a crucial distinction between Israel's right to continue combating Hamas and its obligation to minimize harm to civilians. Although the ruling does not explicitly mention genocide, it cites the Genocide Convention, emphasizing that Israel must immediately cease its military operations in Rafah and any other actions that could lead to the physical destruction of the Palestinian population in Gaza, either in whole or in part. This ruling was supported by thirteen judges, with only two dissenting opinions, including that of former Israeli Supreme Court President Aharon Barak.

The ICJ has emphasized that Israel must take proactive steps to ensure the safety and well-being of civilians in any military operation in Rafah, particularly considering that 800,000 Gazans have been displaced multiple times and are currently living in dire conditions, lacking access to basic necessities like food, water, sanitation, medical care, and proper shelter. Many of these displaced individuals fled Rafah in fear for their lives, with some encouraged to do so by the IDF.

The ICC's arrest warrants against Israeli Prime Minister Benjamin Netanyahu and Defense Minister Yoav Gallant on charges of crimes against humanity are still pending, and it is unlikely that they will result in arrests.[7] The prosecutor's decision to issue warrants for leaders of both Hamas and Israel simultaneously was a misstep and a politically naive move. By doing so, the prosecutor inadvertently equated a designated terrorist organization, Hamas, with a country that remains democratic despite Israel's fragile democratic system. However, this development does not diminish the gravity of the allegations against Israel and the need for the country to conduct a thorough introspection. In a remarkably short period, Israel's international reputation has suffered a significant decline, from enjoying widespread sympathy and support following Hamas's October 7 atrocities to its leaders facing charges of crimes against humanity.

The symbolic and practical implications of enforcing orders to extradite individuals accused of war crimes are multifaceted. Symbolically, extraditing individuals accused of war crimes can send a powerful message about the gravity of the crimes committed and the importance of holding those responsible accountable. It can also demonstrate a commitment to upholding international law and the rule of law, which is essential for maintaining global peace and security. Moreover, extraditing alleged war criminals can help to deter future human rights violations by making it clear that there will be consequences for those who commit such atrocities.

Practically, enforcing orders to extradite alleged war criminals can be challenging due to various obstacles. For example, countries may not cooperate with extradition requests for political or diplomatic reasons, or they may not have the necessary legal mechanisms in place to facilitate the extradition process. Additionally, there may be concerns about the treatment of the accused individuals in the country where they are being sought, including fears about their safety or potential mistreatment.

[7] As of the time of writing in September 2024.

Another challenge is that war crimes are often committed in complex and chaotic environments, making it difficult to gather evidence and build a strong case against the accused. This can lead to lengthy and costly investigations and potential delays or even dismissals of cases. Furthermore, extraditing war criminals can raise ethical concerns. For instance, if an individual is accused of committing war crimes but has fled to a country with a poor human rights record, there may be concerns about their potential torture or mistreatment in that country. In such cases, international pressure may be needed to ensure that the accused individual is treated fairly and humanely.

In some cases, extradition may not be possible because of political or diplomatic constraints. For example, if a country has granted asylum or citizenship to an individual accused of war crimes, it may be difficult to compel their return. In such cases, alternative measures may need to be taken, such as imposing sanctions or diplomatic pressure on the country that has granted asylum or citizenship. Thus, enforcing orders to extradite individuals accused of war crimes is a complex issue that requires careful consideration of both symbolic and practical implications. While extradition can send an important message about accountability and deterrence, it also raises practical challenges and ethical concerns that must be addressed.

Saddam Hussein, the former president of Iraq, was charged with crimes against humanity and genocide by the International Criminal Court (ICC) and the Iraqi High Tribunal (IHT). The ICC did not play a direct role in his trial. In 2005, Saddam Hussein was arrested by American forces in Tikrit, Iraq, and transferred to an Iraqi court for trial. The IHT, a domestic court established by the interim government of Iraq, conducted his trial. Saddam Hussein was charged with crimes against humanity, war crimes, and genocide in connection with his alleged involvement in the Anfal genocide, a campaign of persecution and violence against Kurdish civilians in northern Iraq in the late 1980s. The trial began in 2006 and lasted a few weeks.

In November 2006, Hussein was convicted of crimes against humanity and sentenced to death by hanging. On December 30, 2006, he was executed by hanging at Camp Justice in Baghdad. The ICC did not have jurisdiction over Hussein's case because Iraq was not a member of the ICC at the time (it joined the ICC in 2004), and the crimes alleged to have been committed did not fall within the ICC's jurisdiction under Article 12(2)(a) of the Rome Statute. However, the ICC did issue an arrest warrant for three senior officials from Saddam's regime in 2005 for their alleged involvement in crimes against humanity and war crimes. The warrant was issued under Article 58 of the Rome Statute, which allows the ICC to issue warrants for individuals who are not yet under ICC jurisdiction but may be subject to jurisdiction in the future.

It is worth noting that there has been some controversy over the fairness and legitimacy of Saddam Hussein's trial, with some critics arguing that it did not meet international standards for fair trials. The controversy surrounding the fairness and legitimacy of his trial primarily centered on lack of due process, prejudicial evidence, lack of effective defense, witness intimidation, lack of clear charges, impartiality of the judges, limited international scrutiny, and lack of protection for defense witnesses.

Critics argued that the IHT did not provide a fair and impartial process, as the court was seen as politicized and influenced by US-led occupation authorities and the Iraqi government. The court's independence and impartiality were questioned, as it was seen as a tool for the new Iraqi government to punish its enemies. The prosecution presented evidence that was deemed prejudicial, such as graphic videos of executions and torture, which some argued was intended to inflame emotions rather than present a fair case against Hussein.

Hussein's legal team faced numerous challenges, including restrictions on their ability to question witnesses, access to evidence, and communication with their client. These limitations hindered their ability to effectively defend Hussein. Many witnesses testified against him under threat of reprisal or coercion, which raised concerns about the reliability of their testimony. The charges against Hussein were vague and unclear, making it difficult for him to prepare a defense.

Some critics questioned the impartiality of the judges, as they were appointed by the Iraqi government and had ties to the US-led occupation authorities. The trial was not subject to the same level of international scrutiny and monitoring as a fair trial, raising concerns about its compliance with international human rights standards. Defense witnesses who testified against Hussein faced threats and intimidation, making it difficult for them to come forward and testify.

These concerns led some critics to argue that the trial did not meet international standards for fair trials, as enshrined in the Universal Declaration of Human Rights and other human rights instruments. However, others argued that the trial was a significant step toward accountability for past human rights abuses in Iraq and demonstrated Iraq's commitment to upholding the rule of law.

Benjamin Netanyahu could be in trouble if the United States decides to intervene in his case as it did in the enforcement of the IHT ruling. If Netanyahu were turned over by the Israeli government for war crimes, it would be a highly significant and unprecedented event with far-reaching implications. Potentially, it would mark a major shift in Israel's approach to addressing allegations of war crimes and human rights abuses. Israel has historically been reluctant to prosecute its own leaders or military personnel for alleged human rights violations.

Netanyahu's arrest and prosecution could have significant domestic political implications, potentially leading to government crisis, new elections, international repercussions, or escalating tensions. The government might collapse, as coalition partners might withdraw their support, or Netanyahu's party might face internal splits. Early elections could be called, potentially altering the political landscape and leading to a change in government. The move could enhance Israel's international reputation if it demonstrated a commitment to upholding the rule of law and accountability for leaders. The gesture could revive diplomatic efforts to address the Israeli-Palestinian conflict and other regional issues. Conversely, some countries might view the move as provocative, potentially straining diplomatic relations with Israel.

If such were to happen, Netanyahu would face prosecution in an Israeli court, which must follow due process and fair trial standards. International arrest warrants could follow. Other countries might issue arrest warrants for Netanyahu if they believe he has committed crimes under their jurisdiction. If Netanyahu were to be prosecuted, it could set a precedent for the prosecution of other Israeli military leaders accused of war crimes or human rights abuses. On the other side of the coin, arresting Netanyahu would likely be seen as a significant victory for the Palestinian cause, as it would demonstrate accountability for Israel's actions in the disputed territories. This event could affect relationships between Jewish Israelis and international Jewish organizations, potentially leading to increased scrutiny and criticism from some quarters.

The Importance of Judges

In the context of nonterritorial legal systems like Jewish law and international law, the rule of law warrants interpretation from judges in several ways. Legal texts, such as the Torah or international treaties, can be ambiguous or open-ended, leaving room for interpretation. Judges play a crucial role in clarifying the meaning and application of these texts in specific contexts. Judges must consider the historical, cultural, and social context in which a particular law or principle was written. This helps to ensure that the law is applied in a way that is relevant and effective in the present day.

Nonterritorial legal systems often involve conflicting values, rights, and interests. Judges must balance these competing interests to arrive at a fair and just decision, taking into account the specific circumstances. In areas where there is no explicit text or precedent, judges must fill the gap by applying general principles, analogy, or logical reasoning to reach a decision. In the absence of a central authority or hierarchical structure, judges play a key role in resolving disputes between parties. They must apply the law to the facts of the case, considering the perspectives and arguments presented by each side.

Through their decisions, judges contribute to the development of legal doctrine and precedent, which can shape the trajectory of the legal system over time. In Jewish law, for example, judges may consider additional sources such as Talmudic discussions, commentaries, and responsa literature to inform their decisions. In international law, judges on international tribunals and courts often face similar challenges. Judges must interpret the terms of treaties and conventions to determine their applicability in specific cases. In addition, they must identify and apply customary international law principles, which may not be explicitly stated but may have developed through practice and precedent.

Judges must balance competing interests between states, taking into account factors such as national sovereignty, human rights, and global norms. In both Jewish law and international law, judges play a vital role in ensuring that the rule of law is applied fairly, effectively, and justly. Their interpretations help clarify complex legal concepts, balance competing interests, and guide future cases.

Conclusion

The Jewish tradition is often misperceived as solely a religious phenomenon, but closer examination reveals a rich tapestry of law and jurisprudence at its core. In reality, the Jewish tradition is a legal civilization with a sophisticated system of laws and regulations that shares commonalities with other legal systems, including Roman law, Islamic law, and international law. While the connections with the first two may be evident to rabbinic scholars, the parallels with international law are often overlooked due to the association of international law with Christian civilization. Similarly, international law scholars tend to overlook the relevance of Jewish law.

A comparative analysis of Jewish and international law reveals several striking parallels in their treatment of customary law. Both legal systems lack a single, living legislative authority and operate in a nonterritorial sphere. Furthermore, neither system possesses an enforcing mechanism, rendering them reliant on the trust and observance of the rule of law. This shared characteristic leads jurists within both systems to draw heavily from customary law and practice. In this context, the Talmudic phrase "Go and see what the people are doing" (Hilkhoth Shabbath 23a) takes on new significance. This directive, used by Jewish law experts to incorporate foreign customs and practices into their legal framework, finds a striking parallel in the approach taken by international jurists today. Both seek to understand and adapt to the evolving norms and practices within their respective spheres.

Our central argument is that international law and Jewish law share a crucial similarity in being nonterritorial legal systems, relying heavily on the role of judges to interpret and apply the rule of law. By exploring the commonalities between these two legal systems, scholars of international law and rabbinic jurists can gain valuable insights into how each system can learn from and complement the other. Our book aims to spark a dialogue between scholars from both fields, fostering a long-term collaboration that enables them to share knowledge and expertise to address the complex challenges faced by Jews and non-Jews alike.

The Jewish people have preserved their legal tradition despite persecution, expulsions, and attempted annihilation by political extremists and religious fanatics. The Jewish legal tradition covers a period of almost three thousand years, surviving for more than two millennia after the first commonwealth of the Jews ended. Jewish law has survived for such a long time because of trust in the rule of law and the metaphysical concept *berith*. English jurist John Selden (1584–1654) was astonished at the fact that the Jews subjected themselves throughout their exile to Talmudic national law, without a worldly authority to enforce it. He found that the answer to this enigma lay in "an expectation of an eventual future national ingathering and political restoration of the Jewish State" (Haivry 2017, 118).

As a test subject, one could say that compliance with one's legal culture is the key to maintaining one's ethnic or national identity. During such a long exile from their ancestral homeland, Jews developed a system for examining foreign legal systems and determining whether to incorporate rules from them. This has permitted Jews to respect their host countries' legal culture while preserving and developing their own. Even when Jews did not have a monarchy, they preserved their national identity and ethos by promulgating Talmudic national law. Indeed, the Israelite people became a nation after being redeemed from tyrannical rule by the Egyptians, in the wilderness upon receiving their constitution, the Torah. Thus, even before entering the Promised Land and the establishment of national borders and a monarchy, they had a legal system. Herein lies a very important insight for the debate about the conflict between national politics and international law. One could say that trust in the rule of law takes precedence over political structures. The Jewish hope for restoring a Jewish senate and Jewish state amid trials and tribulations serves as a model for citizens of the world who hope for legitimate global governance based on the rule of law, with equality and sufficiency for all.

Bibliography

Primary Sources

Anghie, Antony. *Imperialism, Sovereignty, and the Making of International Law.* Cambridge: Cambridge University Press, 2004.

European Commission. 2020. "Application of Article 102 TFEU." https://competition-policy.ec.europa.eu/antitrust-and-cartels/legislation/application-article-102tfeu_en#:~:text=Article%20102%20prohibits%20abusive%20behaviour,on%20actual%20or%20potential%20competitors.

Facebook Oversight Board. "Former President Trump's Suspension." January 7, 2021. https://oversightboard.com/decision/FB-691QAMHJ/.

Goodman, Marc. *Future Crimes: A Journey to the Dark Side of Technology—And How to Survive It.* London, UK: Bantam Press, 2015.

Kennedy, David. *A World of Struggle: How Power, Law, and Expertise Shape Global Political Economy.* Princeton, NJ: Princeton University Press, 2016.

Moyn, Samuel. *Not Enough: Human Rights in an Unequal World.* Cambridge, MA: Harvard University Press, 2018.

Neff, Stephen C. *Justice among the Nations: A History of International Law.* Cambridge, MA: Harvard University Press, 2014.

Secondary Sources

Aust, Helmut Philip. "Cities as International Legal Authorities—Remarks on Recent Cities as International Legal Authorities—Remarks on Recent Developments and Possible Future Trends of Research Developments and Possible Future Trends of Research." *Journal of Comparative Law and Policy* 4, no. 1 (2020): 82–88.

Haivry, Ofir. "John Selden and the Jewish Religious Fountainhead of the International Law." In *International Law and Religion: Historical and Contemporary Perspectives*, edited by Martti Koskenniemi, Monica Garcia-Salmones Rovira, and Paolo Amorosa, 111–32. Oxford: Oxford University Press, 2017.

Hannah, Lesley, et al. "E-commerce Giant Amazon Faces Legal Action for Unlawfully Favouring Its Own Product Offers." *Lexology*, October 20, 2022. https://www.lexology.com/library/detail.aspx?g=441d9e62-6477-4e5f-a6 f8-bb1537913b48.

Horwitz, Jeff. "Facebook Says Its Rules Apply to All: Company Documents Reveal a Secret Elite That's Exempt." *The Wallstreet Journal*, September 13, 2021. https://www.wsj.com/articles/facebook-files-xcheck-zuckerberg-elite-rules-11631541353?mod=article_inline.

Koskenniemi, Martti. "The Politics of International Law." *European Journal of International Law* 1 (1990): 4–32.

Nijman, Janne. "The Future of the City and the International Law of the Future." In *Law of the Future and the Future of Law*, edited by Sam Muller, Stavros Zouridis, Morly Frishman, and Laura Kistemaker, 213–29. Brussels, Belgium: Torkel Opsahl Academic EPublisher, 2011.

Paz, Reut Yael. "Hersch Lauterpacht's Rabbinical Approach to International Law." *Goettingen Journal of International Law* 4, no. 2 (2012): 417–45.

"Saudi Arabia: Migrants Workers Who Toiled in Amazon Warehouses Were Deceived and Exploited." *Amnesty International*, October 10, 2023. https://www.amnesty.org/en/latest/news/2023/10/saudi-arabia-migrants-workers-who-toiled-in-amazon-warehouses-were-deceived-and-exploited/.

Staff, Toi. "As Airbnb Set to Go Public, Amnesty International Decries Settlement Listings." *Times of Israel*, December 10, 2020, https://www.timesofisrael.com/as-airbnb-set-to-go-public-amnesty-international-decries-settlement-listings/.

Wells, Georgia, Jeff Horwitz, and Deepa Seetharaman. "Facebook Knows Instagram Is Toxic for Teen Girls, Company Documents Show." *The Wall Street Journal*, September 14, 2021, https://www.wsj.com/articles/facebook-knows-instagram-is-toxic-for-teen-girls-company-documents-show-11631620739?mod=article_inline.

Index

For the benefit of digital users, indexed terms that span two pages (e.g., 52–53) may, on occasion, appear on only one of those pages.